Michael Moran

The Zozimus Papers

A Series of comic and sentimental Stories and Legends

Michael Moran

The Zozimus Papers
A Series of comic and sentimental Stories and Legends

ISBN/EAN: 9783337154271

Printed in Europe, USA, Canada, Australia, Japan

Cover: Foto ©ninafisch / pixelio.de

More available books at **www.hansebooks.com**

THE ZOZIMUS PAPERS.

A SERIES OF

COMIC AND SENTIMENTAL STORIES AND LEGENDS,

BEING THE EDITED, UNEDITED AND PILFERED WORKS OF

MICHAEL MORAN,

THE BLIND STORY-TELLER OF DUBLIN.

———•◦•———

NEW YORK:
P. J. KENEDY,
EXCELSIOR CATHOLIC PUBLISHING HOUSE,
5 BARCLAY STREET.

1889.

PREFACE.

The following humorous and pathetic tales and stories require no recommendation to those who relish innocent and amusing reading. Though all are attributed to the late lamented *Zozimus*, who once made the streets of Dublin vocal with his epigrams and impromptu ballads, it is but candid to say that many of them cannot be traced directly to his authorship, and several of the best, we are aware, were written in the first instance for a weekly journal. However, they are all, without exception, true pictures of Irish life, as it once appeared, nothing being extenuated or set down in malice, and as such we ask for them the kind consideration of the reader.

CONTENTS.

	PAGE
THE "ZOZIMUS" PAPERS	7
THE PROPHECY MAN	16
THE DESERTER	27
THE MATCHMAKER	33
THE GHOST	42
AN IRISH PIC-NIC	51
THE IRISH PARLIAMENT AND THE TURK	69
BOTHERING AN EDITOR	77
A FENIAN TALE	84
HANDY ANDY'S LITTLE MISTAKES	97
PUSS IN BROGUES	106
THE WISE SIMPLETON	116
PEGGY THE PISHOGUE	127
AN IRISH DANCING-MASTER	137
A DANCE AT PAT MALONE'S	146
MIKE DRISCOLL AND THE FAIRIES	161
TOM KEARNEY	181
PADDY CORBETT'S FIRST SMUGGLING TRIP	192
HANNABERRY THE PIPER	206
THE IRISH FIDDLER	214
BARNEY O'GRADY	222
OROHOO, THE FAIRY MAN	227

	PAGE
A Tale of Other Days	237
What Mr. Maguire Saw in the Kitchen	245
The Will	257
Serving a Writ	262
The Gauger Outwitted	266
The Irish Midwife	279
The Will o' the Wisp	304
The Flower of the Well	309

THE "ZOZIMUS" PAPERS.

From the creation of the human race (we may as well begin at the beginning) even unto our own degenerate days, the Unknown Great have formed a very large portion of mankind. How many poets and philosophers sang songs and split syllogistic hairs when the unhappy Cain was building cities by the Euphrates, or the mighty hunter, Nimrod, was developing his young muscle in the sports of the field, it is of course impossible to say; that greatest of all water-cures, the Deluge, has literally washed out every record of their existence. No doubt there were rhymsters and bards without number to lighten the fruitless labor of the builders of the brick tower of Babel, but the calamity that befell those enterprising free-masons and hod-carriers could not have been without its deleterious effect on the children of the muses. What that effect must have been is too painful for contemplation. Imagine a few score of ambitious poetasters, each bawling out at the top of his voice his favorite composition in a strange tongue, unknown to any of his hearers or rival songsters! This, indeed, would be confusion worse confounded.

Then we find matters little mended when we come down to comparatively modern times—that is, the ten or eleven centuries before our era. Where, let us ask, are all the great men who hoodwinked and blarnied the Pharos of Egypt; or those who sat on the sunny sides of the gorgeous palaces and temples of Nineveh and Babylon, surrounded by admiring crowds of princes and courtiers? What has become of all the men who made Greece and her colonies on the borders of the Mediterranean the nurseries of learning, and the favorite summer watering-place of the Nine Muses? Are even their names known to the great majority of enlightened American citizens; or is their knowledge, like the language of the sacred Vedas of India, confined to the occult few, the professors of New England colleges and the hedge-school masters of the remote Kingdom of Kerry?

One name, indeed, has been rescued from oblivion, and if life is preserved to us, we intend to pull to the surface another genius by the drowned locks. Indeed, those two characters, Homer and Moran, had many points in common: both were blind, and both sang their ballads in the public streets for a scanty subsistence, while each in his own way had, during life, to suffer contumely and injustice. Fortunately for the "blind bard of Scio," Lycurgus, the communist of Sparta and the inventor of broth, in his rambles through Asia Minor, a long time after the poet had been carried over the Styx, heard the Homeric ballads sang in the streets, and giving an order to the nearest dealer in *papyrus*, had them stenographed and arranged in sequence for the delectation of his rather savage subjects. Then, and not till then, did

> "Seven cities claim the poet Homer dead,
> Through which the living Homer begged his bread."

To our humble selves falls the onerous but pleasing task of imitating the example of the Spartan ruler, but though we have no claim to that eminent strict constructionist's ability or influence, we have the advantage not only of having heard our hero's ballads sung in the streets of Dublin, in Crampton Court and Jude's *Café;* aye, and even within the classic walls of old Trinity and at the fancy dress balls of the Rotundo, by successful imitators of the great original; but in our callow youth we enjoyed the friendship of the venerable and gifted man. This latter fact enables us to do for Moran what all the biographers and antiquarians in the universe have failed to do for his Greek prototype. We can fix precisely the place and time of his birth, as well as the exact scene of his labors. No seven cities shall, if we can prevent it, wrangle in fruitless rivalry over his birth-place. Himself and all his fame belongs to Dublin, and in the language of a late distinguished Irish advocate, he was, in more than one sense, "racy of its soil." In that fair city celebrated for its Lord Lieutenants and "Lady Lieutenants," its Lions and Unicorns, big policemen and small shopkeepers, *jackeens* and *jokers*, in the year 1840, at Faddle Alley, off Black Pitts, in the Liberties, (we are particular as to the place, for we have no doubt as civilization advances pilgrims by the thousands will throng to gaze and affectionately contemplate the humble and sequestered spot, if the ruthless hand of time spares it so long), the future *improvisatore* first saw the light.

Alas! twas indeed but a short gleam of celestial sunshine that illuminated the windows of the soul of the infant phenomenon. Sickness, that ever haunts the steps of mortals from the cradle to the grave, makes no exception of genius, and when yet two weeks old, those eyes that might have rolled with *divine phrenzy* became forever sightless. Nature, doubtless, when viewing her perfect handiwork, became jealous of the child, and resolved by this infliction to mar his great mental qualities by physical disability. Still when we are deprived of one sense, an increased development of another is generally noticed; and so with Zozimus, for so acute was his hearing and his sense of feeling so delicate, that he easily recognized a mere acquaintance by the sound of his voice, and could perambulate the intricate lanes and streets of the "Liberties" without the guidance of dog or urchin. We remember one exception to this wonderful gift of inhabitiveness.

On a certain very stormy night, as Mr. (now Sir John) Gray, of the Dublin *Freeman's Journal*, was about to cross Essex bridge on his way to the office, he heard through the darkness and the rain a plaintive voice saying:

"Is there any good Christian here that would lead a poor blind man over the bridge?"

"Yes," said the kind-hearted editor, "take my hand and I shall bring you across."

"Thank you, gentle sir," said the poet, as he placed his hand within that of his obliging conductor.

When they had crossed the Liffey to the north side, Mr. Gray stopped and inquired with well assumed gravity:

"Now, Zozimus, why is it you are always so hard on us Protestants? Here am I a heretic, who have taken you safely over the bridge when none of your faith was near to assist you, and yet you say many harsh things against us."

"Sir!" replied the venerable bard, raising up his sightless eyes towards where he supposed heaven might be, in an act of blind devotion, as it were—"Sir! do you not know that we must sometimes, for their own good, pander to the prejudices of an unenlightened public?"

What a blending of humility and wisdom is found in this short answer! We look in vain in the much-lauded pages of Socrates and Plato, of Cicero and Seneca, for anything so replete in sagacity and knowledge of human nature. It furnishes also a key to his system of public instruction, and an explanation of why one so gifted should have preferred the vernacular of Thomas Street and the Coombe to that of more classical English in most of his compositions. Born at a time when the Irish people were sunk in ignorance, he found out as he grew up that they had many of the weaknesses and harmless prejudices which grow out of long years of servitude, so when he had a sound moral to convey or a patriotic sentiment to advance, he made use of these very defects of character to instruct his auditors; and, unlike many modern orators, he was able to impart to them wholesome truths in language they could all understand.

What can be more true to nature as well as to fact than the following ballad composed and sung by the peripatetic bard soon after the celebrated discussion between Rev. Father Thomas Maguire, P.P. of Ballinamore, and Rev. T. D. Gregg, of the Protestant establishment, during which the latter got signally defeated?

MAGUIRE'S TRIUMPH.

"All you that profess to that ancient religion,
    Can boast its foundation from virtue and truth,
Maguire's the champion can trace its origin,
    With any false preacher he's fit to dispute;
The Swifts-ally spouter he's bothered completely,
    The fountain of rancor has leveled him low,
The victory's our own, we'll rejoice late and early,
    That Maguire may conquer wherever he'll go.

"From the sweet county Leitrim to famed Dublin city
    True Catholic doctrine he came to defend,
Those misguided heretics, boys can you pity,
    When to his decisions they were forced to bend;
Their bible cant-tract, was no more but a folly,
    The master of arts on his dunghill may crow,
And fly to the 'Trinity' pack for protection,
    That Maguire may conquer wherever he'll go.

"Each Catholic heart round the green fields of Erin
    Shall nobly re-echo the shamrock shore,
Representing the joys of our holy religion,
    From sweet Dublin city to Ballinamore;
The Tories like dogs may fly to their kennels,
    The foul seed of discord no longer they'll sow,
Let us quarrel no more, but stand firm to each other—
    Father Tom, may you conquer wherever you go.

"This scheme was contrived by the bigoted faction,
    The minds of the people they mean to excite,
For their own selfish ends to drive man to distraction,
    To keep ancient Erin from her lawful right;
But the Catholic Church is triumphant, thank heaven,
    All tempests and dangers she'll still overthrow,
The last dying blow to heresy's given—
    Maguire, may you conquer wherever you go.

"Acclamations of joy through our church is spreading,
    From the seat of Armagh to St. Peter's in Rome,
The call of assassins no more we'll be dreading,
    The Catholic Church has commenced in its bloom;
For the want of sound proofs Tory Gregg you defeated,
    The rank seed of Harry is confounded, you know,
One heaven, one sheepfold by heaven elevated,
    That Maguire may conquer wherever he'll go.

"The Catholic clergy may stand on their altars,
    And challenge the best their foes can produce,
For the minds of the people can never be altered;
    Poor Gregg, your false doctrine is of but little use;
Your name, Father Tom, will be ever enduring,
    Of the infernal proud Satan you have made a show;
Green laurels shall bloom round the chapels of Erin,
    That Maguire may conquer wherever he'll go.

"With joy we'll conclude by the victory proclaiming,
    And toast to Victoria our beautiful queen,
While our kind Lord Lieutenant displays equal justice,
    May he reign triumphant in our land of green;
That the blest Church of Rome may extend through the world;
    As we push round the glass with three cheers let it flow,
To the health of the matchless, unrivaled Maguire,
    May he live long and conquer wherever he'll go."

We admit our inability to understand the logic or appreciate the sentiment of the last verse. What connection could exist between the welfare of "our beautiful queen" and the "equal justice" of the "kind Lord Lieutenant," and the spread of the doctrines of the Church, must remain to us a conundrum. It may be that at the time the poem was given to the public (1838) there had been a fresh stimulus imparted to Dublin loyalty by an increased order for castle livery of "native manufacture;" or that the author, apprehensive of the interference of the police with his chants in praise of the champion of the people, threw in the last few lines as a propitiatory sacrifice to the Molloch of the Castle. Future critics must resolve this delicate enigma; for ourselves, we give it up.

The great Moran was born of poor *but* honest parents, a method of description not very original, but much affected by certain biographers, who think it a strange, nay, wonderful coincidence, that a man's parents may have been poor and yet honest. However, it was a fact in the case of our poet, well known to the public, and, very probably, often inconveniently felt by himself. We wish, for the sake of posterity, that our data regarding his early habits and education were as authentic, for, as a brother poet hath it,

> "Lives of poets all remind us
> We can write dimnation fine,
> Leaving still unsolved behind us
> Query: How are bards to dine?"

What interesting reminiscences must have clustered round his infancy and adolescence, that now can only be left to the imagination! What mud pies he made in the propitious precincts of Faddle Alley! and what spankings he must have received from the maternal brogue! Would that some authentic record had been preserved in the library of the "Silent Sister," or in the Royal Irish Academy, which would tell us of the first dawnings of the genius that was destined not only to astonish his fellow-citizens, but to edify and instruct the whole world—for to what place has his fame not extended? How he listened enraptured to the reading of the good and great bishop of Raphoe's account of Mary of Egypt, and drank in, as eager as the arid sands of the desert do the passing shower, the beautiful and patriotic sentiments of "Come, all ye ancient Britons," "In the year '98," "The Banshee Peelers," and other gems of rustic verse. But, unfortunately, every incident of his life save the mere fact of his entrance into this sublunary sphere, has been forgotten, or suppressed by those who envied his ability without being able to approach it; and we know little of him till he emerged into public life and the streets of Dublin a full-fledged author, composer and musical artist, arrayed in a dress consisting of a long-tailed coat, closely buttoned over the chest (as if to conceal the absence of a shirt), with a cape—the lower parts of the skirts being scalloped like the edge of a monstrous saw, which but allowed the inexpressibles to be revealed. His extremities were encased in a pair of strong brogues, and the *tout ensemble* was crowned by a soft, greasy hat, that had protected the noble head of the venerable man in all weathers for many a year. His only companion, his only weapon of defense and offense—his staff and truncheon—was a long blackthorn stick, which was attached to his wrist by a stout leathern thong, lest, perchance, some profane urchin might snatch it out of his grasp, and leave him open to assault in front and rear.

Thus habited and equipped, he would take his stand on Essex bridge, or in some other thoroughfare, where his appearance never failed to collect a crowd of admirers and patrons. Then a dialogue something like the following would ensue between the bard and his audience:

Zoz. "Gather 'round me, boys; gather 'round me. Well, yez all know St. Patrick was born in Bull Alley, ave he wasn't in France."

FEMALE LISTENER (*loquitor*). "Oh, Kitty Gogarty, glory be to goodness, did you ever hear the like of that afore? Why, he must be a great book-larned man!"

SCAMPS (*in full chorus*). "More power, Zozimus, yer the rale hart ave the rowl;" "Tip huz the T. B. C.;" "There's no damp on the taypot;" "That ye may never die," etc., etc.

It may be well to explain here that the cabalistic letters were the initials of Attorney-General Smith, one of the Crown prosecutors on the trial of O'Connell and six other prominent repealers in 1843. As the result of that inquisition, the imprisonment of the "martyrs," fired the soul of the poet with just indignation; so their liberation, after three months' confinement, called forth some of the noblest strains of the gifted son of song. The first, which is the most valuable on account of its historical and biographical references, ran as follows:

> Ye boys of old Hibernia, attend unto me,
> Whilst I give you the story of young T. B. C.
> Unlike his father, who stood by Father Maguire,
> He prosecuted O'Connell, with spite like hell-fire.
> With him were first-named Fathers Tiernay and Tyrrell,
> But were soon set aside as leading to peril,
> Tom Steele, Richard Barrett, Gavan Duffy and Gray,
> With John O'Connell and our "dear T. M. Ray."
>
> A jury was formed of the right sort,
> Who had the right feeling when called into court,
> And soon pure witnesses were easily found
> To keep the right side—the Royal ground.

Then the learned judge made home his bold charge
Against brave O'Connell and his six at large,
Who to Richmond prison were suddenly sent,
Where some months of confinement they soberly spent.

But when the Writ of Error (with all its records)
Was fully brought up before the House of Lords,
The noble answer was just, rich and rare,
The trial was a "mockery, delusion and snare;"
So then the imprisoned were set fully free,
To the glory and joy of our old countrie;
At least half a million in union did meet,
And had a procession in every street.

It may easily be imagined the effect such a plain, simple, yet forcible ballad like the above, when sung by so skilled a rhetorician as our hero, would have on an intellectual Dublin audience, which is popularly supposed, at least by the good people of that provincial city, to be the most critical of any in Europe, particularly in musical matters.

THE IRISH PROPHECY MAN.

BY WILLIAM CARLETON.

[The warm imagination and playful fancy of the poet were not confined within any limits, and in reciting his stories he wandered from "grave to gay" with the freedom peculiar to his calling, as well as characteristic of the man. His mind was a storehouse of legendary lore from which he could draw at will a tale to suit the taste of his audience. Thus a. one time he would delight his hearers with a description of Donnybrook, given in his own unique way, with all the graces of delivery and action which enhanced so much the value of his lucubrations; at another he would describe a national character with such fidelity to nature and acuteness of observation, as would lead one to imagine that this was his peculiar *forte*. "The Irish Prophecy Man" was a favorite theme with the gifted poet, and when seated by a cheerful fire and in the company of congenial spirits, he delivered it with a ring and *gusto* that must forever remain inimitable. This, like many of his other creations, was gracelessly purloined, and, clothed in a new dress, appeared in the columns of a Dublin magazine. Ah, me! how much must it have lost in symmetry in its transformation.

In the absence of the inimitable version as told by Zozimus, we must present it in the shape which it has assumed under the hand of William Carleton.]

The individual to whom the heading of this article is uniformly applied, stands among the lower classes of his countrymen in a different light and position from any of those previous characters that we have already described to our readers. The intercourse which *they* maintain with the people is one that simply involves the means of procuring subsistence for themselves by the exercise of their professional skill, and their powers of contributing to the lighter enjoyments and more harmless amusements of their fellow-countrymen. All the collateral influences they possess, as arising from the hold which the peculiar nature of this intercourse gives them, generally affect individuals only on those minor points of feeling that act upon the lighter phases of domestic life. They bring little to society beyond the mere accessories that are appended to the general modes of life and manners, and consequently receive themselves as strong an impress from those with whom they mingle, as they communicate to them in return.

Now, the Prophecy Man presents a character far different from all this. With the ordinary habits of life he has little sympathy. The amusements of the people are to him little less than vanity, if not something worse. He despises that class of men who live and think only for the present, without ever once performing their duties to posterity, by looking into those great events that lie in the womb of futurity. Domestic joys or distresses do not in the least affect him, because the man has not to do with feelings or emotions, but with principles. The speculations in which he indulges, and by which his whole life and conduct are regulated, place him far above the usual impulses of humanity. He cares not much who has been married or who has died, for his mind is, in point of time, communing with unborn generations upon affairs of high and solemn import. The past, indeed, is to him something, the future everything; but the present, unless when marked by the prophetic symbols, little or nothing. The topics of his conversation are vast and mighty, being nothing less than the fate of kingdoms, the revolution of empires, the ruin or establishment of creeds, the fall of monarchs, or the rise and prostration of principalities and powers. How can a mind thus engaged descend to those petty subjects of ordinary life which engage the common attention? How could a man hard at work in evolving out of prophecy the subjugation of some hostile state care a farthing whether Loghlin Roe's daughter was married to Gusty Given's son, or not? The thing is impossible. Like fame, the head of the Prophecy Man is always in the clouds, but so much higher up as to be utterly above the reach of any intelligence that does not affect the fate of nations. There is an old anecdote told of a very high and a very low man meeting. "What news down there?" said the tall fellow. "Very little," replied the other: "what kind of weather have you above?" Well indeed might the Prophecy Man ask what news there is below, for his mind seldom leaves those aërial heights from which it watches the fate of Europe and the shadowing forth of future changes.

The Prophecy Man—that is, he who solely devotes himself to an anxious observation of those political occurrences which mark the signs of the times, as they bear upon the future, the principal business of whose life it is to associate them with his own prophetic theories—is now a rare character in Ireland. He was, however, a very marked one. The Shanahus and other itinerant characters had, when compared with him, a very limited beat indeed. Instead of being confined to a parish or a barony, the bounds of the Prophecy Man's travels were those of the kingdom itself; and indeed some of them have been known to make excursions to the Highlands of Scotland, in order, if possible, to pick up old prophecies, and to make themselves, by cultivating an intimacy with the Scottish seers, capable of getting a clearer insight into futurity, and surer rules for developing the latent secrets of time.

One of the heaviest blows to the speculations of this class was the downfall and death of Bonaparte, especially the latter. There are still living, however, those who can get over this difficulty, and who will not hesitate to assure you, with a look of much mystery, that the real "Bonyparty" is alive and well, and will make his due appearance *when the time comes;* he who surrendered himself to the English being but an accomplice of the true one.

The next fact, and which I have alluded to in treating of the

Shanahus, is the failure of the old prophecy that a George the Fourth would never sit on the throne of England. His coronation and reign, however, puzzled our prophets sadly, and indeed sent adrift forever the pretensions of this prophecy to truth.

Having thus, as is our usual custom, given what we conceive to be such preliminary observations as are necessary to make both the subject and the person more easily understood, we shall proceed to give a short sketch of the only Prophecy Man we ever saw who deserved properly to be called so, in the full and unrestricted sense of the term. This individual's name was Barney M'Haighery, but in what part of Ireland he was born I am not able to inform the reader. All I know is, that he was spoken of on every occasion as The Prophecy Man; and that, although he could not himself read, he carried about with him, in a variety of pockets, several old books and manuscripts that treated upon his favorite subject.

Barney was a tall man, by no means meanly dressed; and it is necessary to say that he came not within the character or condition of a mendicant. On the contrary, he was considered as a person who must be received with respect, for the people knew perfectly well that it was not with every farmer in the neighborhood he would condescend to sojourn. He had nothing of the ascetic and abstracted meagreness of the prophet in his appearance. So far from that, he was inclined to corpulency; but, like a certain class of fat men, his natural disposition was calm, but at the same time not unmixed with something of the pensive. His habits of thinking, as might be expected, were quiet and meditative; his personal motions slow and regular; and his transitions from one resting-place to another never of such length during a single day as to exceed ten miles. At this easy rate, however, he traversed the whole kingdom several times; nor was there probably a local prophecy of any importance in the country, with which he was not acquainted. He took much delight in the greater and lesser prophets of the Old Testament; but his heart and soul lay, as he expressed it, "in the Revelations of St. John the Divine."

His usual practice was, when the family came home at night from their labor, to stretch himself upon two chairs, his head resting upon the hob, with a boss for a pillow, his eyes closed, as a proof that his mind was deeply engaged with the matter in hand. In this attitude he got some one to read the particular prophecy upon which he wished to descant; and a most curious and amusing entertainment it generally was to hear the text, and his own singular and original commentaries upon it. That he must have been often hoaxed by wags and wits, was quite evident from the startling travesties of the text which had been put into his mouth, and which, having been once put there, his tenacious memory never forgot.

The fact of Barney's arrival in the neighborhood soon went abroad, and the natural consequence was, that the house in which he thought proper to reside for the time became crowded every night as soon as the hours of labor had passed, and the people got leisure to hear him. Having thus procured him an audience, it is full time that we should allow the fat old Prophet to speak for himself, and give us an insight into futurity.

"Barney, ahagur," the good man his host would say, "here's a lot o' the neighbors come to hear a whirrangue from you on the Prophecies; and, sure, if you can't give it to them, who is there to be found that can?"

"Throth, Paddy Traynor, although I say it that should not say it, there's truth in that, at all evints. The same knowledge has cost me many a weary blisthur an' sore heel in huntin' it up an' down, through mountain an' glen, in Ulsther, Munsther, Leinsther, an' Connaught—not forgettin' the Highlands of Scotland, where there's what they call the 'short prophecy,' or second sight, but wherein there's afther all but little of the Irish or long prophecy, that regards what's to befall the winged woman that flew into the wilderness. No, no—their second sight isn't thrue prophecy at all. If a man goes out to fish, or steal a cow, an' that he happens to be drowned or shot, another man that has the second sight will see this in his mind about or afther the time it happens. Why, that's little. Many a time our own

Irish drames are aiqual to it; an' indeed I have it from a knowledgeable man, that the gift they boast of has four parents—an empty stomach, thin air, a weak head, an' stron whisky, an' that a man must have all these, espishilly the last, before he can have the second sight properly; an' it's my own opinion. Now, I have a little book (indeed I left my books with a friend down at Errigle) that contains a prophecy of the milk-white hind an' the bloody panther, an' a forebodin' of the slaughter there's to be in the Valley of the Black Pig, as foretold by Beal Derg, or the prophet wid the red mouth, who never was known to speak but when he prophesied, or to prophesy but when he spoke."

"The Lord bless and keep us!—an' why was he called the Man wid the Red Mouth, Barney?"

"I'll tell you that; first, bekase he always prophesied about the slaughter and fightin' that was to take place in the time to come; an', secondly, bekase, while he spoke, the red blood always trickled out of his mouth, as a proof that what he foretould was true."

"Glory be to God, but that's wondherful all out. Well, well!"

"Ay, an' Beal Derg, or the Red Mouth, is still livin'."

"Livin'! why, is he a man of our own time?"

"Of our own time! The Lord help you! It's more than a thousand years since he made the prophecy. The case, you see, is this: he an' the ten thousand witnesses are lyin' in an enchanted sleep in one of the Montherlony mountains."

"An' how is that known, Barney?"

"It's known. Every night at a certain hour one of the witnesses—an' they're all sogers, by the way—must come out to look for the sign that's to come."

"An' what is that, Barney?"

"It's the fiery cross; an' when he sees one on aich of the four mountains of the north, he's to know that the same sign's abroad in all the other parts of the kingdom. Beal Derg an' his men are then to waken up, an' by their aid the Valley of the Black Pig is to be set free forever."

"An' what is the Black Pig, Barney?"

"The Prospitarian church, that stretches from Enniskillen to Darry, an' back again from Darry to Enniskillen."

Well, well, Barney, but prophecy is a strange thing to be sure! Only think of men livin' a thousand years!"

'Every night one of Beal Derg's men must go to the mouth of the cave, which opens of itself, an' then look out for the sign that's expected. He walks up to the top of the mountain, an' turns to the four corners of the heavans, to thry if he can see it; an' when he finds that he cannot, he goes back to Beal Derg, who, afther the other touches him, starts up, an' axes him, 'Is the time come?' He replies, 'No; the *man is*, but the *hour is not!*' an' that instant they're both asleep again. Now, you see, while the soger is on the mountain top, the mouth of the cave is open, an' any one may go in that might happen to see it. One man it appears did, an' wishin' to know from curiosity whether the sogers were dead or livin', he touched one of them wid his hand, who started up an' axed him the same question, 'Is the time come?' Very fortunately he said '*No;*' an' that minute the soger was as sound in his trance as before."

"An', Barney, what did the soger mane when he said, 'The man is, but the hour is not'?"

"What did he mane? I'll tell you that. The man is Bonyparty; which manes, when put into proper explanation, the *right side;* that is, the true cause. Larned men have found *that* out."

"Barney, wasn't Columkill a great prophet?"

"He was a great man entirely at prophecy. He prophesied 'that the cock wid the purple comb is to have both his wings clipped by one of his own breed before the struggle come.' Before that time, too, we're to have the Black Militia, an' afther that it is time for every man to be prepared."

"An', Barney, who is the cock wid the purple comb?"

"Why, the Orangemen to be sure. Isn't purple their color, the dirty thieves?"

"An' the Black Militia, Barney, who are they?"

"I have gone far an' near, through north an' through south,

up an' down, by hill an' hollow, till my toes were corned an' my heels in griskins, but could find no one able to resolve that, or bring it clear out o' the prophecy. They're to be sogers in black, an' all their arms an' 'coutrements is to be the same color; an' farther than that is not known *as yet*."

"It's a wondher *you* don't know it, Barney, for there's little about prophecy that you haven't at your finger ends."

"Three birds is to meet (Barney proceeded in a kind of recitative enthusiasm) upon the saes—two ravens an' a dove—the two ravens is to attack the dove until she's at the point of death; but before they take her life, an eagle comes and tears the two ravens to pieces, an' the dove recovers.

"There's to be two cries in the kingdom; one of them is to rache from the Giants' Causeway to the centre house of the town of Sligo; the other is to rache from the Falls of Belcek to the Mill of Louth, which is to be turned three times with human blood; but this is not to happen until a man with two thumbs an' six fingers upon his right hand happens to be the miller."

"Who's to give the sign of freedom to Ireland?"

"The little boy wid the red coat that's born a dwarf, lives a giant, and dies a dwarf again! He's lightest of foot, but leaves the heaviest foot-mark behind him. An' it's he that is to give the sign of freedom to Ireland!"

"There's a period to come when Antichrist is to be upon the earth, attended by his two body servants, Gog and Magog. Who are they, Barney?"

"They are the sons of Hegog an' Shegog, or in other words of Death an' Destruction, and cousin-jarmins to the evil one himself, which of coorse is the raison why he promotes them."

"Lord save us! But I hope that won't be in our time, Barney!"

"Antichrist is to come from the land of Crame o' Tarthar (Crim Tartary), which will account for himself an' his army breathin' fire an' brimstone out of their mouths.

"The prophet of the Black Stone is to come, who was born never to prognosticate a lie. He is to be a mighty hunter, an' instead of riding to his fetlocks *in* blood, he is to ride *upon* it, to the admiration of his times. It's of him it is said 'that he is to be the only prophet that ever went on horseback!'

"Then there's Bardolphus, who, as there was a prophet wid the red mouth, is called 'the prophet wid the red nose.' Ireland was, it appears from ancient books, undher wather for many hundred years before her discovery; but bein' allowed to become visible one day in every year, the enchantment was broken by a sword that was thrown upon the earth, an' from that out she remained dry, an' became inhabited. 'Woe, woe, woe,' says Bardolphus, 'the time is to come when we'll have a second deluge, an' Ireland is to be undher wather once more. A well is to open at Cork that will cover the whole island from the Giants' Causeway to Cape Clear. In them days St. Patrick will be despised, an' will stand over the pleasant houses wid his pasthoral crook in hand, crying out *Cead mille failtha* in vain! Woe, woe, woe,' says Bardolphus, 'for in them days there will be a great confusion of colors among the people; there will be neither red noses nor pale cheeks, an' the divine face of man, alas! will put forth blossoms no more. The heart of the times will become changed; an' when they rise up in the morning, it will come to pass that there will be no longer light heads or shaking hands among Irishmen! Woe, woe, woe, men, women and children will then die, an' their only complaint, like all those who perished in the flood of ould, will be wather on the brain—wather on the brain! Woe, woe, woe,' says Bardolphus, 'for the changes that is to come, an' the misfortunes that's to befall the many for the noddification of the few! an' yet such things must be, for I, in virtue of the red spirit that dwells in me, must prophesy them. In those times men will be shod in liquid fire an' not be burned; their breeches shall be made of fire, an' will not burn them; their bread shall be made of fire, an' will not burn them; their meat shall be made of fire, an' will not burn them; an' why?—Oh, woe, woe, wather shall so prevail that the coolness of their bodies will keep them safe; yea, they shall even get fat, fair, an' be full of health an' strength, by wearing garments wrought out of liquid fire, by eating liquid fire, an' all because they do not drink liquid fire—an' this calamity shall come to pass,' says Bardolphus, the prophet of the red nose.

"Two widows shall be grinding at the Mill of Louth (so saith the prophecy); one shall be taken and the other left."

Thus would Barney proceed, repeating such ludicrous and heterogeneous mixtures of old traditionary prophecies and spurious quotations from Scripture as were concocted for him by those who took delight in amusing themselves and others at the expense of his inordinate love for prophecy.

"But, Barney, touching the Mill o' Louth, of the two widows grindin' there, whether will the one that is taken or the one that is left be the best off?"

"The prophecy doesn't say," replied Barney, "an' that's a matther that larned men are very much divided about. My own opinion is, that the one that is taken will be the best off; betune wars an' pestilences an' famine, the men are to be so scarce that several of them are to be torn to pieces by the women in their struggles to see who will get them for husbands. That time they say is to come."

Such were the speculations upon which the harmless mind of Barney M'Haighrey ever dwelt. From house to house, from parish to parish, and from province to province, did he thus trudge, never in a hurry, but always steady and constant in his motions. He might be not inaptly termed the Old Mortality of traditionary prophecy, which he often chiseled anew, added to, and improved, in a manner that generally gratified himself and his hearers. He was a harmless, kind man, and never known to stand in need of either clothes or money. He paid little attention to the silent business of ongoing life, and was consequently very nearly an abstraction. He was always on the alert, however, for the result of a battle; and after having heard it, he would give no opinion whatsoever until he had first silently compared it with his own private theory in prophecy. If it agreed with this, he immediately published it in connection with his established text; but if it did not, he never opened his lips on the subject.

His class has disappeared, and indeed it is so much the better, for the minds of the people were thus filled with antiquated nonsense that did them no good. Poor Barney, to his great mortification, lived to see with his own eyes the failure of his most favorite prophecies, but he was not to be disheartened even by this; though some might fail, all could not; and his stock was too varied and extensive not to furnish him with a sufficient number of others over which to cherish his imagination and expatiate during the remainder of his inoffensive life.

THE DESERTER.

[In the course of his desultory peregrinations our poet necessarily encountered many a strange and humorous companion, and he seldom was at a loss to discover their salient attractive points, and without any apparent effort, induce them to lay open before him whatever mental treasures they possessed. It was from these humble sources that he gathered the materials for some of his most comical and interesting stories, and that which we next lay before our readers it is supposed was first related to Zozimus by a veteran soldier—a relic of Waterloo—and having received from the poet some of his characteristic touches, afterwards delighted many a charmed audience. Although the form under which we present it to our readers has come through the hands of one of Ireland's most distinguished *littérateurs*, it is yet but a faint reflex of the poet's version, in the absence of which we must be content with that of Lever:]

"Well, it's a good many years ago my father 'listed in the North Cork, just to oblige Mr. Barry, the landlord there; 'For,' says he, 'Phil,' says he, 'it's not a soldier ye'll be at all, but my own man, to brush my clothes and go errands, and the like o' that, and the king, long life to him, will help to pay ye for your trouble—ye understand me.' Well, my father agreed, and Mr. Barry was as good as his word. Never a guard did my father mount, nor as much as a drill had he, nor a roll-call, nor any thing at all, save and except wait on the Captain, his master, just as pleasant as need be, and no inconvenience in life.

"Well, for three years this went on as I'm telling, and the regiment was ordered down to Bantry, because of a report that the 'boys' was rising down there; and the second evening there was a night party patrolling, with Captain Barry, for six hours in the rain, and the Captain, God be marciful to him, tuk cowld and died; more betoken, they said it was drink, but my father says it wasn't; 'For,' says he, 'after he tuk eight tumblers comfortable,' my father mixed the ninth, and the Captain waved his hand this way, as much as to say he'd have no more. 'Is it that ye mean?' says my father, and the Captain nodded. 'Musha, but it's sorry I am,' says my father, 'to see you this way, for ye must be bad entirely to leave off in the beginning of the evening.' And thrue for him, the Captain was dead in the morning.

"A sorrowful day it was for my father, when he died; it was the finest place in the world; little to do; plenty of divarsion; and a kind man he was—when he was sober. Well, then, when the Captain was buried, and all was over, my father hoped they'd be for letting him away; as he said, ' Sure, I'm no use in life to anybody save the man that's gone, for his ways are all I know, and I never was a sodger.' But, upon my conscience, they had other thoughts in their heads; for they ordered him into the ranks to be drilled just like the recruits they took the day before.

"'Musha, isn't this hard?' said my father; ' here I am an ould vitrin that ought to be discharged on a pension, with two-and-six pence a day, obliged to go capering about the barrack-yard practicing the goose step, or some other nonsense not becoming my age nor my habits;' but so it was. Well, this went on for some time, and sure, if they were hard on my father, didn't he have his revenge, for he nigh broke their hearts with his stupidity; oh! nothing in life could equal him; not a thing, no matter how easy, he could learn at all; and so far from caring for being in confinement, it was that he liked best. Every sergeant in the regiment had a trial of him, but all to no good, and he seemed striving so hard to learn all the while, that they were loth to punish him, the ould rogue!

"This was going on for some time, when, one day, news came in that a body of the rebels, as they called them, was coming down from the Gap of Mulnavick to storm the town and burn all before them. The whole regiment was, of course, under arms, and great preparations were made for a battle; meanwhile patrols were ordered to scour the roads, and sentries posted at every turn of the way, and every rising ground, to give warning when the boys came in sight, and my father was placed at the bridge of Drumsnag, in the wildest and bleakest part of the whole country, with nothing but furze mountains on every side, and a straight road going over the top of them.

"'This is pleasant,' says my father, as soon as they left him there alone by himself, with no human crayture to speak to, nor a whisky shop within ten miles of him; 'cowld comfort,' says he, 'on a winter's day; and faix, but I've a mind to give ye the slip.'

"Well, he put his gun down on the bridge, and he lit his pipe, and he sat down under an ould tree, and began to ruminate upon his affairs.

"'Oh, then, it's wishing it well I am,' says he, 'for sodgering; and ill will to the hammer that struck the shilling that 'listed me, that's all,' for he was mighty low in his heart.

"Just then a noise came rattling down near him; he listened, and before he could get on his legs, down comes the General, ould Cohoon, with an orderly after him.

"'Who goes that?' says my father.

"'The round,' says the General, looking about all the time to see where was the sentry, for my father was snug under the tree.

"'What round?' says my father.

"'The grand round,' says the General, more puzzled than afore.

"'Pass on, grand round, and God save you kindly,' says my father, putting his pipe in his mouth again, for he thought all was over.

"'Where are you?' says the General; for sorrow bit of my father could he see yet.

"'It's here I am,' says he, 'and a cowld place I have of it; and av it wasn't for the pipe I'd be lost entirely.'

"The words wasn't well out of his mouth, when the General began laughing till ye'd think he'd fall off his horse; and the dragoon behind him—more by token, they say it wasn't right for him—laughed as loud as himself.

"'Yer a droll sentry,' says the General, as soon as he could speak.

"'Be gorra, it's little fun there's left in me,' says my father, 'with this drilling and parading, and thrampin' about the roads all night.'

"'And is this the way you salute your officer?' says the General.

"'Just so,' says my father, 'sarra a more politeness ever they taught me.'

"'What regiment do you belong to?' says the General.

"'The North Cork,' says my father, with a sigh.

"'They ought to be proud of ye,' says the General.

"'I'm sorry for it,' says my father, sorrowfully, 'for maybe they'll keep me the longer.'

"'Well, my good fellow,' says the General, 'I haven't more time to waste here; but let me teach you something before I go. Whenever your officer passes, it's your duty to present arms to him.'

"'Arrah, it's jokin' ye are,' says my father.

"'No, I'm in earnest,' says he, 'as ye might learn to your cost if I brought you to a court-martial.'

"'Well, there's no knowing,' says my father, 'what they'd be up to; but sure if that's all, I'll do it with all "the veins," whenever yer coming this way again.'

"The General began to laugh again here, but said:

"'I'm coming back in the evening,' says he, 'and mind you don't forget your respect to your officer.'

"'Never fear, sir,' says my father, 'and many thanks to you for your kindness for telling me.'

"Away went the General, and the orderly after him, and in ten minutes they were out of sight.

"The night was falling fast, and one-half of the mountain was quite dark already, when my father began to think they were forgetting him entirely. He looked one way, and he looked another, but sorra bit of a sergeant's guard was coming to relieve him. There he was, fresh and fasting, and daren't go for the bare life. 'I'll give you a quarter of an hour more,' says my father, 'till the light leaves that rock up there; after that,' says he, 'I'll be off, av it cost me what it may!'

"Well, sure enough, his courage was not needed this time; for what did he see at the same moment but the shadow of something coming down the road, opposite the bridge; he looked again; and then he made out the General himself, that was walking his horse down the steep part of the mountain, followed by the orderly. My father immediately took up his musket off the wall, settled his belts, shook the ashes out of his pipe, and put it in his pocket, making himself as smart and neat-looking as he could be, determining, when ould Cohoon came up, to ask him for leave to go home, at least for the night. Well, by this time the General was turning a sharp part of the cliff that looks down upon the bridge, from where you might look five miles round on every side. 'He sees me,' says my father; 'but I'll be just as quick as himself.' No sooner said than done; for coming forward to the parapet of the bridge, he up with his musket to his shoulder, and presented it straight at the General. It wasn't well there, when the officer pulled up his horse quite short, and shouted out, 'Sentry—sentry!'

"'Anan!' says my father, still covering him.

"'Down with your musket, you rascal; don't you see it's the grand round?'

"'To be sure I do,' says my father, never changing for a minute.

"'The ruffian will shoot me,' says the General.

"'Not a fear,' says my father, 'av it doesn't go off of itself.'

"'What do you mean by that, you villain?' says the General, scarce able to speak with fright, for every turn he gave on his horse my father followed with the gun—'What do you mean?'

"'Sure, aint I presenting?' says my father; 'tear an' ages, do you want me to fire next?'

"With that the General drew a pistol from his holster, and took deliberate aim at my father; and there they both stood for five minutes, looking at each other, the orderly, all the while, breaking his heart laughing behind the rock; for, ye see, the General knew av he retreated that my father might fire on purpose, and av he came on that he might fire by chance; and sorra bit he knew what was best to be done.

"'Are ye going to pass the evening up there, grand round?' says my father, 'for it's tired I'm getting houldin' this so long!'

"'Port arms,' shouted the General, as if on parade.

"'Sure I can't, till yer passed,' says my father, angrily, 'and my hand's trembling already.'

"'By Jove! I shall be shot,' says the General.

"'Be gorra, it's what I'm afraid of,' says my father; and the words wasn't out of his mouth before off went the musket, bang, and down fell the General, smack on the ground, senseless. Well, the orderly ran out at this, and took him up and examined his wound; but it wasn't a wound at all, only the wadding of the gun, for my father—God be kind to him—ye see, could do nothing right, and so he bit off the wrong end of the cartridge when he put it in the gun, and by reason there was no bullet in it. Well, from that day after they never got sight of him, for the instant the General dropped, he sprung over the bridge wall, and got away; and what, between living in a lime-kiln for two months, eating nothing but blackberries and sloes, and other disguises, he never returned to the army, but ever after took to a civil situation, and driv a hearse for many years."

THE MATCHMAKER.

[If there was anything which the gifted, but for a time neglected story-teller and *improvvisatore*, loved to dwell on more than another, it was the ancient customs of the people of his own class—customs and habits which even in his day were fast dying out. All that concerned the affections of the peasantry and the humbler denizens of his native city, were to him of much more importance than the simulated love and friendship of what are sometimes called the higher classes. His description of the *Cosherer*, or Matchmaker, which, as soon as it became known, found its way, "with notes and comments," into a Dublin magazine, is particularly good, though the occupation of the Rose Moans is pretty well gone in these latter unsentimental days. We will, however, give the sketch as nearly as possible as he related it, though, of course, somewhat improved by his more accomplished plagiarist.]

One of the best specimens of the Cosherer, or Matchmaker, I ever met was old Rose Mahon, or, as she was called Moan, a name, we doubt, fearfully expressive of the consequences which too frequently followed her negotiations. Rose was a tidy creature of middle size, who always went dressed in a short crimson cloak much faded, a striped red and blue drugget petticoat, and a heather-colored gown of the same fabric. When walking, which she did with the aid of a light hazel staff hooked at the top, she generally kept the hood of her cloak over her head, which gave her whole figure a picturesque effect; and when she threw it back one could not help admiring how well her small but symmetrical features agreed with the dowd cap of white linen, with a plain muslin border, which she wore. A pair of blue stockings and sharp-pointed shoes high in the heels completed her dress. Her features were good-natured and Irish; but there lay over the whole countenance an expression of quickness and sagacity, contracted no doubt by a habitual exercise of penetration and circumspection. At the time I saw her she was very old, and I believe had the reputation of being the last in that part of the country who was known to go about from house to house spinning on the distaff, an instrument which has now passed away, being more conveniently replaced by the spinning-wheel.

The manner and style of Rose's visits were different from those of any other who could come to a farmer's house, or even to an humble cottage, for to the inmates of both were her services equally rendered. Let us suppose, for instance, the whole female part of a farmer's family assembled of a summer evening about five o'clock, each engaged in some domestic employment; in runs a lad who has been sporting about, breathlessly exclaiming, whilst his eyes are lit up with delight, "Mother! mother! here's Rose Moan coming down the boreen!" "Get out, avick; no she's not." "Bad cess to me but she is; that I may never stir if she isn't! Now!" The whole family are instantly at the door to see if it be she, with the exception of the prettiest of them all, Kitty, who sits at her wheel, and immediately begins to croon over an old Irish air which is sadly out of tune; and well do we know, notwithstanding the mellow tones of that sweet voice, why it is so, and also why that youthful cheek in which health and beauty meet is now the color of crimson.

"*Oh, Rosha, acushla, cead millia faille ghud!* (Rose, darlin', a hundred thousand welcomes to you!) Och, musha, what kep' you away so long, Rose? Sure you won't lave us this month o' Sundays, Rose?" are only a few of the cordial expressions of hospitality and kindness with which she is received. But Kitty, whose cheek but a moment ago was carmine, why is it now pale as the lily?

"An' what news, Rose?" asks one of her sisters, "sure you'll tell us everything; won't you?"

"Throth, avillish, *I have no bad news*, anyhow—an' as to tellin' you *all*—Biddy, *thig dumh*, let me alone. No, I have no bad news, God be praised, *but good news.*"

Kitty's cheek is again crimson, and her lips, ripe and red as cherries, expand with the sweet soft smile of her country, exhibiting a set of teeth for which many a countess would barter thousands, and giving out a breath more delicious than the fragrance of a summer meadow. Oh, no wonder, indeed, that the kind heart of Rose contains in its recesses a message to her as tender as ever was transmitted from man to woman!

"An', Kitty, acushla, where's the welcome from *you*, that's my favorite? Now don't be jealous, childre; sure you all know she is, an' ever an' always was."

"If it's not upon my lips, it's in my heart, Rose, an' from that heart you're welcome!"

She rises up and kisses Rose, who gives her one glance of meaning, accompanied by the slightest imaginable smile; and a gentle but significant pressure of the hand, which thrills to her heart and diffuses a sense of ecstasy through her whole spirit. Nothing now remains but the opportunity, which is equally sought for by Rose and her, to hear without interruption the purport of her lover's communication; and this we leave to lovers to imagine.

In some parts of Ireland, however, there occur among the very poorest classes some of the hardest and most penurious bargains in matchmaking that ever were heard of or known. Now strangers might imagine that all this close higgling proceeds from a spirit naturally mean and sordid, but it is not so. The real secret of it lies in the poverty and necessity of the parties, and chiefly in the bitter experience of their parents, who, having come together in a state of destitution, are anxious, each as much at the expense of the other as possible, to prevent their children from experiencing the same privation and misery which they themselves felt. Many a time have matches been suspended or altogether broken off because one party refuses to give his son a slip of a pig, or another his daughter a pair of blankets; and it was no unusual thing for a matchmaker to say, "Never mind; I have it all settled *but the slip.*" One might naturally wonder why those who are so shrewd and provident upon this subject do not strive to prevent early marriages where the poverty is so great. So, unquestionably, they ought, but it is a settled usage of the country, and one, too, which Irishmen have never been in the habit of considering as an evil. We have no doubt that if they once began to reason upon it as such, they would be very strongly disposed to check a custom which has been the means of involving themselves and their unhappy offspring in misery and penury.

Rose, like many others in this world who are not conscious of the same failing, smelt strongly of the shop; in other words, her conversation had a strong matrimonial tendency. No two beings ever lived so decidedly antithetical to each other in this point of view as the Matchmaker and the Keener. Mention the name of an individual or a family to the Keener, and the medium through which her memory passes back to them is that of her professed employment—a mourner at wakes and funerals.

"Don't you know young Kelly of Tamlaght?"

"I do, avick," replies the Keener, "and what about him?"

"Why, he was married to-day mornin' to ould Jack McCluskey's daughter."

"Well, God grant them luck an' happiness, poor things! I do indeed remember his father's wake an' funeral well—ould Risthard Kelly of Tamlaght—a dacent corpse he made for his years, an' well he looked. But indeed I *known* by the color that sted in his cheeks, an' the limbs remainin' soople for the twenty-four hours afther his departure, that some of the family 'ud follow him afore the year was out; an' so she did. The youngest daughter, poor thing, by raison of a cowld she got, overheatin' herself at a dance, was stretched beside him that very day was eleven months; and God knows it was from the heart my grief came for *her*—to see the poor handsome colleen laid low so soon. But when a gallopin' consumption sets in, avourneen, sure we all know what's to happen. In Crockaniska church-yard

they sleep—the Lord make both their beds in heaven this day!"
The very reverse of this, but at the same time as inveterately
professional, was Rose Moan.

"God save you, Rose."

"God save you kindly, avick. Eh!—let me look at you!
Aren't you red Billy M'Guirk's son from Ballagh?"

"I am, Rose. An' Rose, how is yourself an' the world gettin'
an?"

"Can't complain, dear, in such times. How are yez all at
home, alanna?" "Faix, middlin' well, Rose, thank God an'
you. You heard of my grand-uncle's death, big Ned M'Coul?"

"I did, avick, God rest him. Sure it's well I remimber his
weddin', poor man, by the same atoken that I know one that
helped him on with it a thrifle. He was married in a blue coat
and buckskins, and wore a scarlet waistcoat that you'd see three
miles off. Oh, well I remimber it. An' whin he was settin' out
that mornin' to the priest's house—'Ned,' says I, an' I whispered him, 'dhrop a button on the right knee afore you get the
words said.' '*Thighum*,' said he wid a smile, an' he slipped
ten thirteens into my hand as he spoke. 'I'll do it,' said he,
'and thin a fig for the fairies!' becase, you see, if there's a button of the right knee left unbuttoned, the fairies—this day's Friday, God stand betune us and harm!—can do neither hurt nor
harm to sowl or body, an' sure that's a great blessin', avick. He
left two fine slips o' girls behind him."

"He did so—as good-lookin' girls as there's in the parish."

"Faix, an' kind mother for them, avick. She'll be marryin'
agin, I'm judgin', she bein' sich a fresh, good-lookin' woman."

"Why, it's very likely, Rose."

"Throth its natural, achora. What can a lone woman do
wid such a large farm upon her hands, widout having some
one to manage it for her, an' prevint her from bein' imposed
on? But indeed the first thing she ought to do is to marry off
her two girls widout loss of time, in regard that it's hard to say
how a step-father an' thim might agree; and I've often known
the mother herself, when she had a fresh family comin' an her,

to be as unnatural to her fatherless children as if she was a stranger to thim, and that the same blood didn't run in their veins. Not saying that Mary M'Coul will or would act that way by her own; for indeed she's come of a kind ould stock, an' ought to have a good heart. Tell her, avick, when you see her, that I'll spind a day or two wid her—let me see—the day after to-morrow will be Palm Sunday—why, about the Aisther holidays."

"Indeed I will, Rose, with great pleasure."

"An' whisper, dear, jist tell her that I've a thing to say to her—that I had a long dish o' discoorse about her wid *a friend o' mine*. You won't forget now?"

"Oh, the dickens a forget!"

"Thank you, dear; God mark you to grace, avourneen! When you're a little ouldher, maybe I'll be a friend to you yet."

This last intimation was given with a kind of mysterious benevolence, very visible in the complacent shrewdness of her face, and with a twinkle in the eye, full of grave humor and considerable self-importance, leaving the mind of the person she spoke to in such an agreeable uncertainty as rendered it a matter of great difficulty to determine whether she was serious or only in jest, but at all events throwing the onus of inquiry upon him.

The ease and tact with which Rose could involve two young persons of opposite sexes in a mutual attachment, were very remarkable. In truth, she was a kind of matrimonial incendiary, who went through the country holding her torch now to this heart and again to that—first to one and then to another, until she had the parish more or less in a flame. And when we consider the combustible materials of which the Irish heart is composed, it is no wonder indeed that the labor of taking the census in Ireland increases at such a rapid rate. If Rose, for instance, met a young woman accidentally—and it was wonderful to think how regularly these accidental meetings took place—she would address her probably somewhat as follows:

"Arra, Biddy Sullivan, how are you, a-colleen?"

"Faix, bravely, thank you, Rose. How is yourself?"

"Indeed, thin, sorra bit o' the health we can complain of, Bhried, barrin' whin this pain in the back comes upon us. The last time I seen your mother, Biddy, she was complainin' of a *weid*.* I hope she's betther, poor woman?"

"Hut! bad scran to the thing ails her! She has as light a foot as e'er a one of us, an' can dance 'Jackson's mornin' brush' as well as ever she could."

"Throth, an' I'm proud to hear it. Och! och! 'Jackson's mornin' brush!' and it was she that *could* do it. Sure I remimber her wedding-day like yesterday. Ay, far an' near her fame wirt as a dancer; an' the clanest-made girl that ever came from Lisbuie. Like yesterday do I remember it, an' how the squire himself and the ladies from the Big House came down to see herself an' your father, the bride and groom—an' it wasn't on every hill head you'd get sich a couple—dancin' the same 'Jackson's mornin' brush.' Oh! it was far an' her fame wint for dancin' that. An' is there no news wid you, Bhried, at all, at all?"

"The sorra word, Rose; where ud I get news? Sure it's yourself that's always on the fut that ought to have the news for *us*, Rose alive."

"An' maybe I have, too. I was spakin' to a friend o' mine about you the other day."

"A friend o' yours, Rose! Why, what friend could it be?"

"A friend o' mine—ay, an' of yours too. Maybe you have more friends than you think, Biddy—and kind ones, too, as far as wishin' you well goes, 'tany rate. Ay, have you, faix, an' friends that e'er a girl in the parish might be proud to hear named in the one day wid her. Awouh!"

"Bedad we're in luck, thin, for that's more than I know of. An' who may these great friends of ours be, Rose?"

"Awouh! Faix, as dacent a boy as ever broke bread the same boy is, 'And,' says he, 'if I had goold in bushelfuls, I'd think it too little for that girl;' but, poor lad, he's not aisy or

---

*A feverish cold.

happy in his mind in regard o' that. 'I'm afeard,' says he, 'that she'd put scorn upon me, an' not think me her aiquals. An' no more I am,' says he again, 'for where, afther all, would you get the likes of Biddy Sullivan!'—Poor boy! throth, my heart aches for him!"

"Well, can't you fall in love wid him yourself, Rose, whoever he is?"

"Indeed, an' if I was at your age, it would be no shame to me to do so; but, to tell you the thruth, the sorra often ever the likes of Paul Heffernan came across me."

"Paul Heffernan! Why, Rose," replied Biddy, smiling with the assumed lightness of indifference, "is that your beauty? If it is, why, keep him, an' make much of him."

"Oh, wurrah! the differ there is between the hearts an' tongues of some people—one from another—an' the way they spaik behind others' backs! Well, well, I'm sure that wasn't the way he spoke of you, Biddy; an' God forgive you for runnin' down the poor boy as you're doin'. Trogs! I believe you're the only girl would do it."

"Who, me? I'm not runnin' him down. I'm neither runnin' him up nor down. I have neither good nor bad to say about him—the boy's a black sthranger to me, barrin' to know his face."

"Faix, an' he's in consate wid you these three months past, an' intinds to be at the dance on Friday next, in Jack Gormly's new house. Now, good-bye, alanna; keep your own counsel till the time comes, an' mind what I said to you. It's not behind every ditch the likes of Paul Heffernan grows. *Bannaght lhath!* My blessin' be wid you!"

Thus would Rose depart just at the critical moment, for well she knew that by husbanding her information and leaving the heart something to find out, she took the most effectual steps to excite and sustain that kind of interest which is apt ultimately to ripen, even from its own agitation, into the attachment she is anxious to promote.

The next day, by a meeting similarly accidental, she comes in contact with Paul Heffernan, who, honest lad, had never probably bestowed a thought upon Biddy Sullivan in his life.

"*Morrow ghud*, Paul!—how is your father's son, ahager?"

'*Morrow ghuteka*, Rose!—my father's son wants nothin' but a good wife, Rosha.'

An' it's not every set day or bonfire night that a good wife is to be had, Paul—that is, a *good* one, as you say; for, throth, there's many o' them in the market, sich as they are. I was talkin' about you to a friend of mine the other day—an', trogs, I'm afeard you're not worth all the abuse we gave you."

"More power to you, Rose! I'm oblaged to you. But who is the friend in the mane time?"

"Poor girl! Throth, when your name slipped out an her, the point of a rush would take a drop of blood out o' her cheek, the way she crimsoned up. 'An', Rose,' says she, 'if ever I know you to breathe it to man or mortual, my lips I'll never open to you to my dyin' day.' Trogs, whin I looked at her, an' the tears standin' in her purty black eyes, I thought I didn't see a betther favored girl, for both face and figure, this many a day, than the same Biddy Sullivan."

"Biddy Sullivan! Is that long Jack's daughter of Cargah?"

"The same. But, Paul, avick, if a syllable o' what I tould you——"

"Hut, Rose! honor bright! Do you think me a *stag*, that I'd go and inform on you?"

"Whisper, Paul; she'll be at the dance on Friday next in Jack Gormly's new house. So *bannaght lhath*, an' think o' what I betrayed to you."

Thus did Rose very quietly and sagaciously bind two young hearts together, who probably might otherwise have never for a moment even thought of each other. Of course, when Paul and Biddy met at the dance on the following Friday, the one was the object of the closest attention to the other, and each being prepared to witness strong proofs of attachment from the opposite party, everything fell out exactly according to their expectations.

THE GHOST.

[No one was more deeply versed in "old folk lore" than the gifted poet, and his versatility in this regard was only equaled by the readiness with which he gratified his eager audiences. Fairy legends and ghost stories formed no inconsiderable portion of his vast mental treasures, and the gravity with which he related the latter added not a little to their intrinsic merit.

The story which we here present to our readers was a favorite one with the poet, who solemnly averred (and who but a churl would doubt his word?) that the events narrated happened to a particular friend of his own. That it was a favorite with his hearers also is evidenced by the fact that, unlike many of his lucubrations which are lost to us forever, it was saved from such an untimely and deplorable fate by Charles Lever, who, like all others that preyed on the forgiving poet, appropriated it to himself, and put it in the mouth of Mickey Free. Not content with this, the novelist gave it some fresh touches, not, we think, to its improvement. We prefer, therefore, to give it as nearly as possible in the words of the lamented Zozimus, and without further preface we will lay it before our readers.]

"Well, I believe your honor heard me tell long ago how my father left the army, and the way that he took to another line of life that was more to his liking. And so it was, he was happy as the day was long; he drove a hearse for Mr. Callaghan of Cork for many years, and a pleasant place it was; for ye see, my father was a cute man and knew something of the world; and though he was a droll devil, and could sing a funny song when he was among us boys, no sooner had he the big black cloak on him, and the weepers, and he seated on the high box with the six long-tailed blacks before him, you'd really think it was his own mother was inside, he looked so melancholy and miserable. The sexton and grave-digger was nothing to my father; and he had a look about his eye—to be sure there was a reason for it—that you'd think he was up all night crying, though it's little indulgence he took that way.

"Well, of all Mr. Callaghan's men, there was none so great a favorite as my father; the neighbors were all fond of him.

"'A kind crayture every inch of him,' the women would say. 'Did ye see his face at Mrs. Delany's funeral?'

"'True for you,' another would remark; 'he mistook the road with grief, and stopped at a shebeen-house instead of Kilmurry church.'

"I need say no more, only one thing, that it was principally among the farmers and the country people my father was liked so much. The great people and the quality—I ax your pardon —but sure isn't it true, Mister Charles, they don't fret so much after their fathers and brothers, and they care little who's driving them, whether it was a decent, respectable man like my father, or a chap with a grin on him like a rat-trap? And so it happened that my father used to travel half the county, going here and there wherever there was trade stirring; and, faix, a man didn't think himself rightly buried if my father wasn't there; for ye see he knew all about it; he could tell to a quart of sperits what would be wanting for a wake; he knew all the good cryers for miles around; and I've heard it was a beautiful sight to see him standing on a hill, arranging the procession as they walked into the church-yard and giving the word like a captain.

"'Come on, the *stiff*—now the friends of the *stiff*—now the pop'lace.'

"'That's what he used to say; and, troth, he was always repeating it when he was a little gone in drink—for that's the time his spirits would rise—and he'd think he was burying half Munster.

"And sure it was a real pleasure and a pride to be buried in them times; for av it was only a small farmer with a potato garden, my father would come down with the black cloak on him, and three yards of crape behind his hat, and set all the children crying and yelling for half a mile round; and then the way he'd walk before them with a spade on his shoulder, and sticking it down in the ground, clap his hat on the top of it to make it look like a chief mourner. It was a beautiful sight."

"But, Mike, if you indulge much longer in this flattering recollection of your father, I'm afraid we shall lose sight of the ghost entirely."

"No fear in life, your honor, I'm coming to him now. Well, it was this way it happened:—In the winter of the great frost, about forty-two or forty-three years ago, the priest of Tulloughmuray took ill and died; he was sixty years priest of the parish, and mightily beloved by all the people, and good reason for it; a pleasanter man and a more social crayture never lived—'twas himself was the life of the whole country-side. A wedding nor a christening wasn't lucky av he wasn't there, sitting at the top of the table, with as much kindness in his eye as would make the fortunes of twenty hypocrites if they had it among them. And then he was so good to the poor; the Priory was always full of ould men and ould women, sitting around the big fire in the kitchen, so that the cook could hardly get near it. There they were eating their meals and burning their shins, till they were speckled like a trout's back, and grumbling all the time; but Father Dwyer liked them, and he would have them.

"'Where have they to go,' he'd say, 'av it wasn't to me? Give Molly Kinshela a lock of that bacon. Tim, it's a cowld morning.'

"Ah, that's the way he'd spake to them; but sure goodness is no warrant for living, any more than devilment; and so he got cowld in his feet at a station, and he rode home in the heavy snow without his big coat—for he gave it away to a blind man on the road—and in three days he was dead.

"I see you're getting impatient; so I'll not stop to say what grief was in the parish when it was known; but troth there never was seen the like before; not a crayture would lift a spade for two days, and there was more whisky sold in that time than at the whole spring fair. Well, on the third day the funeral set out, and never was the equal of it in them parts: first, there was my father; he came special from Cork with the six horses all in new black, and plumes like little poplar trees; then came Father Dwyer, followed by the two coadjutors in beautiful surplices, walking bare-headed, with the little boys of the Priory school, two and two."

"Well, Mike, I'm sure it was very fine; but for heaven's sake spare me all these descriptions, and get on to the ghost."

"Faith, your honor's in a great hurry for the ghost; maybe you won't like him when ye have him, but I'll go faster if you please. Well, Father Dwyer, ye see, was born at Aghan-lish, of an ould family, and he left it in his will that he was to be buried in the family vault; and, as Aghan-lish was eighteen miles up the mountains, it was getting late when they drew near. By that time the great procession was all broke up and gone home. The mourners stopped to dine at the 'Blue Bellows' at the cross-roads; the little boys took to pelting snow-balls; there was a fight or two on the way besides; and in fact, except an ould deaf fellow that my father took to mind the horses, he was quite alone. Not that he minded that same; for when the crowd was gone my father began to sing a droll song, and tould the deaf chap that it was a lamentation. At last they came in sight of Aghan-lish. It was a lonesome, melancholy-looking place, with nothing near it except two or three ould fir-trees, and a small slated house with one window, where the sexton lived, and even that same was shut up, and a padlock on the door. Well, my father was not over-much pleased at the look of matters; but, as he was never hard put to know what to do, he managed to get the coffin into the vestry; and then, when he unharnessed the horses, he went to an ould disolate and desarted house in the neighborhood, where he prepared to make himself comfortable for the night; and then he made a roaring fire on the ould hearth—for there was plenty of bog fir there—closed the windows with the black cloaks, and wrapping two round himself, he sat down to cook a little supper he brought with him in case of need.

"Well, you may think it was melancholy enough to pass the night up there alone, with the wind howling about on every side, and the snow-drift beating against the walls; but, as the fire burned brightly, and the little plate of rashers and eggs smoked temptingly before him, my father mixed a jug of the strongest punch, and sat down as happy as a king. As long as he was eating away, he had no time to be thinking of anything else; but when all was done and he looked about him, he began to feel very low and melancholy in his heart. There was the mourning cloaks that he had stuck up against the windows moving backward and forward like living things; and, outside, the wild cry of the plover as he flew past, and the night-owl sitting in a nook of the old house. 'I wish it was morning, anyhow,' said my father, 'for this is a lonesome place to be in; and, faix, he'll be a cunning fellow that catches me passing the night this way again.' Now there was one thing distressed him most of all: my father used always to make fun of the ghosts and sperits the neighbors would tell of, pretending there was no such thing; and now the thought came to him, 'Maybe they'll revenge themselves on me to-night, when they have me up here alone;' and with that he made another jug stronger than the first, and tried to remember a few prayers in case of need; but somehow his mind was not too clear, and he said afterwards he was always mixing up old songs and toasts with the prayers, and when he thought he had just got hold of a beautiful psalm, it would turn out to be 'Tatter Jack Walsh,' or 'Limping James,' or something like that. The storm, meanwhile, was rising every moment, and parts of the old house were falling, as the wind shook the ruin; and my father's sperits, notwithstanding the punch, were lower than ever.

"'I made it too weak,' said he, as he set to work on a new jorum; and troth this time that was not the fault of it, for the first sup nearly choked him.

"'Ah!' said he now, 'I knew what it was; this is like the thing; and, Mr. Free, you are beginning to feel easy and comfortable; pass the jug; your very good health and song. I'm a little hoarse, it's true, but if the company will excuse—'

"And then he began knocking on an ould table with his knuckles, as if there was a room full of people asking him to sing: In short, my father was drunk as a fiddler; the last brew finished him, and he began roaring away all kinds of droll songs, and telling all manner of stories, as if he was at a great party.

"While he was capering this way about the room, he knocked down his hat, and with it a pack of cards he put into it before leaving home, for he was mighty fond of a game.

"'Will ye take a hand, Mr. Free?' said he, as he gathered them up and sat down beside the fire.

"'I'm convanient,' said he, and began dealing out as if there was a partner forninst him.

"When my father used to get this far in the story, he became very confused. He says that once or twice he mistook the liquor and took a pull at the bottle of potteen instead of the punch; and soon after that he slipped down on the ground and fell fast asleep. How long he lay that way he could never tell. When he awoke and looked up, his hair nearly stood on end with fright. What do you think he seen forninst him, sitting at the other side of the fire, but a real ghost; there he was, devil a lie in it, wrapped up in one of the mourning cloaks, trying to warm his hands at the fire.

"'*Salve hoc nomine patri!*' said my father, crossing himself; 'av you're a ghost, God presarve me!'

"'Good evening t'ye, Mr. Free,' said the ghost; 'and av I might be bould, what's in the jug?'—for ye see me father had it under his arm fast, and never let it go when he was asleep.

"'Potteen, sir,' said my father, for the ghost didn't look pleased at his talking Latin.

"'Ye might have the politeness to ax if one had a mouth on him,' then says the ghost.

"'Sure, I didn't think the like of you would taste sperits.'

"'Try me,' said the ghost; and with that he filled out a glass and tossed it off like a Christian.

"'Beamish!' says the ghost, smacking his lips.

"'The same,' says my father; 'and sure what's happened you has not spoilt your taste.'

"'If you'd mix a little hot,' says the ghost, 'I'm thinking it would be better; the night is mighty sevare.'

"'Anything that your honor pleases,' says my father, as he began to blow up a good fire to boil the water.

"'And what news is stirring?' says the ghost.

"'Not a word, your honor; times is bad; except the measles, there's nothing in our parts.'

"'And we're quite dead hereabouts, too,' says the ghost.

"'There's some of us so, anyhow,' says my father, with a sly look. 'Taste that, your honor.'

"'Pleasant and refreshing,' says the ghost; 'and now, Mr. Free, what do you say to a little spoil five, or beggar my neighbor?'

"'What will we play for?' says my father; for a thought just struck him—'maybe it's some trick of the devil to catch my soul.'

"'A pint of Beamish,' says the ghost.

"'Done,' says my father; 'cut for deal; the ace of clubs; you have it.'

"Now the whole time the ghost was dealing the cards my father never took his eyes off of him, for he wasn't quite aisy in his mind at al'; but when he saw him turn up the trump and take a strong drink afterwards, he got more at case, and began the game.

"How long they played it was never rightly known; but one thing is sure, they drank a cruel deal of spirits; three quart bottles my father brought with him were all finished, and by that time his brain was so confused with the liquor, and all he lost—for somehow he never won a game—that he was getting very quarrelsome.

"'You have your own luck of it,' says he, at last.

"'True for you; and, besides, we play a great deal where I come from.'

"'I've heard so,' says my father. 'I lead the knave, sir, spades; bad cess to it, lost again.'

"Now it was really very distressing; for by this time, though they only began for a pint of Beamish, my father went on betting till he lost the hearse and all the six horses, mourning cloaks, plumes and everything.

"'Are you tired, Mr. Free? maybe you'd like to stop?'

"'Stop! faith it's a nice time to stop; of course not.'

"'Well, what will ye play for now?'

"The way he said these words brought a trembling all over my father, and his blood curdled in his heart. 'Oh, murther!' says he to himself, 'it's my sowl he is wanting all the time.'

"'I've mighty little left,' says my father, looking at him keenly, while he kept shuffling the cards quick as lightning.

"'Mighty little; no matter, we'll give you plenty of time to pay, and if you can't do it, it shall never trouble you as long as you live.'

"'Oh, you murthering devil!' says my father, flying at him with a spade that he had behind his chair, 'I've found you out.'

"With one blow he knocked him down; and now a terrible fight began, for the ghost was very strong too; but my father's blood was up, and he'd have faced the devil himself then. They rolled over each other several times, the broken bottles cutting them to pieces and the chairs and tables crashing under them. At last the ghost took the bottle that lay on the hearth, and leveled my father to the ground with one blow; down he fell, and the bottle and the whisky were both dashed into the fire; that was the end of it, for the ghost disappeared that moment in a blue flame that nearly set fire to my father as he lay on the floor.

"Och! it was a cruel sight to see him next morning, with his cheek cut open, and his hands all bloody, lying there by himself;

all the broken glass and the cards all round him. My father couldn't speak a word for days afther, and as for the sexton, it was a queer thing, but when they came to call him in the morning, he had two black eyes, and a gash over his ear, and he never knew how he got them. It was easy enough to know the ghost did it; but my father kept the secret, and never told it to any man, woman or child in them parts."

AN IRISH "PIC-NIC."

Of all the pleasant interludes in the drama of life, a sod party, where everything goes right, is one of the pleasantest. What talking! what fuss! what discussions! what direfully important arrangements for a week beforehand! what a puzzle how to divide the various necessaries into such relatively fair proportions that no individual should feel more burdened than another. I do not mean one of those parties where all the trouble and expense fall upon one unfortunate individual, who, consequently, can derive no pleasure from the affair, except that of seeing others enjoying themselves—a very great pleasure, doubtless, considered abstractly, but rather too refined for every-day mortals—no; but a regular pic-nic, where lots are drawn, and each supplies whatever may be written on the slip that she or he holds, and furnishes a quota of the trouble, as well as of the provisions; one individual, nevertheless, being the director.

What a hurry-skurry on the morning of the eventful day! Then the assembling of the carriages and other vehicles at the place of rendezvous.

"Dear me," said Mrs. Harvey, on the morning of the day appointed for her pic-nic, having consulted her watch for the twentieth time; "dear me, where is Mr. Sharpe? What can possibly delay Mrs. Molloy? Well, well, how hard it is to get people to be punctual!"

"Oh, mamma, maybe they'll meet us at Howth; we had better set off. If they come here, they can be directed to follow us, you know. Do, pray, mamma, let us move.

"Oh, my dear, we must send a messenger to Mr. Sharpe. If

he missed us, or took huff at our going without him (and you know he's very tetchy), it would be such a dreadful inconvenience, for he has to supply the knives and forks, spoons and glasses, and he would think nothing of leaving us in the lurch, if he took it into his head; and Mrs. Molloy is so forgetful, that she might come without the roast beef, and never think of it until it would be missed at table. George, dear, will you step over to Mr. Sharpe's, and tell him that the company is assembled? And, Mr. O'Brien, will you permit me to send your servant to Mrs. Molloy with a similar message?"

"Certainly, madam, with the greatest pleasure."

And now the little annoyances inseparable from all sublunary enjoyments begin.

"John has received a severe hurt, my dear. In packing some bottles, one of them broke, and a piece of it has cut his wrist. I have sent him to the apothecary's to get it dressed."

"Mercy on us! I hope he's not seriously injured. He won't be obliged to stay at home, surely?"

"I am afraid he must, my dear."

"If he does, everything will go wrong, he is such a careful creature, and so completely up to everything on a sod party, and has everything so orderly and regular, and all without fuss or hurry. Oh, dear! we shall be sadly off without him."

Mr. Sharpe was announced, and a slight, small, dapper little personage made his appearance. A physiognomist of the very least discernment must at once have pronounced him to be a satirical, irritable, genuine lover of mischief, for mischief's sake— mirthful after his own fashion, and as merry as a grig upon a gridiron, when every face about him should be drawn to a half yard in length by some unforeseen annoyance, or petty disaster. He rubbed his hands, congratulating the ladies on the fineness of the day. "Heavenly day—fine road—Bay of Dublin will be seen to such advantage—sea so smooth—coast of Wicklow splendid—Killiney will look so bold!"—talk—talk—talk; he stunned every person with his extraordinary volubility.

Mr. O'Brien's servant entered. "Please, ma'am, Mrs. Molloy

is coming." Scarcely was the message delivered when the lady made her appearance.

"Oh, my dear Mrs. Harvey, I hope I haven't kept you waiting long. I totally forgot that this was the day appointed for your party, until Sparks reminded me of it by calling me up."

"Make no apologies, my dear madam: we haven't waited at all. Mr. Sharpe has but just arrived, and our number is now complete. Have you everything packed?"

"Packed! Why, do you think we'll have rain?—had I better get my cloak and umbrella? But, sure, I can go in your carriage, and as I shan't be exposed on an outside car, I won't want them."

"My dear Mrs. Molloy, it is the beef I allude to. Is *it* packed?"

"The beef! What beef?"

"Why, dear me, you surely haven't forgotten that a six-rib piece of roast beef was to be supplied by you?"

"I—declare—I—never—once—thought of it. Well, now, that's odd."

Mr. Sharpe's countenance fell. The discovery had been made too timely to please him.

"What's best to be done now? I can purchase beef somewhere as we go along, and we'll get it dressed at Howth, in some cabin or another."

"Phwee—oo," whistled Mr. Robert O'Gorman; "what the deuce would we do with ourselves for five or six hours, at the least, that such a piece would take to roast, without anything to keep its back warm in an open cabin? I'll tell you what, ma'am; give me the money, and I'll get as much cold roast beef as you like, from Mulholland."

"Who is Mulholland?"

"Oh, 'tis no matter; I'll get the meat, if you want it."

"Very well, Mr. O'Gorman, do so, and you'll oblige me; here is a guinea. But why not tell who Mulholland is?"

Mr. O'Gorman bolted, without making any reply.

Now, the fact of the matter was simply this, that Mulholland was a sort of second-hand caterer, who purchased the meat that was sent unused from the dining hall of Trinity College, and supplied it again to such students as felt too economically inclined to attend commons, and thus save money from the parental allowances, for other, and better (?) uses. To this class did Mr. O'Gorman sometimes belong.

In a very short time he re-appeared.

"You were not long, Mr. O'Gorman; did you succeed in getting a suitable piece?"

"Suitable? If sixteen pounds will suit you, I have got that; and I gave him the change of the guinea," addressing Mrs. Malloy, "for himself, ma'am, for his trouble in packing it, and the loan of the basket, which, of course, he can't expect in reason ever to see again. Nobody would bring home an empty basket."

"The change of the guinea for himself! Why, Mr. O'Gorman, instead of giving him more than he asked, you should have cut him down in his price. The change of the guinea for himself! Oh, gracious! did any one ever hear of the like! Oh, dear me! the change for himself! Oh, dear!" and in a gentle repetition or two, in an under-tone, Mrs. Molloy's surprise died away, like a retiring echo; for the bustle of departure claimed all attention now.

It has been but too frequently remarked, that a party of pleasure is seldom wholly unembittered by pain, and our party was doomed not to be an exception to the rule; although the point had been mooted, and the question discussed, at the first meeting (an evening party at Mrs. Harvey's), where the preliminaries were arranged, and it had been voted unanimously that our party should be pleasant, and agreeable, and happy, from the start to the return; and further, that nothing should go astray; and that if any person should be disagreeable, he or she should be voted out; with fifty other resolutions, that the secretary was unable to record, in consequence of the movers and seconders, the president and audience, secretary and all, talking rapidly and vehemently together, until order was suddenly restored by Mr. O'Gorman (who had the loudest voice, and the knack of making himself heard above any uproar, acquired by a long and regular course of practice in the upper gallery of Crow Street theatre) shouting out, "Order-r-r-r-r, ladies and gentlemen, order-r-r-r-r! The rule of this society is, that not more than *six* shall speak at a time: and I feel it to be my duty, madam, to call upon you, for the sake of regularity, to preserve this rule inviolate. This party of pleasure, madam, is to be a party of pleasure unlike all the parties of pleasure that have gone before it. Pleasure, madam, is to be the beginning, pleasure the middle, and pleasure the end of it; and I shall conclude, madam, by saying that I have the pleasure of wishing that it may be so."

Mr. O'Gorman unfortunately had not the celebrated wishing-cap on his head at the time.

Mr., Mrs., and Miss Harvey, a maiden sister of Mr. Harvey, Mrs. Molloy, Mr. Sharpe, Mr. O'Brien, his mother and three sisters, Mr. O'Donnell and his daughter, O'Gorman, Fitzgerald, Sweeny, Costello, and two or three more college men, completed the muster roll of the party. The vehicles consisted of Mr. Harvey's and Mr. O'Brien's carriages, Mr. O'Donnell's jaunting-car, an outside jarvey that O'Gorman had brought, and Mr. Sharpe's gig.

Poor John's wrist had been so sadly hurt that he could not attend, and the gentlemen gave every assurance to Mrs. Harvey that he would not be missed by her, they would make themselves so useful.

Everything was at length announced to be ready. A basket, covered with oiled silk, swinging conspicuously from the axle-tree of the gig, rendered it unnecessary to ask Mr. Sharpe if he had all the requisites prepared; and Mrs. Harvey, having cast the last scrutinizing glance around, gave the long-wished-for word to "take places."

Now, all this time there were four hearts bent upon one object, and four heads at work planning how to attain it. The youngest of the Misses O'Brien was the sprightliest girl of the party; and although Miss O'Donnell might dispute the prize for beauty with her, the former was the most admired by the young men upon the present occasion, and Messrs. O'Gorman, Fitzgerald, Sweeny, and Costello, had each resolved to attach himself to her, if possible.

The first-mentioned, who was a general favorite, had contrived most successfully to keep near her during breakfast, and pretty nearly to engross her attention during the subsequent time that had elapsed previously to the discovery of Mrs. Molloy's forgetfulness, by telling her tales of college life, and adventures replete with wonders, that might have caused the renowned Sinbad the sailor himself, or the equally celebrated Baron Munchausen, to stare, and bite the bitter nail of envy, while they could not withhold their meed of applause from one who was their master at the marvelous, and could give them lessons in the sublime art of invention.

It was Bob's anxiety to get on the road that made him tender his service, in the supplying of the beef; and the certainty that he had completely ingratiated himself with the young lady, by his stories, at which she had laughed most heartily, made him feel very little uneasiness at the prospect of a few minutes' separation, especially when she knew that he had only absented himself for the purpose of expediting the arrangements that were to give him an opportunity of catering for her amusement for the remainder of the day. When he returned and saw her surrounded by the other three, he resolved to let them go on quietly, and trusted to snatch her from them by some stratagem, just at the last moment.

Now, it must be confessed that Miss Kate would have much preferred the rattling, noisy, lying, merry, mischievous scamp, as her companion, to any other, because she loved laughing, and he supplied her plentifully with food for mirth; and she was very well inclined, and quite resolved within herself, to second any bold attempt that he might make to rescue her from the trio by which she was surrounded. Great was her chagrin to see that he took no manner of trouble about the matter, but apparently occupied himself with the elder Miss Harvey. What a taste he must have! thought she, to attach himself to the old maid of the party ; and it was with something of pettishness that she stood, or rather jumped up, when the order to move was given. Her glove fell. Fitzgerald and Costello stooped, or rather dashed themselves down from opposite sides at the same instant to secure the prize ; their heads came in contact, with a crash resembling that caused by two cracked pitchers being jolted together, and so loud as to astonish the hearers ; and they recoiled from the collision into a sitting posture, one under the table, and the other under the piano.

When Xantippe, the wife of that great philosopher Socrates, had failed in her efforts to vex him by abuse, her last resource was to break some article of crockery upon his head : it is recorded that he coolly wiped his face, which had been deluged by the contents, merely saying, "After thunder comes rain." Now, I'd be bound that if we could ascertain what Socrates said to himself at the time, we should find that for all his smooth face and soft words he inwardly took some desperate liberties with the heathen deities, aud pitched Xantippe, crockery, and all the makers of it, to Pluto, and all the infernal gods, in a hurry. However, he kept his countenance, which is more than can be said of Frank Costello, or Dick Fitzgerald, or of Mr. Sharpe, who nearly went into convulsions with laughter ; indeed, to do him justice, his was not the only laughter, for no one could resist the excitement to risibility contained in the picture before them. At the first moment each of the gentlemen had uttered a loud exclamation savoring strongly of impiety ; then, immediately recollecting the presence of ladies, they muttered what might have been supposed by the charitable to be half-suppressed prayers, but that their countenances were strangely discordant with pious thoughts, for each with his hand on his head, his teeth set, his lips apart and tightly drawn, and his eyes glaring with pain and vexation, sat looking, or rather grinning, like a hyena, at the other. That keen sense of the ridiculous which always comes upon us so inopportunely, made them at length get up, and the condolences offered on all sides, in the most tender inflections of voice, but with countenances which but too plainly showed how great was the effort to suppress laughter, excited their anger against one another most terribly; nor was it likely to be the more readily allayed by seeing Dan Sweeny walking off with the prize, the contention for which had caused their misfortune. It was with difficulty they could be kept from fighting. Leaving them to settle the matter as they pleased, Sweeny conducted the lady to her carriage, close to which a new scene awaited them.

On the step of the hackney jaunting-car sat O'Gorman, with his left foot upon his right knee, alternately rubbing his shin very gently, and hugging the leg as if it was a baby, groaning, and screwing his face into the most hideous grimaces. After the scene they had just witnessed, this was irresistible, and Miss Kate laughed long and heartily. Bob looked at her, made a more hideous grimace than before, groaned, rubbed more violently, and then giving himself a most ludicrous twist, grinned, rubbed, and groaned again.

"Why—ha-ha-ha!—Mr. O'Gorman, what—ha-ha-ha!—has happened you?"

"Oh, ah! oh! may the d—— I beg your pardon. But, oh, hif! to the—och, I mean bad luck to all wood and iron! Ilif, oh! I attempted to jump upon this rascally step, when my foot slipped off, and down I came, scraping all the skin off my shin bone. Oh! bad luck to it—to the step, I mean."

The manner in which he said this, made all who heard him laugh more, but he did not seem to be in the least degree disconcerted; and as to being angry, there was not a trace of it on his countenance.

Sweeny, who prided himself upon being quite a ladies' man, and who was just then immensely elated at having distanced all his competitors, but especially O'Gorman, whose retirement from the competition he considered to be a tacit acknowledgment of inferiority, offered a jesting sort of condolence to him, and recommended him strongly to rub the injured part with vinegar, or whiskey, or salt and water; it might smart a little at first, to be sure, and make him grin and roar somewhat, but it would be well in no time! But in the midst of his badinage, Miss

O'Brien missed her parasol, and he was obliged to run back to the drawing-room to look for it.

As soon as he had disappeared within the hall door, O'Gorman sprang to his feet, and drawing the parasol from the breast of his coat, tendered it, and his arm, to the young lady, saying, with the greatest exultation, "Hoaxed, by jingo! alas! poor Sweeny. Come, Miss Kate, your brother is so taken up with Miss O'Donnell, that he can't attend to anything, or anybody. Never mind your mother; she can't bawl out at us, you know; and if she attempted to scold, she'd be voted out. I've got Sharpe's gig—come, jump up, and we'll have such a day! Oh, but haven't I done them all brown! Hurrah for Howth, and the sky over it! Oh, you little darling!" added he, restraining himself with considerable difficulty from giving her a hug and a kiss, as she laughingly complied with his invitation, and seated herself with him in the gig, just as Sweeny returned, protesting himself unable to find the parasol. "Oh, it got tired waiting for you, and came of itself. But I say, Sweeny, capital receipt that of yours for sore shins; quite cured mine in a moment—first application. Hullo! here, you will probably want a pocket handkerchief during the day; I'll lend you one;" and Bob threw him his own. "I picked his pocket in the drawing-room," said he, turning to his delighted companion; "I was determined that he should go back for something; and here's yours, which I secured also. Now, then, if we follow those rumbling machines, we shall be smothered with dust, so we had better show them the way." Chick, chick—and poor Mrs. O'Brien could scarcely believe her eyes when she saw her daughter whirl past her in a gig with one of the most incorrigible scapegraces in the University.

He took good care that they should not be recalled, for he was out of sight in a twinkling; nor did the party get a view of him again until they had passed Clontarf, when they found him walking the horse quietly, in order that they might overtake him.

In those days the favorite resort for parties of pleasure was the rocky shore of Howth, facing Killiney, and our party had selected a spot which was well known to two or three of them. It was a little hollow in the rocks, where the mould had collected, and was covered with a smooth, close sod. Its form resembled a horseshoe, the open being to the sea; and the rock descended at that side perpendicularly six or seven feet to the water. There was just room enough for the party to seat themselves comfortably, so that every one could enjoy the seaward view. It was a considerable distance from the place where the vehicles should stop; indeed, the hill intervened and should be crossed, so that it was no trifling matter to carry a large basket or hamper to it.

O'Gorman resolved not to encumber himself with anything that might divide his attention with his charming partner; and, accordingly, when they had pulled up, calling to the driver of the jarvey, "Here, Murphy," said he, "you'll take charge of the basket that's slung under the gig, and follow the rest when they're ready."

"Oh, to be sure, sir, sartinly," was the reply, and away went Bob to show the scenery to Miss Kate, from various points quite unknown to her before, leaving the remainder of the party to settle matters as they pleased.

Murphy's assistance was required by the servants who were unlading the carriages first; and each gentleman, taking a basket or bundle, and even the ladies charging themselves with some light articles, they set forward, leaving two or three heavy hampers to the servants' charge.

All having at length departed, except Mr. O'Donnell's servant, who had been left in charge of the vehicles, and Murphy, who was to take the gig basket, the latter proceeded to unstrap it. As he shook it in opening the buckles, some broken glass fell upon the road.

"Oh! miallia murther! what's this? My sowl to glory, if half the bottom isn't out ov the basket. Och, hone, oh! Masther Bob, bud you are the raal clip. By gannies, he's dhruv till he's dhruv the knives and forks clane through; the dickens a one there's left; an' as for the glasses, be my sowl he'd be a handy fellow that ud put *one* together. Oh! marcy sa' me! here's a purty mess. Musha! what's best to be done, at all, at all?"

"Take it to them, anyhow," answered his companion, "and show it to them."

"Arrah, what's the use of hawkin' it over the mountain? Can't I jist go an' tell what's happened?"

"Take care you wouldn't have to come back for it," said the other, "an' have two journeys instead of one. Maybe they wouldn't b'lieve you, thinkin' it was only a thrick that that limb o' th' ould boy put you up to."

The prospect of a second journey, on such a hot day, not being particularly agreeable, Murphy took up the shattered basket and proceeded.

Having yet two hours to spare, the party resolved to consume them by sauntering about until the hour appointed for dinner, which being come, and all having assembled at one point, near the Bailey, they proceeded together to the chosen spot, where they found Murphy awaiting them with a most rueful countenance. He had been vainly trying to invent some plausible excuse for his patron, as he dreaded that all the blame would be thrown upon Bob's hard driving at setting out.

"The bottom's fell out o' the blaggard rotten ould bashket, ma'am, an' the knives an' forks has fell an the road."

"Oh, well," said Mr. Sharpe (who did not seem to be either so astonished or angry as one might have expected), "give them a rub in a napkin; a little dust won't do them any harm."

"Why, thin, the sorra a one o' them there is to a rub," said Murphy, "barrin' this one crukked ould fork."

Despite his loss, Mr. Sharpe could not refrain from laughing when Murphy held up an article, which had certainly been packed for a joke, it was so distorted, one prong being tolerably straight, but the other sticking out as if it was going to march. However, collecting himself, he asked sternly, "Do you mean to tell me that all the knives and forks were lost upon the road?"

"Jist so, sir," was the reply.

"The glass; is it safe?"

"Bruck, sir—all in smithereens; sorra as much ov id together as ud show what the patthern was."

"And the spoons," roared Mr. Sharpe, as if the thought had only just struck him.

"Spoons! sir. Oh, be my sowl you'd better look for thim yourself; here's the bashket."

"This is a costly party to me," said Mr. Sharpe, "but it can't be helped now; so don't let my loss cause any diminution of your pleasure or enjoyment."

Every one looked with perfect admiration at Mr. Sharpe, surprised at his magnanimity, and Mrs. Harvey thought that she must have altogether mistaken his character hitherto; but she would not have thought so, had she known that he had purposely procured a rotten basket, with the bottom partially broken, in which he had packed a quantity of broken glass, and in which he (of course) had *not* packed either spoons, knives, or forks, except the very one which Murphy had held up; and it was to prevent examination or inquiry that he had been so voluble upon his arrival in the morning. But had his loss been, as the company supposed, real instead of fictitious, he must have been gratified, nay, delighted, at the dismay which gradually spread itself over almost every countenance, at the prospect of having to eat a dinner without knives, forks, or spoons, and to drink without glasses, or even cups.

"Gentlemen," said Mr. Harvey, "have you got penknives with you? I have forgotten mine."

So had every one else except Mr. Sharpe. He would willingly have kept it secret, but he knew that if he should attempt to use it himself, it would be seen; so he made a virtue of necessity, and lent it to Mr. Harvey for the purpose of carving the roast beef!

The dinner was now nearly arranged, and the last basket, in which Mulholland had packed the roast beef, was opened. The remnant of an old college gown was first dragged forth, and Mr.

O'Brien's servant, to whom the task was assigned, looked in, tittered, looked again, and then drew forth two long, large ribs, with a piece of meat about the size of a cricket ball attached to the ends of them. Having laid them on the dish, he dipped again, and produced, with another titter, a shapeless lump of meat without any bone—(he would be a clever anatomist that could tell what part of the beast it had been.) Another dip, and with a roar of laughter he raised and deposited on the dish four ribs, from which nearly every morsel of meat had been cut.

"What is the meaning of this, Mr. O'Gorman?" said Mrs. Harvey, who was quite disconcerted at the turn things had taken, and was now seriously disposed to be angry.

"My dear madam," said he, "it may look a little unsightly, but it is all prime meat, depend upon it. It was dressed yesterday for the College dining-hall."

"You don't mean, surely, to call bare bones *meat*, sir?"

"My dear madam," said Bob, "you will find that there is as much meat without bone as will compensate. Mulholland is a very honest fellow in that respect."

Some laughed, some were annoyed, some were disgusted; but by degrees hunger asserted its rights, and reconciled them a little, especially when O'Gorman pointed out how much easier it would be to carve the small pieces with a *penknife*, than if they had but one large one.

"Well," said Mrs. Harvey, "I have long indulged the hope of having a *pic-nic* party so perfectly arranged that nothing should go astray; and so far have I been from succeeding, that I really do think there never was a more unfortunate, irregular affair. I really do not know what to say, and I feel quite incompetent to preside. Mr. O'Gorman, as you have the happy knack of making the best of everything, I believe you are the person best qualified in this company to make the most of the matter, and we must rely on your ingenuity."

"Thank you, ma'am. That is as much as to say, 'Bob, as you have treated us to broken meat, and lost the knives and forks, you will please to carve!' Well, nabocklish, this isn't a round table, like Prince Arthur's, for it's little more than half round, and we have old Howth at the head, and old Neptune at the foot of it; but, for the rest, we don't stand upon precedence, and therefore I need not change my place, to preside. Mr. Harvey, I'll trouble you for the penknife—I beg pardon—the carver —hem! and that specimen of antediluvian cutlery, the '*crukked ould fork*.' Thank you—shove over the beef now. Ods marrow-bones and cleavers! what a heap! Gentlemen, you had better turn up your cuffs as a needful preliminary; and, perchance, an ablution may also be necessary—you can get down to the water here, at this side."

As soon as the party had re-assembled, after having washed their hands, he again addressed them.

"Mr. Sharpe and Mr. Harvey, will you please drag that turkey asunder? Mr. O'Brien, will you tear a wing off that fowl for Miss O'Donnell? Fitz, gnaw the cord off one of those ale bottles; draw the cork with your teeth, and send the bottle round. The corkscrew was with the knives."

"Draw my teeth with the cork, you mean; I had rather knock off the neck, thank you," said Fitz, about to suit the action to the word.

"No, no," cried Bob, "do you forget that we must drink out of the bottles; do you want the ladies to cut their pretty lips with the broken glass, you Mohawk! Though, faith," said he, in an undertone, to his fair companion, "I could almost wish such an accident to happen to some one that I know, that I might have an opportunity of exhibiting my devotion, by sucking the wound"

"A prize! a prize!" cried he, jumping up and running a little distance. He returned with five or six Malahide oyster shells, that had been bleaching on the cliff, where they had been thrown by some former party. Two of them were top shells. "Here," said he, throwing one to Sweeny, "is a carver for that ham; make haste and put an edge on it, on the rock. Ladies, here are primitive drinking goblets for you. Miss O'Brien, the pleasure of a *shell* of wine with you."

"I have put a very good edge on the shell," said Sweeny, "but I can't cut the ham with it, it slides about so."

"Psha! take a grip of it by the shank, can't you? What are you afraid of, you omedhaun? Hold it fast, and don't let it slide. Costello, break up that loaf and send it round. Mr. O'Donnell, will you have the goodness to hold one of these ribs for me. Oh, faith, finger and thumb work won't do; you must take it in your fist, and hold it tight; now pull—bravo! Beau Brummell would be just in his element here. Be my sowl, as Paddy Murphy says, I think if he saw us, he'd jump into that element to get away."

Mr. Sharpe was now in his glory; he had, with Mr. Harvey's assistance, torn up the turkey; and seeing that Bob had decidedly the worst job on the table, he asked him for beef. Mr. Harvey joined in the joke, and put in also; but their man was too able for them.

"As you are in partnership in the turkey business, in which you have been so successful," said he, "you had better continue so, in the general provision line," handing them a piece sufficient to satisfy two; and prevent them from calling again.

"Bill" (to one of the college men), "here's a shell for you to cut the crust of that pie, and help it. Jem" (to another), "Miss Kate O'Brien wishes for some of that chicken that you are trying to dislocate, as gently as if you were afraid of hurting it, or greasing your fingers."

"What part?" said Jem.

"A little of the soul, if you please," said Kate, with a maliciously demure face.

"Here it is for you, Miss Kate, soul and body;" and he handed it to her.

"The mirth and fun (now) grew fast and furious."

No water fit for drinking could be procured, and the consequence was, that the ale, porter and wine, were swallowed too abundantly by the gentlemen. Songs were called for, and O'Gorman was in the midst of the "Groves of Blarney," when Costello shouted out, "A porpoise! a porpoise!"

Up jumped the whole party, and up also jumped the table-cloth, which Mr. O'Donnell and Mr. Sharpe had fastened to their coats or waistcoats.

They sat directly facing the opening to the water, with Mrs. Harvey between them; so that when, by their sudden start up, they raised the cloth, it formed an inclined plane, down which dishes, plates, pies, bread and meat glided, not majestically, but too rapidly, into the sea. Then, oh, what a clamor!

Above the jingling of broken bottles and plates, the crash of dishes, and the exclamation of the gentlemen, arose the never-failing shriek of the ladies. And then came a pause, whilst they silently watched the last dish as it gracefully receded from their view.

"Oh, faith!" said Mrs. Harvey (surprised by her emotion into using a gentle oath), "I think it is time to go home *now.*"

"Faith," said O'Gorman, "it is time to leave the dinner-table at all events, since the things have been removed; but as to going home, we have so little to carry, or look after, besides ourselves and—hic—the ladies, that I think, with all respect to Mrs. Harvey, we may—hic—take it easy. I wish I could get a drink of water to cure this hic—hiccough; for I am certain, Miss O'Brien, I need not assure you—indeed I can appeal to you to bear witness—hic—that it was the *want,* not the quantity of liquid, that has brought it on."

The "want," however, had made Bob's eyes particularly and unusually luminous; nor did Kate take his proposition "to launch all the hampers and baskets, after their recent contents, into the sea," to be any additional proof of his self-possession; and when, with a caper and whoop, he sent Mulholland's basket to the fishes, her suspicions that he was slightly elevated became considerably strengthened.

"Mrs. Harvey," said Mr. Sharpe, "you think your party unfortunate. I have been upon a great many parties of this kind, and I assure you I have seen far more unpleasant affairs—(Gentlemen, here are a few bottles of wine that have escaped the watery fate of their unhappy companions). Now, the very last party that I was on last season, three or four of the gentlemen quarreled (pass the wine, if you please), and one of them, in the scrimmage, was knocked over the rocks into the sea."

"Mercy on us, Mr. Sharpe! was he drowned?"

"Why, no, but his collar-bone was broken, and his shoulder dislocated. But a worse accident happened coming home."

"What was it?"

"Poor Singleton had come, with his wife and two nieces, in a job carriage; the driver got drunk, and overturned the whole concern, just where the road branches off down to the strand; they rolled over the cliff, and fell about twenty feet; the horses were both killed, and the whole party dreadfully injured, barely escaping with life. Then, the quarrel after dinner (by which Jones got his collar-bone broken) led to a duel on the following morning, in which one of the parties, Edwards, fell; and his antagonist, young O'Neill, got a bullet in his knee, which has lamed and disfigured him for life. Pass the wine, gentlemen."

"No! no! no!" screamed Mrs. Harvey, on whom the above delectable recital had had the desired effect, and who was worked into a desperate state of terror, "no more wine, gentlemen, if you please. Come, ladies, we must return at once, before evening closes in."

Each lady being perfectly satisfied that the gentleman who had fallen to her lot would keep sober, whatever *others* might do, demurred to the early retreat; but Mrs. Harvey was too much frightened at the prospect of returning with gentlemen and drivers drunk, not to be determined; and, accordingly, with much growling, and the most general dissatisfaction, the party broke up.

"I am done with *pic-nics*—I'll never have anything to say to one again," said the disappointed directress. "There never was any affair more perfectly arranged, never was so much care taken to have things regular. I never proposed to myself such enjoyment as I expected this day."

"My dear Mrs. Harvey," said O'Gorman, to whose countenance the last four or five shells of wine had imparted an air of the most profound wisdom, "my dear Mrs. Harvey, 'the whole art of happiness is *contentment.*' This is the great secret of enjoyment in this life—this is the talisman that clothes poverty in imperial robes, and imparts to the hovel a grandeur unknown to the halls of princes—this is the true philosopher's stone, for which alchemists so long have sought in vain, that converts all it touches into gold—this is the cosmetic that beautifies the ill-favored wife, and the magic wand that bestows upon the frugal board the appearance of surpassing plenty—this is the shield of adamantine proof, on which disappointment vainly showers its keenest darts— this is the impregnable fortress, ensconced in which, we may boldly bid defiance to the combined forces of sublunary ills—and whether it be announced from the pulpit or the cliff, by the dignified divine or the college scamp; be it soothingly whispered in the ear of the deposed and exiled monarch, or tendered as comfort to the discomfited authoress of a *pic-nic*, it still retains, in undiminished force, its universality of application"——

Here Mr. Sweeny facetiously gave him a slap on the crown of the hat, which drove it down, and stuck it gracefully over his eye, thereby breaking the thread of his discourse. He then addressed the fair Catherine; but all his eloquence and profundity were unavailing to induce her to return with him in the gig. She would listen to nothing but the carriage, and as room could not be made for him inside, he mounted the box, leaving the gig to any one that pleased to have it. Nor was it long untenanted. Frank Costello and Bill Nowlan mounted together, and were found in it next morning fast asleep, in the stable-lane behind Mr. Sharpe's house, the horse having found his way home when left to his own guidance.

The remainder of the party arrived as safely, but somewhat more regularly, in the evening of their eventful day, and all dissatisfied except Mr. O'Gorman.

THE IRISH PARLIAMENT AND THE TURK.

Until England dragged the sister kingdom with herself into the ruinous expenses of the American War, Ireland owed no debt. There were no taxes, save local ones; the Irish Parliament, being composed of resident gentlemen interested in the prosperity and welfare of their country, was profuse in promoting all useful schemes; and no projector who could show any reasonable grounds for seeking assistance, had difficulty in finding a patron.

Amongst other projectors whose ingenuity was excited by this liberal conduct, was one of a very singular description—a Turk who had come over, or, as the *on dit* went, had *fled* from Constantinople. He proposed to establish, what was greatly wanted at that time in the Irish metropolis, "hot and cold sea-water baths," and, by way of advancing his pretensions to public encouragement, offered to open free baths for the poor on an extensive plan, giving them, as a doctor, attendance and advice *gratis* every day in the year. He spoke English very intelligibly; his person was extremely remarkable, and the more so as he was the first Turk who had ever walked the streets of Dublin in his native costume. He was in height considerably above six feet, rather pompous in his gait, and apparently powerful; an immense black beard covering his chin and upper lip. There was at the same time something cheerful and cordial in the man's address, and, altogether, he cut a very imposing figure. Everybody liked Doctor Achmet Borumborad; his Turkish dress, being extremely handsome, without an approach to the tawdry, and crowned with an immense turban, drew the eyes of every passer-by, and

I must say that I have never seen a more stately looking Turk since that period.

The eccentricity of the doctor's appearance was, indeed, as will be readily imagined, the occasion of much idle observation and conjecture. At first, whenever he went abroad, a crowd of people, chiefly boys, was sure to attend him, but at a respectful distance; and if he turned to look behind him, the gaping boobies fled, as if they conceived even his looks to be mortal. These fears, however, gradually wore away, and were entirely shaken off on the fact being made public that he meant to attend the poor; which undertaking was, in the usual spirit of exaggeration, soon construed into an engagement, on the part of the doctor, to cure *all disorders whatever!* and hence he quickly became as much admired and respected as he had previously been dreaded.

My fair readers will perhaps smile when I assure them that the persons who seemed to have the least apprehension of Doctor Borumborad, or rather to think him "a very nice Turk," were the ladies of the metropolis. Many a smart, snug little husband, who had been heretofore considered "quite the thing," despotic in his own house, and peremptory commandant of his own family, was now regarded as a wretched, contemptible, close-shaven pigmy, in comparison with the immensity of the doctor's figure and whiskers; and what is more extraordinary, his good humor and engaging manners gained him many friends even among the husbands themselves! he thus becoming, in a shorter period than could be imagined, a particular favorite with the entire city, male and female.

Doctor Achmet Borumborad having obtained footing thus far, next succeeded surprisingly in making his way amongst the members of Parliament. He was full of conversation, yet knew his proper distance; pregnant with anecdote, but discreet in its expenditure; and he had the peculiar talent of being humble without the appearance of humility. A submissive Turk would have been out of character, and a haughty one excluded from society: the doctor was aware of this, and regulated his demeanor with remarkable skill upon every occasion—and they were numerous—whereon, as a "lion," he was invited to the tables of the great. By this line of conduct he managed to warm those who patronized him into violent partisans; and accordingly little or no difficulty was experienced in getting a grant from Parliament for a sufficient fund to commence his great metropolitan undertaking.

Baths were now planned after Turkish models. The money voted was most faithfully appropriated; and a more ingenious or useful establishment could not be found in any metropolis. But the cash, it was soon discovered, ran too short to enable the doctor to complete his scheme; and on the ensuing session a further vote became necessary, which was by no means opposed, as the institution was good, fairly executed, and charitably applied. The worthy doctor kept his ground—session after session he petitioned for fresh assistance, and never met with refusal; his profits were good, and he lived well; whilst the baths proved of the utmost benefit, and the poor received attention and service from his establishment without cost. An immense cold bath was constructed to communicate with the river; it was large and deep, and entirely renewed every tide. The neatest lodging rooms for those patients who chose to remain during a course of bathing were added to the establishment, and always occupied. In short, the whole affair became so popular, and Doctor Achmet acquired so many friends, that the annual grants of Parliament were considered nearly as matters of course.

But alas! fortune is treacherous, and prosperity unstable. Whilst the ingenious Borumborad was thus rapidly flourishing, an unlucky though most ludicrous incident threw the poor fellow completely aback, and, without any fault on his part, nearly ruined both himself and his institution.

Preparatory to every session it was the doctor's invariable custom to give a grand dinner at the baths to a large number of his patrons, members of Parliament who were in the habit of proposing and supporting his grants. He always on these occasions procured some professional singers, as well as the finest wines in Ireland, endeavoring to render the parties as joyous and convivial as possible. Some nobleman, or commoner of note, always acted for him as chairman, the doctor himself being quite unassuming.

At the commencement of a session whereupon he anticipated this patronage, it was intended to increase his grant, in order to meet the expenses of certain new works, etc., which he had executed on the strength of the ensuing supply; and the doctor had invited nearly thirty of the leading members to a grand dinner in his spacious saloon. The singers were of the first order; the claret and champagne excellent; and never was the Turk's hospitality shown off to better advantage, or the appetites of his guests administered to with greater success. The effects of the wine in time began to grow obvious. The elder and more discreet members were for adjourning, whilst the juveniles declared they would stay for another dozen; and Doctor Borumborad accordingly went down himself to his cellar, to select and send up a choice dozen, by way of *bonne bouche*, for " finishing " the refractory members of Parliament.

In his absence, Sir John S. Hamilton took it into his head that he had taken enough, and rose to go away, as is customary in these days of freedom when people are so circumstanced; but at that period men were not always their own masters on such occasions, and a general cry arose of, "Stop Sir John! stop him! the *bonne bouche!* the *bonne bouche!*" The carousers were on the alert instantly; Sir John opened the door and rushed out. The ante-chamber was not lighted; some one or two and twenty staunch members stuck to his skirts—when *splash* at once comes Sir John, not into the street, but into the great *cold bath*, the door of which he had retreated by in mistake! The other Parliament men were too close upon the baronet to stop short like the horse of a Cossack: in they went by fours and fives; and one or two, who, on hearing the splashing of the water, cunningly threw themselves down on the brink to avoid popping in, operated directly as stumbling-blocks to those behind, who thus obtained their full share of a *bonne bouche* none of the parties had bargained for.

When Doctor Borumborad re-entered, ushering a couple of servants laden with a dozen of his best wine, and missed all his company, he thought some devil had carried them off; but perceiving the door of his noble, deep, cold salt-water bath open, he with dismay rushed thither, and espied eighteen or nineteen Irish Parliament men either floating like so many corks upon the surface, or scrambling to get out like mice who had fallen into a basin! The doctor's *posse* of attendants were immediately set at work, and every one of the honorable members extricated: the quantity of salt water, however, which had made its way into their stomachs was not so easily removed, and most of them carried the beverage home to their own bed-chambers.

It was unlucky, also, that as the doctor was a Turk, he had no Christian wardrobe to substitute for the well-soaked garments of the honorable members. Such dresses, however, as he had, were speedily put into requisition: the bathing attendants furnished their quota of dry apparel; and all were speedily distributed amongst the swimmers, some of whom exhibited in Turkish costume, others in bathing shifts, and when the clothes failed, blankets were pinned around the rest. Large fires were made in every room; brandy and mulled wine liberally resorted to; and as fast as sedan-chairs could be procured, the Irish Commoners were sent home, cursing all Turks and infidels, and denouncing a crusade against anything coming from the same quarter of the globe as Constantinople.

Poor Doctor Achmet Borumborad was distracted and quite inconsolable! Next day he duly visited every suffering member, and though well received, was acute enough to see that the ridicule with which they had covered themselves was likely to work out eventually his ruin. His anticipations were well founded: though the members sought to hush up the ridiculous parts of the story, they became, from that very attempt, still more celebrated. In fact, it was too good a joke to escape the embellishments of Irish humor, and the statement universally circulated was—that "Doctor Borumborad had nearly drowned nineteen members of Parliament, because they would not promise to vote for him!"

The poor doctor was now assailed in every way. Among other things, it was asserted that he was the Turk who had strangled the Christians in the Seven Towers at Constantinople! Though everybody laughed at *their own* inventions, they believed those of *other people;* and the conclusion was, that no more grants could be proposed, since not a single member was stout enough to mention the name of Borumborad! the laugh, indeed, would have overwhelmed the best speech ever delivered in the Irish Parliament.

Still the new works must be paid for, although no convenient vote came to make the necessary provision: the poor doctor was therefore cramped a little, but notwithstanding his embarrassment he kept his ground well, and lost no private friends except such as the wearing-off of novelty estranged. He continued to get on; and at length a new circumstance intervened to restore his happiness, in a way as little to be anticipated by the reader as was his previous discomfiture.

Love had actually seized upon the Turk above two years before the accident we have been recording. A respectable surgeon of Dublin, of the name of Hartigan, had what might be termed a very "neat" sister, and this lady had made a lasting impression on the heart of Borumborad, who had no reason to complain of his suit being treated with disdain, or even indifference. On the contrary, Miss Hartigan liked the doctor vastly, and praised the Turks in general, both for their dashing spirit and their beautiful whiskers. It was not, however, consistent either with her own or her brother's Christianity to submit to the doctor's tremendous beard, or think of matrimony, till "he had shaved the chin at least, and got a parson to turn him into a Christian, or something of that kind." Upon those terms only would she surrender her charms and her money, for some she had, to Doctor Achmet Borumborad, however amiable.

The doctor's courtship with the members of Parliament having now terminated, so far at any rate as further grants were concerned, and a *grant* of a much more tender nature being now within his reach, he began seriously to consider if he should not at once capitulate to Miss Hartigan, and exchange his beard and his Alcoran for a razor and the New Testament. After weighing matters deliberately, love prevailed, and he intimated by letter, in the proper vehemence of Asiatic passion, his determination to turn Christian, discard his beard, and, throwing himself at the feet of his beloved, vow eternal fidelity to her in the holy bands of matrimony. He concluded by requesting an interview in the presence of the young lady's confidant, a Miss Owen, who resided next door. His request was granted, and he repeated his proposal, which was duly accepted, Miss Hartigan stipulating that he should never see her again until the double promise in his letter was fully redeemed, upon which he might mention his own day for the ceremony. The doctor, having engaged to comply, took leave.

On the evening of the same day a gentleman was announced to the bride elect with a message from Doctor Achmet Borumborad. Her confidential neighbor was immediately summoned, the gentleman waiting meantime in a coach at the door. At length Miss Hartigan and her friend being ready to receive him, in walked a Christian gallant, in a suit of full-dress black, and a very tall, fine-looking Christian he was! Miss Hartigan was surprised; she did not recognize her lover, particularly as she thought it impossible he could have been made a Christian before the ensuing Sunday! He immediately, however, fell on his knees, seized and kissed her lily hand, and on her beginning to expostulate, cried out at once, "Don't be angry, my dear creature! to tell the honest truth, I am as good a Christian as the archbishop; I'm your own countryman, sure enough! Mr. Patrick Joyce from Kilkenny county—not a Turk any more than yourself, my sweet angel!" The ladies were astonished; but astonishment did not prevent Miss Hartigan from keeping her word, and Mr. and Mrs. Joyce became a very loving and happy couple.

The doctor's great skill, however, was supposed to lie in his beard and faith; consequently, on this *denouement*, the baths declined. But the honest fellow never had done any discreditable or improper act—none, indeed, was ever laid to his charge; he fully performed every engagement with the Parliament whilst he retained the power to do so.

His beauty and portly appearance were considerably diminished by his change of garb. The long beard and picturesque dress had been half the battle; and he was, after his transformation, but a plain, rather coarse, but still brave-looking fellow. An old memorandum-book reminded me of these circumstances, as it noted a payment made to him by me on behalf of my elder brother, who had been looking in the bath-house at the time of the "swimming match."

This little story shows the facility with which public money was formerly voted, and at the same time the comparatively fortunate financial state of Ireland at that period, when the public purse could afford a multiplicity of such supplies without any tax or imposition whatsoever being laid upon the people to provide for them.

BOTHERING AN EDITOR.

However astonished I had been at the warmth by which I was treated in London, I was still less prepared for the enthusiasm which greeted me in every town through which I passed. There was not a village where we stopped to change horses whose inhabitants did not simultaneously pour forth to welcome me with every demonstration of delight. That the fact of four horses and a yellow chaise should have elicited such testimonies of satisfaction was somewhat difficult to conceive; and, even had the important news that I was the bearer of dispatches been telegraphed from London by successive postboys, still the extraordinary excitement was unaccountable. It was only on reaching Bristol that I learned to what circumstance my popularity was owing. My servant Mike, in humble imitation of election practices, had posted a large placard on the back of the chaise, announcing, in letters of portentous length, something like the following:

"Bloody news! Fall of Ciudad Rodrigo! Five thousand prisoners and two hundred pieces of cannon taken!"

This veracious and satisfactory statement, aided by Mike's personal exertions, and an unwearied performance on the trumpet he had taken from the French dragoon, had roused the population of every hamlet, and made our journey from London to Bristol one scene of uproar, noise and confusion. All my attempts to suppress Mike's oratory or music were perfectly unavailing. In fact, he had pledged my health so many times during the day—he had drunk so many toasts to the success of the British arms—so many to the English nation—so many in honor of Ireland—and so many in honor of Mickey Free himself, that all respect for my authority was lost in his enthusiasm for my greatness, and his shouts became wilder, and the blasts from the trumpet more fearful and incoherent; and finally, on the last stage of our journey, having exhausted as it were every tribute of his lungs, he seemed (if I were to judge by the evidence of my ears) to be performing something very like a hornpipe on the roof of the chaise.

Happily for me there is a limit to all human efforts, and even *his* powers at length succumbed; so that, when we arrived at Bristol, I persuaded him to go to bed, and I once more was left to the enjoyment of some quiet. To fill up the few hours which intervened before bedtime, I strolled into the coffee-room. The English look of every one and everything around had still its charm for me; and I was contemplating, with no small admiration, that air of neatness and propriety so observant—from the bright-faced clock, that ticked unwearily upon the mantelpiece, to the trim waiter himself, with noiseless step, and that mixed look of vigilance and vacancy. The perfect stillness struck me, save when a deep voice called for "another brandy-and-water," and some more modestly-toned request would utter a desire for ' more cream." The attention of each man, absorbed in the folds of his voluminous newspaper, scarcely deigning a glance at the new comer who entered, were all in keeping, giving in their solemnity and gravity a character of almost religious seriousness to what, in any other land, would be a scene of riotous noise and discordant tumult. I was watching all these with a more than common interest, when the door opened, and the waiter entered with a large placard. He was followed by another with a ladder, by whose assistance he succeeded in attaching the large square of paper to the wall, above the fireplace. Every one about rose up, curious to ascertain what was going forward; and I myself joined in the crowd around the fire. The first glance of the announcement showed me what it meant; and it was with a strange mixture of shame and confusion I read:

"Fall of Ciudad Rodrigo; with a full and detailed account of the storming of the great breach—capture of the enemy's cannon, etc.—by Michael Free, 14th Light Dragoons."

Leaving the many around me busied in conjecturing who the aforesaid Mr. Free might be, and what peculiar opportunities he might have enjoyed for his report, I hurried from the room and called the waiter.

"What's the meaning of the announcement you've just put up in the coffee-room? Where did it come from?"

"Most important news, sir; exclusively in the columns of the *Bristol Telegraph;* the gentleman has just arrived ——"

"Who, pray? What gentleman?"

"Mr. Free, sir, No. 13—large bedroom—blue damask—supper for two—oysters—brandy and water—mulled port."

"What do you mean? Is the fellow at supper?"

Somewhat shocked by the tone I ventured to assume towards the illustrious narrator, the waiter merely bowed his reply.

"Show me to his room," said I; "I should like to see him."

"Follow me, if you please, sir—this way—what name shall I say?"

"You need not mind announcing me—I'm an old acquaintance—just show me the room."

"I beg pardon, sir, but Mr. Meckins, the editor of the *Telegraph*, is engaged with him at present; and positive orders are given not to suffer any interruption."

"No matter; do as I bid you. Is that it? Oh! I hear his voice. There, that will do. You may go down stairs; I'll introduce myself."

So saying, and slipping a crown into the waiter's hand, I proceeded cautiously towards the door, and opened it stealthily. My caution was, however, needless; for a large screen was drawn across this part of the room, completely concealing the door; closing which behind me, I took my place beneath the shelter of this ambuscade, determined on no account to be perceived by the parties.

Seated in a large arm-chair, a smoking tumbler of mulled port before him, sat my friend Mike, dressed in my full regimentals, even to the helmet, which, unfortunately, however, for the effect, he had put on back foremost; a short "dudeen" graced his lip, and the trumpet, so frequently alluded to, lay near him.

Opposite him sat a short, puny, round-faced little gentleman, with rolling eyes and a turned-up nose. Numerous sheets of paper, pens, etc., lay scattered about; and he evinced, by his air and gesture, the most marked and eager attention to Mr. Free's narrative, whose frequent interruptions, caused by the drink and the oysters, were viewed with no small impatience by the anxious editor.

"You must remember, captain, time's passing; the placards are all out; must be at press before one o'clock to-night; the morning edition is everything with us. You were at the first parallel, I think."

"Not a one o' me knows. Just ring that bell near you. Them's elegant oysters; and you're not taking your drop of liquor. Here's a toast for you; 'May'—— Whoop!—raal Carlingfords, upon my conscience. See, now, if I won't hit the little black chap up there, the first shot."

Scarcely were the words spoken, when a little painted bust of Shakspeare fell in fragments on the floor as an oyster-shell laid him low.

A faint effort at a laugh at the eccentricities of his friend was all the poor editor could accomplish, while Mike's triumph knew no bounds.

"Didn't I tell you? But come, now—are you ready? Give the pen a drink, if you won't take one yourself."

"I'm ready, quite ready," responded the editor.

"Faith, an it's more nor I am. See now, here it is: The night was murthering dark; you could not see a stim."

"Not see a—what?"

"A stim, bad wind to you; don't you know English? Hand me the hot water. Have you that down yet?"

"Yes. Pray proceed."

"The fifth division was ordhered up, bekase they were fighting chaps; the Eighty-eighth was among them; the Rangers—— Oh! upon my word, we must drink the Rangers. Here, not a one o' me will go on till we give them all the honors—hip— begin."

"Hip!" sighed the luckless editor, as he rose from his chair, obedient to the command.

"Hurra—hurra—hurra! Well done! there's stuff in you yet, ould foolscap! The little bottle is empty—ring again, if you plaze. Arrah, don't be looking miserable and dissolute that way. Sure I'm only getting myself up for you."

"Really, Mr. Free, I see no prospect of our ever getting done."

"The saints in heaven forbid," interrupted Mike, piously; "the evening's young, and drink plenty. Here, now, make ready!"

The editor once more made a gesture of preparation.

"Well, as I was saying," resumed Mike, "it was pitch dark when the columns moved up, and a cold, raw night, with a little thin rain falling. Have you that down?"

"Yes. Pray go on."

"Well, just as it might be here, at the corner of the trench I met Dr. Quill. 'They're waiting for you, Mr. Free,' says he, 'down there. Picton's asking for you.' 'Faith and he must wait,' says I, 'for I'm terrible dry.' With that, he pulled out his canteen and mixed me a little brandy-and-water. 'Are you taking it without a toast?' says Doctor Maurice. 'Never fear,' says I; 'here's Mary Brady'——"

"But, my dear sir," interposed Mr. Meekins, "pray *do* remember this is somewhat irrelevant. In fifteen minutes it will be twelve o'clock."

"I know it, ould boy, I know it. I see what you're at. You were going to observe how much better we'd be for a broiled bone."

"Nothing of the kind, I assure you. For heaven's sake, no more eating and drinking."

"No more eating nor drinking! Why not? You've a nice notion of a convivial evening. Faith, we'll have the broiled bone sure enough, and, what's more, a half gallon of the strongest punch they can make us; an' I hope that, grave as you are, you'll favor the company with a song."

"Really, Mr. Free——"

"Arrah! none of your blarney. Don't be misthering me. Call me Mickey—Mickey Free, if you like better."

"I protest," said the editor, with dismay, "that here we are two hours at work, and haven't got to the foot of the great breach."

"And wasn't the army three months and a half in just getting that far, with a battering train, and mortars, and the finest troops ever was seen? and there you sit, a little fat creature with your pen in your hand, grumbling that you can't do more than the British army. Take care you don't provoke me to beat you; for I am quiet till I'm roused. But, by the Rock o' Cashel——"

Here he grasped the brass trumpet with an energy that made the editor spring from his chair.

"For mercy's sake, Mr. Free——"

"Well, I won't; but sit down there, and don't be bothering me about sieges, and battles, and things that you know nothing about."

"I protest," rejoined Mr. Meekins, "that had you not sent to my office intimating your wish to communicate an account of the siege, I never should have thought of intruding myself upon you. And now, since you appear indisposed to afford the information in question, if you will permit me, I'll wish you a very good night."

"Faith, and so you shall, and help me to pass one too; for not a step out o' that chair shall you take till morning. Do ye think I am going to be left here by myself, all alone?"

"I must observe——" said Meekins.

"To be sure, to be sure," said Mickey; "I see what you mean. You're not the best of company, it's true; but at a pinch like this—— There now, take your liquor."

"Once for all, sir," said the editor, "I would beg you to recollect that on the faith of your message to me I have announced an account of the storming of Ciudad Rodrigo for our morning edition. Are you prepared, may I ask, for the consequences of my disappointing ten thousand readers?"

"It's little I care for one of them. I never knew much of reading myself."

"If you think to make a jest of me," interposed Mr. Meekins, reddening with passion.

"A jest of you! Troth it's little fun I can get out of you; you're as tiresome a creature as ever I spent an evening with. See now, I told you before not to provoke me. We'll have a little more drink; ring the bell. Who knows but you'll turn out better by and by?"

As Mike rose at these words to summon the waiter, Mr. Meekins seized the opportunity to make his escape. Scarcely had he reached the door, however, when he was perceived by Mickey, who hurled the trumpet at him with all his force, while he uttered a shout that nearly left the poor editor lifeless with terror. This time, happily, Mr. Free's aim failed him, and, before he could arrest the progress of his victim, he had gained the corridor, and, with one bound, cleared the first flight of the staircase, his pace increasing every moment as Mick's denunciations grew louder and louder, till at last, as he reached the street, Mr. Free's delight overcame his indignation, and he threw himself upon a chair and laughed immoderately.

A FENIAN TALE.

On a certain day a fair and a gathering were held at Bineadar, by the seven ordinary and seven extraordinary battalions of the Fenians of Erinn. In the course of the day, on casting a look over the broad expanse of the sea, they beheld a large, smooth-sided, and proud-looking ship ploughing the waves from the east and approaching them under full sail. When the capacious vessel touched the shore and lowered her sails, the Fenians of Erinn counted upon seeing a host of men disembark from her; and great was their surprise when one warrior, and no more, came out of the ship and landed on the beach. He was a hero of the largest make of body, the strongest of champions, and the finest of the human race; and in this wise was the kingly warrior equipped:— an impenetrable helmet of polished steel encased his ample and beautiful head, a deep-furrowed, thick-backed, sharp-edged sword hung at his left side; and a purple bossed shield was slung over his shoulder. Such were his chief accoutrements; and armed in this fashion and manner did the stranger come into the presence of Finn MacCoole and the Fenians of Erinn.

It was then that Finn, the King of the Fenians, addressed the heroic champion, and questioned him, saying, " From what quarter of the globe hast thou come unto us, O goodly youth ? or from which of the noble or ignoble races of the universe art thou sprung? Who art thou?"

" I am," answered the stranger, " Ironbones, the son of the King of Thessaly; and so far as I have traveled on this globe, since the day that I left my own land, I have laid every country, peninsula and island, under contribution to my sword and my arm: this I have done even to the present hour; and my desire is to obtain the crown and tribute of this country in like manner; for if I obtain them not, I purpose to bring slaughter of men and deficiency of heroes and youthful warriors on the seven ordinary and seven extraordinary battalions of the Fenian host. Such, O king, is the object of my visit to this country, and such is my design in landing here."

Hereupon uprose Conán the Bald, and said, "Of a truth, my friend, it seems to me that you have come upon a foolish enterprise, and that to the end of your life, and the close of your days, you will not be able to accomplish your purpose; because from the beginning of ages until now, no man ever heard of a hero or ever saw a champion coming with any such mighty design to Ireland, who did not find his match in that same country."

But Ironbones replied: "I make but very little account of your speech, Conán," said he; "for if all the Fenian heroes who have died within the last seven years were now in the world, and were joined by those who are now living, I would visit all of them with the sorrow of death and show all of them the shortness of life in one day; nevertheless I will make your warriors a more peaceable proposal. I challenge you then, O warrior, to find me a man among you who can vanquish me in running, in fighting or in wrestling; if you can do this, I shall give you no further trouble, but return to my own country without loitering here any longer."

"And pray," inquired Finn, "which of those three manly exercises that you have named will it please you to select for the first trial of prowess?"

To this Ironbones answered, "If you can find for me any one champion of your number who can run faster than I can, I will give you no further annoyance, but depart at once to my own country."

"It so happens," said Finn, "that our Man of Swiftness, Keelte MacRonan, is not here at present to try his powers of running with you; and as he is not, it were better, O hero, that you should sojourn here a season with the Fenians, that you and they may mutually make and appreciate each other's acquaintance by means of conversation and amusements, as is our wont. In the meanwhile I will repair to Tara of the Kings in quest of Keelte MacRonan; and if I have not the good fortune to find him there, I shall certainly meet with him at Ceis-Corann of the Fenii, from whence I shall without delay bring him hither to meet you."

To this Ironbones agreed, saying that he was well satisfied with what Finn proposed; and thereupon Finn proceeded on his way towards Tara of the Kings, in search of Keelte. Now it fell out that as he journeyed along he missed his way, so that he came to a dense, wide and gloomy wood, divided in the midst by a broad and miry road or pathway. Before he had advanced more than a very little distance on this road, he perceived coming directly towards him an ugly, detestable-looking giant, who wore a gray frieze coat, the skirts of which reached down to the calves of his legs, and were bespattered with yellow mud to the depth of a hero's hand; so that every step he made, the lower part of that coat struck with such violence against his legs as to produce a sound that could be distinctly heard a full mile of ground off. Each of the two legs that sustained the unwieldy carcass of this horrible hideous monster was like the mast of a great ship, and each of the two shoes that were under his shapeless, horny, long-nailed hoofs, resembled a roomy long-sided boat; and every time he lifted his foot, and at every step that he walked, he splashed up from each shoe a good barrelful of mire and water on the lower part of his body. Finn gazed in amazement at the colossal man, for he had never before seen any one so big and bulky; yet he would have passed onward and continued his route, but the giant stopped and accosted him, and Finn was under the necessity of stopping also, and exchanging a few words with the giant.

The giant began in this manner: "What, ho! Finn Mac Coole," said he, "what desire for traveling is this that has seized on you, and how far do you mean to go upon this journey?"

"Oh," said Finn, "as to that, my trouble and anxiety are so great that I cannot describe them to you now, and indeed small is the use," added he, "it would be of to me to attempt doing so; and I think it would be better for you to let me go on my way without asking any more questions of me."

But the giant was not so easily put off. "O Finn," said he, "you may keep your secret if you like, but all the loss and the misfortune attending your silence will be your own; and when you think well upon that, maybe you would not boggle any longer about disclosing to me the nature of your errand."

So Finn, seeing the huge size of the giant, and thinking it advisable not to provoke him, began to tell him all that had taken place among the Fenians of Erinn so short a time before. "You must know," said he, "that at the meridian hour of this very day the great Ironbones, the son of the King of Thessaly, landed at the harbor of Bineadar, with the view of taking the crown and sovereignty of Ireland into his own hands; and if he does not obtain them with the free and good will of the Irish, he threatens to distribute death and destruction impartially among the young and old of our heroes; howbeit he has challenged us to find a man able to surpass him in running, fighting or wrestling, and if we can find such a man, then he agrees to forego his pretensions, and to return to his own country without giving us further trouble; and that," said Finn, "is the history I have for you."

"And how do you intend to oppose the royal warrior?" asked the giant: "I know him well, and I know he has the vigor in his hand and the strength in his arm to carry every threat he makes into effect."

"Why, then," said Finn, in answer to this, "I intend to go to Tara of the Kings for Keelte MacRonan, and if I do not find him there, I will go to look for him at Ceis-Corann of the Fenii; and it is he," said he, "whom I mean to bring with me for the purpose of vanquishing this hero in running."

"Alas!" said the giant, "weak is your dependence and feeble your champion for propping and preserving the monarchy of Ireland; and if Keelte MacRonan be your *Tree of Defiance*, you are already a man without a country."

"It is I, then," said Finn, "who am sorry you should say so; and what to do in this extremity I cannot tell."

"I will show you," replied the gigantic man: "just do you say nothing at all, but accept of me as the opponent of this champion; and it may happen that I shall be able to get you out of your difficulty."

"Oh," said Finn, " for the matter of that, it is my own notion that you have enough to do if you can carry your big coat and drag your shoes with you one half mile of ground in a day, without trying to rival such a hero as Ironbones in valor or agility."

"You may have what notions you like," returned the giant, "but I tell you that if I am not able to give battle to this fighting hero, there never has been and there is not now a man in Ireland able to cope with him. But never mind, Finn MacCoole, let not your spirits be cast down, for I will take it on myself to deliver you from the danger that presses on you."

"What is your name?" demanded Finn.

"Bodach-an-Chota-Lachtna (the Churl with the Grey Coat) is my name," the giant answered.

"Well, then," said Finn, "you will do well to come along with me." So Finn turned back, and the Bodach went with him; but we have no account of their travels till they reached Bineadar. There, when the Fians beheld the Bodach attired in such a fashion and trim, they were all very much surprised, for they had never before seen the like of him; and they were greatly overjoyed that he should make his appearance among them at such a critical moment.

As for Ironbones, he came before Finn, and asked him if he had got the man who was to contend with him in running. Finn made answer that he had, and that he was present among them; and thereupon he pointed out the Bodach to him. But as soon as Ironbones saw the Bodach, he was seized with astonishment, and his courage was damped at the sight of the gigantic proportions of the mighty man, but he pretended to be only very indignant, and exclaimed, "What! do you expect me to demean myself by engaging in a contest with such an ugly, greasy, hateful-looking Bodach as that? It is myself that will do no such thing!" said he; and he stepped back and would not go near the Bodach.

When the Bodach saw and heard this, he burst into a loud, hoarse, thunderous laugh, and said, "Come, Ironbones, this will not do; I am not the sort of person you affect to think me; and it is you that shall have proof of my assertion before tomorrow evening; so now, let me know," said he, "what is to be the length of the course you propose to run over, for over the same course it is my intention to run along with you; and if I do not succeed in running that distance with you, it is a fair conclusion that you win the race, and in like manner if I do succeed in outstripping you, then it stands to reason that you lose the race."

"There is sense and rationality in your language," replied Ironbones, for he saw that he must submit, "and I agree to what you say, but it is my wish not to have the course shorter or longer than three score miles."

"Well," said the Bodach, "that will answer me too, for it is just three score miles from Mount Loocra in Munster to Bineadar; and it will be a pleasant run for the pair of us; but if you find that I am not able to finish it before you, of course the victory is yours."

Ironbones replied that he would not contradict so evident a proposition, whereupon the Bodach resumed: "What it is proper for you to do now," said he, "is to come along with me southward to Mount Loocra this evening, in order that we may make ourselves acquainted with the ground we are to go over to-morrow on our return; and we can stop for the night on the Mount, so that we may be able to start with the break of day." To this also Ironbones acceded, saying it was a judicious speech, and that he had nothing to object to it.

Upon this the two competitors commenced their journey, and little was the delay they made till they arrived at Mount Loocra in Munster. As soon as they had got thither, the Bodach again addressed Ironbones, and told him that he thought their best plan would be to build a hut in the adjoining wood, that so they might be protected from the inclemency of the night: "for it seems to me, O son of the King of Thessaly," said he, "that if we do not, we are likely to have a hard couch and cold quarters on this exposed hill."

To this Ironbones made reply as thus: "You may do so, if you please, O Bodach of the Big Coat, but as for me, I am Ironbones, and care not for dainty lodging, and I am mightily disinclined to give myself the trouble of building a house hereabouts only to sleep in it one night and never see it again; howbeit, if you are desirous of employing your hands there is nobody to cross you; you may build, and I shall stay here until you have finished."

"Very good," said the Bodach, "and build I will; but I shall take good care that a certain person who refuses to assist me shall have no share in my sleeping-room, should I succeed in making it as comfortable as I hope to do;" and with this he betook himself into the wood, and began cutting down and shaping pieces of timber with the greatest expedition, never ceasing until he had got together six pair of stakes and as many of rafters, which, with a sufficient quantity of brushwood and green rushes for thatch, he carried, bound in one load, to a convenient spot, and there set them up at once in regular order; and this part of his work being finished, he again entered the wood, and carried from thence a good load of dry green sticks, which he kindled into a fire that reached from the back of the hut to the door.

While the fire was blazing merrily he left the hut, and again addressing his companion, said to him: "O son of the King of Thessaly, called by men Ironbones, are you provided with provisions for the night, and have you eatables and drinkables to keep you from hunger and thirst?"

"No, I have not," said Ironbones proudly; "it is myself that used never to be without people to provide victuals for me when I wanted them," said he.

"Well, but," said the Bodach, "you have not your people near you now, and so the best thing you can do is to come and hunt with me in the wood, and my hand to you, we shall soon have enough of victuals for both of us."

"I never practiced pedestrian hunting," said Ironbones; "and with the like of you I never hunted at all, and I don't think I shall begin now," said he, in a very dignified sort of way.

"Then I must try my luck by myself," said the Bodach; and off again he bounded into the wood, and after he had gone a little way he roused a herd of wild swine and pursued them into the recesses of the wood, and there he succeeded in separating from the rest the biggest and fattest hog of the herd, which he soon ran down and carried to his hut, where he slaughtered it, and cut it into two halves, one of which he placed at each side of the fire on a self-moving holly-spit. He then darted out once more, and stopped not until he reached the mansion of the Baron of Inchiquin, which was thirty miles distant, from whence he carried off a table and a chair, two barrels of wine, and all the bread fit for eating he could lay his hands on, all of which he brought to Mount Loocra in one load. When he again entered his hut, he found his hog entirely roasted and in nice order for mastication; so he laid half the meat and bread on the table, and sitting down, disposed of them with wonderful alacrity, drinking at the same time precisely one barrel of the wine, and no more, for he reserved the other, as well as the rest of the solids, for his breakfast in the morning. Having thus finished his supper, he shook a large number of green rushes over the floor, and laying himself down, soon fell into a comfortable sleep, which lasted until the rising of the sun next morning.

As soon as the morning was come, Ironbones, who had got neither food nor sleep the whole night, came down from the mountain's side and awoke the Bodach, telling him that it was time to commence their contest. The Bodach raised his head, rubbed his eyes, and replied: "I have another hour to sleep yet, and when I get up I have to eat half a hog and drink a barrel of wine; but as you seem to be in a hurry, you have my consent to proceed on your way before me; and you may be sure I will follow you." So saying, he laid his head down and fell again a-snoring, and upon seeing this, Ironbones began the race by himself, but he moved along heavily and dispiritedly, for he began to have great dread and many misgivings, by reason of the indifference with which the Bodach appeared to regard the issue of the contest.

When the Bodach had slept his fill he got up, washed his hands and face, and having placed his bread and meat on the table, he proceeded to devour them with great expedition, and then washed them down with his barrel of wine, after which he collected together all the bones of the hog and put them into a pocket in the skirt of his coat. Then setting out on his race in company with a pure and cool breeze of wind, he trotted on and on, nor did he ever halt in his rapid course until he had overtaken Ironbones, who, with a dejected air and drooping head, was wending his way before him. The Bodach threw down the bare bones of the hog in his path, and told him he was quite welcome to them, and that if he could find any pickings on them he might eat them. "For," said he, "you must surely be hungry by this time, and myself can wait until you finish your breakfast."

But Ironbones got into a great passion on hearing this, and he cried, "You ugly Bodach with the Big Coat, you greasy, lubberly, uncouth tub of a man, I would see you hanged, so I would, before you should catch me picking such dirty common bones as these—hogs' bones, that have no meat on them at all, and have moreover been gnawed by your own long, ugly, boarish tusks."

"Oh, very well," replied the Bodach, "then we will not have any more words about them for bones, but let me recommend to you to adopt some more rapid mode of locomotion, if you desire to gain the crown, sovereignty and tribute of the kingdom of Ireland this turn, for if you go on at your present rate, it is second best that you will be after coming off, I'm thinking." And having spoken, off he darted as swift as a shadow, or a roebuck, or a blast of wind rushing down a mountain declivity on a March day, Ironbones in the mean time being about as much able to keep pace with him as he was to scale the firmament; nor did he check his own speed until he had proceeded thirty miles on the course. He then stopped for awhile to eat of the blackberries which grew in great abundance on the way, and while he was thus employed, Ironbones came up with him and spoke to him. "Bodach," said he, "ten miles behind us I saw one skirt of your gray coat, and ten miles further back again I saw another skirt; and it is my persuasion, and I am clearly of the opinion, that you ought to return for those two skirts without more to do, and pick them up."

"Is it the skirts of this big coat that I have on me you mean?" asked the Bodach, looking down at his legs.

"Why, to be sure it is them that I mean," answered Ironbones.

"Well," said the Bodach, "I certainly must get my coat skirts again, and so I will run back for them if you consent to stop here eating blackberries until I return."

"What nonsense you talk!" cried Ironbones. "I tell you I am decidedly resolved not to loiter on the race, and my fixed determination is not to eat any blackberries."

"Then move on before me," said the Bodach, upon which Ironbones pushed onward, while the Bodach retraced his steps to the different spots where the skirts of his coat were lying, and having found them and tacked them to the body of the coat, he resumed his route and again overtook Ironbones, whom he thus addressed: "It is needful and necessary that I should acquaint you of one thing, O Ironbones, and that is that you must run at a faster rate than you have hitherto used, and keep pace with me on the rest of the course, or else there is much likelihood and considerable probability that the victory will go against you, because I will not again have to go back either for my coat-skirts or anything else;" and having given his companion this warning, he set off once more in his usual manner, nor did he stop until he reached the side of a hill, within ten miles of Bincadar, where he again fell a-plucking blackberries, and ate an extraordinary number of them. When he could eat no more, his jaws being tired and his stomach stuffed, he took off his great coat, and handling his needle and thread, he sewed it into the form of a capacious sack, which he filled with blackberries; this he slung over his shoulders, and then off he scampered for Bineadar, greatly refreshed, and with the speed of a young buck.

In the mean time, Finn and his troops were awaiting in great doubt and dread for the result of the race, though, without knowing who the Bodach was, they had a certain degree of confidence in him; and there was a champion of the Fenians on the top of the Hill of Howth, who had been sent thither by Finn, and had been there from an early hour of the morning to see which of the competitors would make his appearance first in view. When this man saw the Bodach coming over the nearest eminence, with his heavy burden on his back, he thought that to a certainty it was Ironbones whom he beheld, and fled back quite terrified to Finn and the troops, telling them Ironbones was coming up, carrying the Bodach, dead, over his shoulders. This news at first depressed Finn and the troops; but Finn by and by exclaimed, "I will give a suit of armor and arms to the man who brings me better news than that!" whereupon one of the heroes went forth, and he had not proceeded far when he espied the Bodach advancing toward the outposts of the troops, and knowing him at a glance, he flew back to Finn and announced to him the glad tidings.

Finn thereupon went joyfully out to meet the Bodach, who speedily came up and threw down his burden, crying out aloud, "I have good and famous news for all of you; but," added he, "my hunger is great, and my desire for food pressing; and I cannot tell you what has occurred until I have eaten a very large quantity of oatmeal and blackberries. Now, as for the latter, that is, the blackberries, I have got them myself in this big sack, but the oatmeal I expect to be provided for me by you; and I hope that you will lose no time in getting it, and laying it before me, for I am weak for the want of nutriment, and my corporeal powers are beginning to be exhausted." Upon hearing this Finn replied, that his request should be at once attended to, and in a little space of time, accordingly, there was spread under the Bodach a cloth of great length and breadth, with a vast heap of oatmeal in the middle of it, into which the Bodach emptied out all the blackberries in his bag; and having stirred the entire mass about for some time with a long pole, he commenced eating and swallowing with much vigor and determination.

He had not long been occupied in this way before he descried Ironbones coming towards the troops with his hand on the hilt of his sword, his eyes flaming like red coals in his head, and ready to commence slaughtering all before him because he had been vanquished in the contest. But he was not fated to put his designs into execution, for when the Bodach saw what wickedness he had in his mind, he took up a handful of the oatmeal and blackberries, and dashing it towards Ironbones with an unerring aim, it struck him so violently upon his face that it sent his head spinning through the air half a mile from his body, which fell to the ground and there remained writhing in all the agonies of its recent separation, until the Bodach had concluded his meal. The Bodach then rose up and went in quest of the head, which, after a little searching about, he found; and casting it from his hands with an unerring aim, he sent it bowling along the ground all the half mile back again, until coming to the body it stopped and fastened itself on as well as ever, the only difference being that the face was now turned completely round to the back of the neck, while the back of the head was in front.

The Bodach having accomplished this feat much to his satisfaction, now grasped Ironbones firmly by the middle, threw him to the ground, tied him hand and foot so that he could not stir, and addressed him in these words: "O Ironbones, justice has overtaken you; the sentence your own vain mind had passed on others is about to be pronounced against yourself; and all the liberty that I feel disposed to leave you is the liberty of choosing what kind of death you think it most agreeable to die of. What a silly notion you did get into your noddle, surely, when you fancied that you, single-handed, could make yourself master of the crown, sovereignty, and tributes of Ireland, even though there had been nobody to thwart your arrogant designs but myself! But take comfort and be consoled, for it shall never be said of the Fians of Ireland that they took mortal vengeance on a single foe without any warriors to back him; and if you be a person to whom life is a desirable possession, I am willing to allow you to live, on condition that you will solemnly swear by the sun and moon that you will send the chief tributes of Thessaly every year to Finn MacCoole here in Ireland."

With many wry faces did Ironbones at length agree to take this oath; upon which the Bodach loosed his shackles and gave him liberty to stand up; then having conducted him towards the seashore, he made him go into the ship, to which, after turning its prow from the shore, he administered a kick in the stern, which sent it seven miles over the waters at once. And such was the manner in which Ironbones executed his vainglorious project, and in this way it was that he was sent off from the shores of Ireland, without victory, honor or glory, and deprived of the power of ever again boasting himself to be the first man on the earth in battle or combat.

But on the return of the Bodach to the troops, the sun and the wind lighted up one side of his face and his head in such a way that Fin and the Fians at once recognized him as Manannan Mac Lir, the Tutelary Fairy of Cruachan, who had come to afford them his assistance in their exigency. They welcomed him accordingly with all the honor that was due to him, and feasted him sumptuously for a year and a day. And these are the adventures of the Bodach-an-Chota-Lachtna.

HANDY ANDY'S LITTLE MISTAKES.

When Handy Andy grew up to be "a brave lump of a boy," his mother thought he was old enough to do something for himself, so she took him one day along with her to the Squire's, and waited outside the door until chance might give her "a sight of the Squire afore he wint out or afore he wint in," and after spending her entire day in this idle way at last the Squire made his appearance, and Judy presented her son, who kept scraping his foot, and pulling his forelock, that stuck out like a piece of ragged thatch from his forehead, making his obeisance to the Squire, while his mother was sounding his praises for "bein' the handiest crayture alive—an' so willin'—nothin' comes wrong to him."

"I suppose the English of all this is, you want me to take him," said the Squire.

"Throth, an' yer honor, that's just it—if your honor would be plased."

"What can he do?"

"Anything, your honor."

"That means *nothing*, I suppose," said the Squire.

"Oh, no, sir. Everything, I mane, that you would desire to do."

"Can he take care of horses?"

"The best of care sir," said the mother, while the miller, who was standing behind the Squire, waiting for orders, made a grimace at Andy, who was obliged to cram his face into his hat to hide the laugh, which he could hardly smother from being heard as well as seen.

"Let him come, then, and help in the stables, and we'll see what we can do."

"May the Lord—"

"That'll do—there now, go."

"Oh, sure, but I'll pray for you, and—"

"Will you go?"

"And may the angels make your honor's bed this blessed night, I pray."

"If you don't go, your son shan't come."

Judy and her hopeful son turned to the right about in double-quick time, and hurried down the avenue.

The next day Andy was duly installed into his office of stable-keeper; and, as he was a good rider, he was soon made whipper-in to the hounds, and Andy's boldness in this capacity soon made him a favorite with the Squire, who scorned the attentions of a valet, and let any one that chance threw in his way bring his boots, or his hot water for shaving, or his coat whenever it *was* brushed. One morning, Andy, who was very often the attendant on such occasions came to his room with hot water. He tapped at the door.

"Who's that?" said the Squire, who had just risen.

"It's me, sir."

"Oh—Andy, come in."

"Here's the hot water, sir," said Andy, bearing an enormous tin can.

"Why, what the deuce brings that tin can here? You might as well bring the stable bucket."

"I beg you pardon, sir," said Andy, retreating.

In two minutes more Andy came back, and tapping at the door, put in his head cautiously, and said "The maids in the kitchen, your honor, says there's not so much hot wather ready."

"Did I not see it a moment since in your hand?"

"Yes, sir, but that's not nigh the full o' the shtable-bucket."

"Go along, you stupid thief! and get me some hot water directly."

"Will the can do, sir?"

"Aye, anything, so make haste."

Off posted Andy, and back he came with the can.

"Where'll I put it, sir?"

"Throw this out," said the Squire, handing Andy a jug containing some cold water, meaning the jug to be replenished with the hot.

Andy took the jug, and the window of the room being open, he very deliberately threw the jug out. The Squire stared with wonder, and at last said:

"What did you do that for?"

"Sure you *towld* me to throw it out, sir."

"Go out of this, you thick-headed villain!" said the Squire, throwing his boots at Andy's head, along with some very neat curses. Andy retreated, and thought himself a very ill-used person.

Though Andy's regular duty was "whipper-in," yet he was liable to be called on to attend at table, when the number of guests required that all the subs. should be put in requisition, or rode on some distant errand for the "mistress," or drove out the nurse and children on the jaunting car, and many were the mistakes, delays or accidents that occurred.

The first time Andy was admitted into the mysteries of the dining-room, great was his wonder. The butler took him in to give him some previous instructions, and Andy was so astonished at the sight of the assembled glass and plate, that he stood with his mouth and eyes wide open, and scarcely heard a word that was said to him. After the head man had been dinning his instructions into him for some time, he said he might go until his attendance was required. But Andy moved not; he stood with his eyes fixed by a sort of fascination on some object that seemed to rivet them with the same unaccountable influence which the rattlesnake exercises over its victim.

"What are you looking at?" said the butler.

"Them things, sir," said Andy, pointing to some silver forks.

"What things do you mean?"

"These things, sir," said Andy, taking up one of the silver

forks, and turning it round and round in his hand in utter astonishment, while the butler grinned at his ignorance, and enjoyed his own superior knowledge.

"Well," said Andy, after a long pause, "the devil be from me if ever I seen a silver spoon split that way before."

The butler gave a hoarse laugh, and made a standing joke of Andy's split spoon; but time and experience made Andy less impressed with wonder at the show of plate and glass, and the split spoons became familiar as "household words" to him; yet still there were things in the duties of table attendance beyond Andy's comprehension—he used to hand cold plates for fish, and hot plates for jelly, etc. But "one day," as Zanga says, "one day" he was thrown off his centre in a remarkable degree by a bottle of soda-water.

It was when that combustible was first introduced into Ireland as a dinner beverage that the occurrence took place, and Andy had the luck to be the person to whom a gentleman applied for some soda-water.

"Sir," said Andy.

"Soda-water," said the guest, in that subdued tone in which people are apt to name their wants at the dinner-table.

Andy went to the butler. "Mr. Morgan, there's a gintleman—"

"Let me alone, will you?" said Mr. Morgan.

Andy manœuvred round him a little longer, and again essayed to be heard. "Mr. Morgan—"

"Don't you see I'm as busy as I can be? Can't you do it yourself?"

"I dunna what he wants."

"Well, go an' ax him," said Mr. Morgan.

Andy went off as he was bidden, and came behind the thirsty gentleman's chair, with "I beg your pardon, sir."

"Well," said the gentleman.

"I beg your pardon, sir, but what's this you axed me for?"

"Soda-water!"

"What, sir?"

"Soda-water; but perhaps you have not any."

"Oh, there's plenty in the house, sir. Would you like it hot, sir?"

The gentleman laughed, and supposing the new fashion was not understood in the present company, said: "Never mind."

But Andy was too anxious to please to be so satisfied, and again applied to Mr. Morgan.

"Sir!" said he.

"Bad luck from you! Can't you let me alone?"

"There's a g'ntleman wants some soap and wather."

"Some what?"

"Soap and wather, sir."

"The sorrow sweep you! soda-water, you mane. You'll get it under the sideboard."

"Is it in the can, sir?"

"No, you dhunderhead! in the bottles."

"Is this it, sir?" said Andy, producing a bottle of ale.

"No, bad cess to you! the little bottles."

"Is it the little bottles with no bottoms, sir?"

"I wish *you* wor in the bottom o' the say," said Mr. Morgan, who was fuming and puffing, and rubbing down his face with a napkin as he was hurrying to all quarters of the room, or, as Andy said in praising his activity, that he was "like bad luck, everywhere."

"There they are," said Mr. Morgan at last.

"Oh, them bottles that wont stand," said Andy, "sure them's what I said, with no bottoms to them. How'll I open it? It's tied down."

"Cut the cord, you fool."

Andy did as he was desired; and he happened at the time to hold the bottle of soda-water on a level with the candles that shed light over the festive board from a large silver branch, and the moment he made the incision, bang went the bottle of soda-water, knocking out two of the lights with the projected cork, which, performing its parabola the length of the room, struck the Squire himself in the eye at the foot of the table; while the hostess at the head had a cold bath down her back. Andy, when he saw the soda-water jumping out of the bottle, held it from him at arm's length; every fizz it made exclaiming, "Ow!—ow —ow!" and, at last, when the bottle was empty, he roared out, "Oh, Lord!—it's all gone!"

Great was the commotion; few could resist laughter, except the ladies, who all looked at their gowns, not liking the mixture of satin and soda-water. The extinguished candles were relighted—the Squire got his eye open again; and the next time he perceived the butler sufficiently near to speak to him, he said in a low and hurried tone of deep anger, "Send that fellow out of the room," but, within the same instant, resumed his former smile, that beamed on all around as if nothing had happened.

Andy was expelled the *sallé a manger*, and when the butler held up Andy's ignorance to ridicule, by telling how he asked for "soap and wather," he was given the name of "suds," and was called by no other for months after.

Even in his outdoor functions, Andy's evil genius haunted him, and he put his foot in a piece of business which was so simple as to defy almost the chance of Andy making any mistake about it; but Andy was very ingenious in his own particular line.

"Ride into the town and see if there's a letter for me," said the Squire one day to our hero.

"Yes, sir."

"You know where to go?"

"To the town, sir."

"But do you know where to go in the town?"

"No, sir."

"And why don't you ask, you stupid thief?"

"Sure I'd find out, sir."

"Didn't I often tell you to ask what you're to do, when you don't know?"

"Yes, sir."

"And why don't you?"

"I don't like to be throublesome, sir."

"Confound you," said the Squire.

"Well," continued he, "go to the post-office. You know the post-office, I suppose?"

"Yes, sir, where they sell gun-powdher."

"You're right for once. Go then to the post-office and ask for a letter for me. Remember—not gunpowder, but a letter."

"Yes, sir," said Andy, who got astride of his hack, and trotted away to the post-office. On arriving at the shop of the postmaster (for that person carried on a brisk trade in groceries, etc.), Andy presented himself at the counter and said, "I want a letther, if you plaze."

"Who do you want it for?" said the postmaster, in a tone which Andy considered an aggression upon the sacredness of private life; so Andy, in contempt of the prying impertinence of the postmaster, repeated his question.

"I want a letther, sir, if you plaze."

"And who do you want it for?" repeated the postmaster.

"What's that to you?" said Andy.

The postmaster told him he could not give him a letter till he gave the direction.

"The directions I got was to get a letther here; that's the directions."

"Who gave you those directions?"

"The masther."

"And who's your master?"

"What consarn is that of yours?"

"Why, you stupid rascal, if you don't tell me his name how can I give you a letther?"

"You could give it if you liked; but you're fond of axin' impident questions, bekase you think I'm simple."

"Go along out o' this! Your master must be as great a goose as yourself, to send such a messenger."

"Bad cess to your impidence," said Andy, "is it Squire Egan you dare say goose to?"

"Oh, Squire Egan's your master, then?"

"Yes; have you anything to say agin it?"

"Only that I never saw you before."

"Faith, thin, you'll never see me again, if I have me own consint."

"I won't give you any letter for the Squire, unless I know you're his servant. Is there any one in town knows you?"

"Plinty. It's not every one is as ignorant as you." Just at this moment a person to whom Andy was known came in, and vouched to the postmaster that he might give Andy the letter.

"Have you one for me?"

"Yes, sir," said the postmaster, producing one—"fourpence." The gentleman paid the four-pence postage, and left the shop with his letter.

"Here's a letter for the Squire," said the postmaster; "you've to pay me eleven-pence postage."

"What ud I pay eleven-pence for?"

"For postage."

"To the puck wid you. Didn't I see you give Mr. Dunphy a letther for four-pence this minit, and a bigger letther than this? and now you want me to pay eleven-pence for this scrap of a thing. Do you think I'm a fool?"

"No, but I'm sure of it," said the postmaster.

"Well, you're welkum to be sure, sir—but don't be delayin' me now; here's four-pence for you, and gi' me the letther."

"Go along, you stupid thief," said the postmaster, taking up the letter and going to serve a customer with a mouse-trap.

Meanwhile Andy lounged up and down the shop, every now and then saying, "Will ye gi' me the letther?"

He waited over half an hour, and left, when he found it impossible to get common justice for his master. The Squire in the mean time was getting impatient for his return, and when Andy made his appearance, asked if there was a letter for him.

"There is, sir," said Andy.

"Then give it to me."

"I haven't it, sir."

"What do you mean?"

"He wouldn't give it to me."

"Who wouldn't give it to you?"

"That ould chate beyant in the town—wantin' to charge double for it."

"Maybe it's a double letter. Why didn't you pay what he asked, sir?"

"Arrah, sir, why would I let you be chated? It's not a double letther at all; not above half the size o' one Mr. Dunphy got before my face for four-pence apiece."

"Go back, you scoundrel! or I'll horsewhip you; and if you're longer than an hour I'll have you ducked in the horse-pond."

Andy vanished and made a second visit to the post-office. When he arrived two other persons were getting letters, and the postmaster was selecting the epistles for each from a large parcel; at the same time many shop customers were waiting to be served.

"I'm come for that letther," said Andy.

"I'll attend to you by and by."

"The masther's in a hurry."

"Let him wait till his hurry's over."

"He'll murther me if I'm not back soon."

"I'm glad to hear it."

Meanwhile Andy's eye caught the heap of letters which lay on the counter; so while certain weighing of soap and tobacco was going forward, he contrived to become possessed of two letters from the heap, and, having effected that, waited patiently enough till it was the great man's pleasure to give him the missive directed to his master.

Then did Andy bestride his hack, and, in triumph at his trick on the postmaster, rattled along the road homewards, as fast as the beast could carry him. He came into the Squire's presence, his face beaming with delight, and an air of self-satisfied superiority in his manner, quite unaccountable to his master, until he pulled forth his hand, which had been grubbing up his prizes from the bottom of his pocket, and holding three letters over his head, while he said, "Look at that!" he next slapped them down under his broad fist on the table before the Squire, exclaiming, "Well! if he did make me pay eleven-pence, by gor, I brought your honor the worth o' your money, anyhow."

PUSS IN BROGUES.

At the foot of a hill, in a lonely district of the County Cork about a dozen miles from my native village, there lived, in old times, a poor man named Larry Roche. He was, they say, descended from that family of the Roches once so mighty in the south of Ireland, and some branches of which still retain a considerable degree of their former consequence and respectability. Poor Larry, however, although the blood of kings might flow through his veins, was neither rich nor respectable. Yet Larry was not discontented with his situation; and, although sometimes he might feel disposed to envy those on whom fortune smiled, yet, on cool reflection, he would console himself with the consideration that it was not every one was born with a silver spoon in his mouth. Thus rolled away Larry's days in poverty and contentment. In the shooting season his time was occupied in following his master over heath and hillock with his game-bag on his shoulder, while the rest of his time was spent in chatting with the crones of the vicinity about his family connections, or the fairies of Glendharig, or squabbling with his good woman and her young ones; for Larry was married, and as his wife was exactly a counterpart of himself, every hour of course gave fresh cause for that bickering and disagreement so often the result of untimely and ill-assorted marriages.

The only domestic animal in or about Larry Roche's cabin was a ferocious-looking old black tom-cat, far bigger and stronger than any cat ever seen in that part of the country. His fur was black, he had strong whiskers, his nails were like a tiger's, and at the end of his tail was fixed a claw or "gaff" as sharp and hooked as a falcon's beak; his eyes also flashed by night with an appalling glare, and his cry was a savage howl, baffling all description, and unlike any sound ever heard from any other animal. He was as singular in his habits, too, as in his appearance. He was never known to demand a morsel of food; and if offered any, he would reject it with indignation. Every evening at twilight he left the fireside, and spent the night scouring over moor and heather, and at daybreak would return from his foray, gaining access through the low chimney of the cabin, and be found in the morning in his usual position on the hob-stone. There he would sit from morning till night; and when Larry and Betty and the "childre" were chatting in a group around the fire, the cat would watch them intently, and if the nature of their conversation was such as to excite laughter or merriment, he would growl in a low tone, evidently dissatisfied; but if their dialogues were held in a jarring, angry strain, as sometimes happened, he would purr hoarsely and loudly, whilst the wagging of his tail testified the pleasure he felt in their feuds and dissensions. The family had often been advised to make away with him, but superstitious awe or family prejudice prevented them; and although the whole neighborhood averred that "he was no right thing," yet for the reasons I have stated his owners could never be induced to make any attempt to banish or destroy him.

One dreary evening in October, Larry returned from his day's wandering with the squire over the bleak bogs, and although it rained, and the wind blew bitterly, he appeared in much better spirits than was usual with him on similar occasions. His wife wondered, and made more than usual preparations to please him. She trimmed the fire, and assisted him in taking off his dripping clothes, and then commenced pouring out her sympathy for his sufferings.

"Oh, never mind," said Larry, "I have good news."

"Arrah, sit down," said Betty, "and tell us what it is."

Larry sat down, and putting his hand in his pocket, pulled out a glittering gold coin.

"Arrah, Larry, avourneen, what's that?" asked the woman.

"Faith, it's a rale yellow boy; a good goold guinea," replied

Larry. "The squire gev it to me, and tould me to buy a pair of brogues with it, and drink his health with the balance."

"Och, musha! then, long life to him," vociferated Betty; "and, Larry, a-hagur, will you buy the brogues?"

"Feix and I will," said Larry, "and another rattling pair for yourself, a-chorra."

"Ay, daddy, and another pair for me," shouted young Larry.

"And another for me," cried Thady.

"And another for me," chuckled Charley.

"Ay, and two pair for me," cried the black cat, speaking in a wild, unearthly tone from the hob-stone, and breaking forth into a horrible laugh.

"The sorrow knock the daylights out of yez all," cried Larry, without seeming to take any notice of the strange circumstance, though his heart died within him with terror and surprise.

"Lord have mercy on us!" faintly ejaculated Betty, signing her brow, whilst all the children started up in terror, and ran behind their parents in the chimney-corner.

All this time the cat remained silent on the hob; but his aspect, at all times terrible, now seemed perfectly monstrous and hideous. For some time a death-like silence was preserved, but at last Larry plucked up courage to address the speaking animal.

"In the name of God," he began, "what business have you with brogues?"

"Ask me no questions," replied the cat, "but get me the brogues as soon as possible."

"Oh, by all means," replied Larry, quite gently, "you must have them; and why did you not ask them long ago, and you should have got them?"

"My time was not come," replied Puss, briefly.

"Well," resumed Larry, "to-morrow is Sunday, and at daybreak I will start off to my gossip, Phadruig Donovan's, in Mill Street, to engage the brogues; he is the best broguemaker in the county, and he's my first gossip besides."

"I know all that," said the cat, as he leaped up the chimney, on his departure to the scene of his midnight wanderings. "Good night, Larry, and don't forget your engagement;" and he disappeared through the gathering gloom, to the great relief of poor Larry and his terrified family.

That was a sad and uneasy night with poor Larry and his wife and children. They did not go to bed at all, but sat trembling at the fire, expecting every moment that the black imp would return with legions of fiends to carry them away, body and bones, to the regions below. Numerous were the plans proposed for getting rid of their old companion, but all were rejected—some as inefficient, others as impracticable; and the only point on which they could finally agree, was, that their days were numbered, and that perhaps before morning their blood would be streaming on the hearth-stone, and their souls wandering through mire and morass, the prey of troops of fiends.

At last the morning dawned, and as Larry, disconsolately enough, was preparing to set forward on his journey to Mill Street, the cat jumped down the chimney, and took his usual place on the hob.

"Well, I am going now," said Larry; "have you any directions to give about the brogues?"

The cat did not reply, but uttered a hideous growl, which fell heavily on the poor fellow's heart; so, kissing his wife and children, and commending them to the protection of God, he set out on his sorrowful journey.

He had not gone far when he perceived through the dim gray of the morning a human figure approaching; and on advancing a little nearer, he found that it was a very old man, of extremely diminutive stature and forbidding aspect. He wore an old gray coat and an equally old woolen cap, and his thin white hair descended to his knees; he was bare-foot, and carried a walking-stick in his hand.

"Good morrow, and God save you, Larry Roche," said the old man as he came up.

"A bright morning to you," answered Larry.

"How is every rope's length of you, Larry, and how is the woman and the childre at home?" demanded the stranger.

"Faix, purty well, considherin'," replied Larry; "but you have a great advantage of me."

"How's that?" said the old man.

"Why, because you know me so well, while I have no more knowledge of you than of the man in the moon."

"Och, I'd know your skin in a tan-yard," said the old chap, laughing. "But is it possible you don't know me?"

"Faix, if God Almighty knows no more about you than I do, the devil will have a prey of you one of these days," replied Larry.

"Well, say no more about that," said the old fellow, rather angrily. "But where are you going this blessed Sunday morning, Larry?"

"To Mill Street," said Larry.

"All the ways—musha! what's taking you to Mill Street, Larry?"

"My feet and my business," said Larry, something piqued at the old fellow's inquisitive importunity.

"You are very stiff this morning, Larry," said the stranger with a grin.

"I am worse than that," said the poor fellow; "the heart within me is sick and sore."

"And what troubles you now, Larry?"

Larry hereupon told the whole of his strange misfortunes to the stranger, ending with a deep "ochone," and wishing, if it was the will of God, that "his four bones were stretched in the church-yard of Kilebawn."

"You'll be there time enough for your welcome, maybe," said the old chap, "but that's neither here nor there. What will you do with the black cat?"

"Och, sweet bad luck to all the cats alive, both black and white," imprecated Larry.

"That cat's a devil—a fiend," said the stranger; "and more than that, he intends to murder you and your family this very night."

Larry groaned, whilst the stranger's hideous countenance was convulsed with half-suppressed laughter.

"Well, Larry," said he again, "I am your friend, and I have power to save you and yours, on one condition; and that is, that you will stop up the window in the back wall of your cabin."

"Faith and I'll do that with a heart and a half," said Larry. "But what do you want that for?"

"I'll tell you that another time," said the little man.

"Go home now, and say you can't proceed to Mill Street without taking the wife and children with you, to leave the measure of their feet for the brogues. Tell the cat also that he must come too, to have his fit taken; then tie him up in a bag, and bring him with you; fasten this hair around your neck," added the old man, at the same time extracting a single white hair from his head, "and all the imps of hell cannot hurt you. But mind and don't open your lips from the time you leave home till you come to this spot; and when you arrive here with the cat, sit down and wait the event."

A thick fog now suddenly rose, and the old man was hidden from the sight of Larry, who, greatly overjoyed, returned to his cabin to execute the orders he had got, and was met by his wife, who was trembling for his safe return, but did not expect him sooner than night.

"Musha! Larry agragal, you're welcome," she exclaimed; "and what in the name of God turned you back?"

"I am coming for you and the gorsoons; you must all come to Mill Street to have your measure taken for the brogues."

"And must I go too?" asked the cat.

"Faix you must," said Larry; "if natural Christians couldn't be fitted without bein' on the spot, it's hard to expect that you could."

"And how am I to travel?" he asked.

"In the bag on my back," replied Larry. "I'll whip you through the country like a dinner to a hog, and man or mortal shall never be the wiser, if the broguemaker keeps his tongue quiet."

"I'll go bail he will," said Puss, "for I'll kill him the very night the brogues is brought home."

"Lord have mercy on him!" ejaculated Larry, his heart sinking within him.

"Pray for yourself—maybe you want mercy as well as him," said the cat.

The preparations were soon completed, and the cat being put into the bag, Larry tied the mouth of it firmly with a piece of cord, and then slung it on his shoulder; and, after acquainting his wife with his adventure with the old man on "Moin-more," he departed, whistling the air of "Thamama Thulla."

He soon gained the spot where he had parted with the old man, and looking round and perceiving nobody, he sat down on the green fern, still holding the bag which contained his terrible fellow-traveller.

"What stops you, Larry?" asked the cat.

Larry recollecting the old man's injunction, spoke not, but continued whistling.

"Does anything ail you, Larry?"

"Whoo, hoo, phoo, hoo—Thamemo Chodladh."

"Is Betty and the childre to the fore?"

"Thamemo Chodladh."

"Bad cess to you and your 'Thamemo Chodladh,'" cried the cat.

"That the prayers may fall on the preacher," said Larry to himself.

The cat now began to make desperate efforts to escape from the bag, whilst Larry redoubled his exertions to detain him. His attention, however, was soon arrested by the cry of hounds, and on looking westward, he perceived, rapidly approaching over the morass, a big black horse, and accompanied by a numerous pack of black dogs.

"Ochone," thought Larry, "now I am coached of all ever happened me. Here is the chap's black friends coming to rescue him, and they won't leave a toothful a-piece in my carcass."

"Let me go, Larry," said the cat, "let me go, and I'll show you where there's a cart-load of gold buried in the ground." But Larry remained silent, and meantime the horseman and hounds came up.

"Good morrow and good luck, Larry Roche," said the black equestrian, with a grim smile.

"Good morrow, kindly," said Larry.

"Is that a fox you have in the bag, Larry?"

"No, in troth," said Larry, "though I believe he is not much honester than a fox."

"I must see what it is, anyhow," said the sable horseman, with a gesticulation which convinced Larry at once that he was the fellow he had seen before.

So Larry opened the bag, and out jumped Puss, and away with him over the bog like a flash of lightning. The wild huntsman hallooed his dogs, and the pursuit commenced, but the cat was soon surrounded and torn to pieces.

"Now," said the horseman, "I must bid you farewell;" and off he went; and then Larry returned home with the happy tidings, and the squire's guinea was spent in the purchase of sundry bottles of "Tom Corcoran's" best potteen; but we must do Larry the justice to say that his agreement with the old man was punctually performed, and the back window stopped as effectually as mud and stones could do it.

A few nights after, Larry was aroused from his sleep by the merry tones of bagpipes at his fireside, and getting up he perceived the kitchen illuminated with a bright, reddish glare, whilst on the hob-stone he saw, snugly seated, the ever-remembered little old man, playing a set of bagpipes, to the delightful tones of which hundreds of little fellows with red caps and red small clothes were capering about the floor.

"God bless the man and the work," said Larry; "and warm work yez have ov it this hour ov the night."

The little fellow hereupon set up a shout, and rushing to the door, flew through it, one of them striking poor Larry a box on the right eye, which blinded it.

"Good night, Misthur Larry," said the piper; "and how is your four bones? and how is the good woman that owns you?"

"Och, no fear at all ov the woman," replied Larry; "and as for my bones, they are well enough; but, faith, my right eye, I believe, is in whey in my head."

"Well, it will teach you how to speak to your betters in future," said the little piper; "never mintion the holy name again, when talking to the 'good people.'

"But, Larry, listen: I'll now tell you why I wanted you to stop up your back window.

"You must know that this cabin of yours stands on the middle of a fairy pass. We often come this way in our wanderings through the air in cold nights, and often we wished to warm ourselves at your fireside; but as there was a window in the back of your cabin, we had not power to stop, but were compelled to pursue our journey. Now that the window is stopped, we can come in and remain as long as we wish, and resume our journey through the door by which we enter. We pass this way almost every night, and you need never feel in the least apprehensive of injury so long as you let us pursue our pastimes undisturbed."

"I'll be bound me or mine shall never annoy one of yez," said Larry.

"That's a good fellow, Larry," said the little chap; "and now take those pipes and play us a tune."

"Och, the devil a chanter I ever fingered," said Larry, "since I was christened."

"No matter," said the little fellow; "I'll go bail you'll play out of the soot."

Larry "yoked" on the pipes, and lilted up in darling style a merry tune, whilst the old chap was ready to split with laughing.

"What's the name of that tchune?" said Larry.

"*Caith-na-brogueen*," replied the fairy piper; "a tune I composed in memory of your escape from the cat; a tune that will soon become a favorite all over Munster."

Larry handed back the pipes; the little man placed them in a red bag, and, bidding his host "good night," dashed up the chimney.

The next night, and almost every following night, the din of fairy revels might be heard at Larry Roche's fireside, and Larry himself was their constant companion in their midnight frolics. He soon became the best performer on the bagpipes in the south of Ireland, and after some time surrendered his cabin to the sole occupation of the "good people," and wandered with his family through all the Munster counties, and was welcome, and kindly treated wherever he came. After some time, the cabin from neglect fell, and offered no further impediment to the fairy host in their midnight wanderings, whilst Larry followed a life of pleasure and peace, far from the scene of his former perils and privations.

The cat, of course, was never seen after; but the peasantry of the neighborhood say that the screams of the infernal fiend, mingled with the deep howlings of hell-hounds and the savage yellings of the sable hunter, may be distinctly heard in horrid chorus amongst the fens and morasses of the broad Moin-more.

THE WISE SIMPLETON.

A very long time ago, somewhere in the western part of the province of Munster, lived, in a small and wretched cabin, a poor widow, named Moireen Mera. She had three sons, two of whom were fine young men; but the third—and of him we shall soon hear a good deal—though strong and active, was of a lazy disposition, which resulted, as his mother at least always thought, not so much from any fault of his own, as from his natural foolishness of character; in fact, she really considered him as of that class called in Ireland "naturals." But before we say anything of the third son, let us trace the histories of his two elder brothers.

Now the first, whose name was Mihal More, or Michael Big Fellow, never let his mother rest one moment until she had consented to his starting, in order that he might, as he said, should he fall in with a good master, return, and perhaps make her comfortable for the remainder of her days.

To this plan, after much hesitation, Moireen Mera at length agreed, and the day was fixed by Mihal for starting. "And, mother," said he, "though you have but little left, and it is wrong to deprive you of it, if you *would* but bake me a fine cake of wheaten bread, and if you *could* but spare me one of the hens —ah! that would be too much to ask!—against the long road; could you, mother?"

"Why not, Michael? I could never refuse you anything; and you will want the cake and hen badly enough. And, Mihal *avick asthore!* if you *should* ever meet *one of the good people*, or anything you may think *isn't right*, pass it by, and say not a word."

It was evening when he began his expedition, nor did he stop on the road till daylight returned, when he found himself in the centre of a wood, and very faint and hungry. Seeing a convenient-looking rock near a place where he thought it most probable he should find water, he seated himself, with the intention of satisfying his hunger and thirst.

He had not been many moments engaged in eating some of his bread, and had just commenced an attack on the hen, by taking off one of her wings, when there came up to him a poor greyhound, which looked the very picture of starvation. Greyhounds are proverbially thin, but this was thinner than the thinnest, and, it was easy to see, had doubtlessly left at home a very large family.

Mihal More was so very intent on eating that he heeded not the imploring look of the poor greyhound, and it was not till, wonderful to say, she addressed him in *intelligible Irish*, that he deigned to notice her. But when the first word came from her mouth, he was sure she must be one of those against any communication with whom his mother had so emphatically warned him, and accordingly determined to apply her maxim strictly to the occurrence.

"You are a traveller, I see," said the greyhound, "and were doubtless weary and fainting with hunger when you took your seat here. I am the mother of a numerous and helpless family, who are even now clamorous for subsistence; this I am unable to afford them, unless I am myself supported. *You* have now the means. Afford it to me, then, if only in the shape of a few of the hen's small bones; I will be forever grateful, and may perhaps be the means of serving you in turn when you most want and least expect it."

But Mihal continued sedulously picking the bones, and when he had finished, he put them all back into his wallet, still resolving to have nothing to do whatever with this fairy, represented, as he imagined, by the greyhound.

"Well!" said she piteously, "since you give *me* nothing, follow me. You are perhaps in search of service; my master, who knows not my faculty of speech, lives near; *he* may assist you.

And see," continued she, as he followed, "behold that well. Had you relieved me, it was in my power to have changed its contents, which are of *blood*, to the finest virgin honey; but the honey is beneath the blood, neither can it now be changed! However, try your fortune, and if you are a reasonably sensible fellow, I may yet relent, and be reconciled to you."

Mihal still answered not a word, but followed the greyhound, until she came to the gate of a comfortable farmer's residence. She entered the door, and Mihal saw her occupy her place at the side of the fire, and that she was quickly besieged by a number of clamorous postulants, whose wants she seemed but poorly adequate to supply.

At a glance he perceived that the house contained a master and a mistress; but an old lady in the chimney corner, having by her a pair of crutches, made him quail, by the sinister expression of her countenance. Still, nothing daunted, he asked the master of the house at once for employment.

"Plenty of employment have I, friend, and good wages," answered he, " but I am a man of a thousand; and I may also say, not one man in a thousand will stop with me in this house."

"And may I ask the reason of this, sir?" said Mihal, taking off his hat respectfully.

" I will answer you immediately; but first follow me into my garden. There," said he, pointing to a heap of bones which lay bleaching on the ground, "*they* are the bones of those unfortunate persons who have followed in my service; if now, therefore, you should so wish, you have my full permission to depart unhurt; if you will brave them, hear now the terms on which I must be served."

"Sir," answered Mihal, "you surprise me. I have travelled far, have no money, neither any more to eat; say, therefore, your terms; and if I can at all reconcile myself to them, I am prepared to stop here."

" You must understand, then," said the farmer, " that I hold my lands by a very unusual tenure. This is not my fault. However, you will find *me* an indulgent master to *you*, at all events;

for, in fact, you may chance to be my master as much as I yours, or perhaps more, for *these* are the terms:

"If *I*, at any time, first find fault with any one thing *you* may say or do, *you* are to be solemnly bound to take this (pointing to an immense and sharp axe), and forthwith, without a word, strike *me* till *I* shall be dead; but should *you*, at any one time, first find fault with one of *my* words or actions, *I* must be equally bound to do the very same dreadful thing to *yourself*. Blame *me* not, therefore, should *you* find fault with *me*, for it will be my destiny, nay, my duty, to do as I have described; and, on the contrary, if it happen *otherwise*, I must be ready to submit to my fate. Consider, and reply."

"Oh, my master!" said Mihal More, "I have but the alternative of starvation; I am in a strangely wild country, without a friend. I *must* die if I proceed, and nothing more dreadful than death can happen to me here. I therefore throw myself upon your compassion, and agree to your terms."

They then returned to the house, and Mihal felt somewhat refreshed, even by the smell alone of the savory viands which the mistress was then preparing for the afternoon's repast; the greyhound, too, cast occasionally wistful glances towards the operations going forward.

At length the dinner hour being all but arrived, the old lady in the chimney-corner then opened her lips for the first time since Mihal had come in, and expressed a wish to go out and take a walk; "for," said she, "I have not been out for some weeks, ever since our last servant left us. What is your name, my man?" So he told her. "Come, then," said she, "Mihal, and assist me about the garden, for I am completely cramped."

Mihal muttered a few words about dinner, hunger, and so on, but was interrupted by the farmer, who said, "Mihal, you *must* attend my mother; she has sometimes strange fancies. Besides, remember our agreement. *Do you find fault with me?*"

"Oh, by no means, sir," said Mihal, frightened; "I must do my business, I suppose."

The dinner was actually laid out on the plates to every one

when Mihal and the old lady walked out. No sooner had they done so, than the greyhound, before she could be prevented, pounced on his dinner, and devoured it in a moment!

The old lady thought it proper to walk for some hours in the garden; and now was Mihal very hungry, for he had tasted nothing since he had finished the hen early that morning; he almost began to wish that he had relieved the greyhound.

No sooner had they entered the house than the accursed old lady seized a large cake of wheaten bread, which was baking on the embers, and, hastily spreading on it a coat of butter, directed Mihal to attend her again into the garden! He could say nothing, for his master's eyes were on him. He was completely bewildered. In despair he went with the old lady, and as it was a lovely moonlight night, she stopped out an unusual time, and it was very late when they came in.

Mihal stretched himself, quite fainting, on the bed, but slept not a wink. How I wish, now, thought he, that I had given the greyhound not only the small bones, but even half my hen!

The next morning the family early assembled for breakfast, and again were the cakes put down to bake over the glowing fire. *Again* did the old lady seize one, and command Mihal into the garden!

He was now completely exhausted; and, determining to expostulate with his master when he came in, went up to him, craving some food.

"No," said the farmer; "we never eat except at stated times, and my mother keeps the keys."

"Ah, sir, have pity on me!" answered Mihal; "how can I exist or do your business?"

"*And can you blame me?*" said the master.

Mihal, now quite losing sight of the agreement, and confused by the question, put in so treacherous a manner, answered, "that of course he could not but blame any person who would permit such infamous conduct."

Here was the signal. Mihal, in his enfeebled state, was no match for the sturdy farmer; in a moment his head was rolling on the floor by a vigorous stroke of the fatal axe, while grins of satisfaction might be seen playing on the countenances both of the old lady *and her greyhound.*

But when, in the course of a year, Mihal did not appear, the widow's grief was unbounded. How was she, then, astonished, when "the fool," as he was yet always called, although his real name was Rooshkulum, actually volunteered to do the same! Nothing could stop him; go he would. So the cake was baked, the hen was killed and roasted, and Rooshkulum, "the fool," set out on *his* expedition. And *there*, at the rock in the wood, was that very same greyhound; and as soon as she had looked him in the face, he said, "Why, poor thing! I have here what I cannot eat, and you seem badly to need it; here are these bones and some of this cake."

It was *then* the greyhound addressed him. "Come with me," said she; "lo! here is the well, of which *your brother* could not drink: behold! here is the honey on top, clear and pure, but the blood is far beneath!"

When "the fool" had satisfied himself at this well, he followed the greyhound to the farmer's house. It *may* be barely possible that by the road he received from her some excellent advice.

The conversation that ensued when Rooshkulum arrived at the farmer's, and offered himself for his servant, was much of the same nature as I have before detailed while relating the former part of my story. "But," said Rooshkulum the fool, "I will not bind myself to these terms forever; I might get tired of you, or you of me; so, if you please, I will agree to stop with you for certain till we both hear the cuckoo cry when we are together."

To this they agreed, and went into the house. However, just before they stepped in, the farmer asked Rooshkulum his name.

"Why," said he, "mine is a very curious name: it is so curious a name, indeed, that you would never learn it; and where is the occasion of breaking your jaws every minute trying to call me 'Pondracalcuthashochun,' which *is* my real name, when you may as well call me always 'the Boy?'"

"Well! that will do," answered the master.

The dinner was now prepared, and laid out on the plates, and the old tricks about to be played. Rooshkulum, as with the others, could not find fault, for, fool as he was, he knew the consequences. As he went out with the old lady, she too inquired his name.

"Why, really," said he to her, "mine is a name that no one, I venture to say, was ever called before. All my brothers and sisters died, and my father and mother thought that perhaps an unusual queer kind of name might have luck, so they called me '*Mehane*.'"

And, reader, if thou understandest not our vernacular, know that "Mehane" signifies in English "myself."

They spent some hours, as usual, in the garden, and Rooshkulum returned tired and exhausted. But when he expected to get his supper, and when she again brought him out, and ate the fine hot buttered cake before his very eyes, it was more than flesh and blood could stand. However, he pretended not to mind it in the least, but was very civil to the old lady, amusing her by his silly stories. "And now, ma'am," said he, "let's walk a little way down this sunny bank before we go in."

Certain it was that the sun did happen to shine on the bank at that very time, but it was to what were *growing* on it that he wished to direct her close attention; for when he came to a certain place where there was a cavity filled by a rank growth of nettles, thistles and thorns, he gave his charge such a shove as sent her sprawling and kicking in the midst of them, uttering wild shrieks, for the pain was great.

But Rooshkulum had no notion of helping her out, and ran into the house, which was some distance away, desiring the farmer to run, for that his mother *would* walk there, and had fallen into a hole, from which he could not get her. And then the farmer ran, and cried, "Oh, mother, where are you? what has happened?"

"Alas, my son! here I am down in this hole! Help me out! I am ruined, disfigured for life!"

THE WISE SIMPLETON. 123

"And *who* is it," said the farmer, "that has dared to serve you thus?"

"Oh," said she, "it was Mehane! *Mehane a veil Mehane!*" (Myself has ruined myself!)

"Who?" said the farmer as he helped her out.

"Oh, it was *Mehane*," answered she; "*Mehane a veil Mehane!*"

"Well, then," said the farmer, "I suppose it can't be helped, as it was yourself that did it. So here, 'Boy!' take her on your back, and carry her home; it was but an accident!"

So Rooshkulum carried her off and put her to bed, she all the time crying out, "Ah! but it was *Myself* that ruined Myself!" till her son thought her half cracked. She was quite unable to rise next morning; so Rooshkulum "the fool" made an excellent and hearty breakfast, which he took care also to share with the greyhound.

But then the old lady called her son to her bedside, and explained how that it was "the Boy" who had done the mischief, "And I command you," said she, "to get rid of him, and for that purpose desire him at once to go and make 'cuisseh na cuissheh na guirach' (the road of the sheeps' feet), that you have long been intending to do, and then to send him with the flock over the road to the land of the giant; we shall then never see him more; and it is better to lose even a flock of sheep than have him longer here, now that he has discovered our trick."

The farmer called Rooshkulum to him, and taxed him with what he had done to his mother.

"And," said Rooshkulum, "*could you blame me?*"

"Why, no," answered the farmer, remembering *his* part of the agreement, "*I don't blame you*, but you must never do it any more. And now you must take these (pointing to the sheep), and because the bog is soft on the road to the 'land of the giant,' you must make 'the road of the sheeps' feet' for them to go over, and come back when they are fat, and the giant will support you while you are there. *Do you blame me for that?*"

"No," said Rooshkulum, driving away the sheep.

But, contrary to all their expectations, in an hour's time in marched Rooshkulum, covered with bog dirt and blood. "Oh!" said he, "I have had hard work since, and made a good deal of the road of the sheep's legs; but indeed, there are not half enough legs after all, and you must give me more legs, if you would wish the road made firm."

"And, you rascal, do you tell me you have cut off the legs of all my fine sheep?"

"Every one, sir; did you not desire me? *Do you blame me?*"

"Oh, dear no! by no means! Only take care, and don't do it any more."

They went on tolerably for a few days, for they were afraid of Rooshkulum, and let him alone, till one morning the farmer told him he was going to a wedding that night, and that he might go with him.

"Well," said Rooshkulum, "what is a wedding? what will they do there?"

"Why," answered the farmer, "a wedding is a nice place, where there is a good supper, and two people are joined together as man and wife."

"Oh, is that it? I should like much to see what they'll do."

"Well, then, you must promise me to do what I'll tell you with the horses when we are going."

"Why, what shall I do?"

"Oh, only when we are going, *don't take your eyes from the horses* till we get there; then have your *two eyes* on my plate, and *an eye* on every other person's plate; and *then* you'll see what they'll do."

Rooshkulum said nothing. They went to the wedding; but when they sat down to supper, all were surprised to find a round thing on their plates, covered with blood, and not looking very tempting. But the farmer soon guessed the sad truth, and calling Rooshkulum aside, he sternly asked him what he had done.

"*Can you blame me?*" answered the provoking Rooshkulum; "did you not desire me not to take the eyes from the horses till I got here, and to put them on the plates, and two on your own plate, and that I would see what they would do then?"

"*Oh, don't imagine I blame you,*" said the farmer; "but I meant your own eyes all the time; and, mind me, *don't do it any more!*"

They were all by this time heartily sick of Rooshkulum, especially the old lady, who had never left her bed; and one morning, feeling something better, she called the farmer to her bedside, and addressed him thus:—"You know, my son, that your agreement with that rascal will terminate when you both shall hear the cuckoo. Now, in my youth I could imitate the cuckoo so well that I have had them flying round me. Put me up, therefore, in the big holly bush; take him along with you to cut a tree near; I will then cry 'cuckoo!' 'cuckoo!' and the agreement will be broken!" said she chuckling to herself.

This seemed a capital idea; so the farmer lifted his mother out of bed, and put her up into the holly bush, calling Rooshkulum to bring the big axe, for that he intended to fell a tree. Rooshkulum did as he was desired, and commenced cutting down a certain tree, which the farmer pointed out. And not long had he been thus engaged when the old lady in the holly bush cried out "cuckoo!" "Hah! what's that?" said the farmer; "that sounds like the cuckoo!"

"Oh, that cannot be," said Rooshkulum, "for this is winter!" But now the cuckoo was heard beyond a doubt.

"Well," said Rooshkulum, "before I'm done with you, I'll go and see this cuckoo."

"Why, you stupid fool!" said the farmer, "no man ever saw the cuckoo."

"Never mind!" said Rooshkulum, "it can be no harm to look. Wouldn't you think, now, that the cuckoo was speaking out of the holly bush?"

"Oh, not at all!—perhaps she is five miles away. Come away at once and give up your place. Did we not both hear her?"

"Stop!" said Rooshkulum; "stay back! don't make a noise! There! did not you see something moving? Ay! THAT must be the cuckoo!"

So saying, he hurled the axe into the holly bush with his

whole force, cutting away the branches, scattering the leaves and berries, and with one blow severing the head from the shoulders of the farmer's mother!

"Oh!" said the farmer, "my poor old mother! Oh, what have you done, you villain! You have murdered my mother!"

"And," said Rooshkulum (seemingly surprised), "*I suppose you* BLAME *me for this, do you?*"

And *now* was the farmer taken by surprise, and in the heat of his passion answered, "How dare you, you black-hearted villain, ask me such a question? Of course I do! Have you not murdered my mother? Alas! my poor old mother."

"Oh, very well!" said Rooshkulum, as the farmer continued looking at his mother, and lamenting, "perhaps you also remember our own little agreement. I have but too good reason to think that you and your accursed old mother, by your schemes, caused the death of my fine brother. But now for the fulfillment of my share of the bargain!"

In a moment the axe descended on his head; and Rooshkulum, *the wise simpleton*, having now got rid of his enemies, took possession of all the farmer's property, returned home for his mother, and lived free from care or further sorrow for the remainder of his happy life; but he never forgot the services of the greyhound and never allowed her to want.

PEGGY THE PISHOGUE.

"And now, Mickey Brennan, it's not but I have a grate regard for you, for troth you're a dacint boy, and a dacint father and mother's child; but you see, avick, the short and the long of it is, that you needn't be looking after my little girl any more."

Such was the conclusion of a long and interesting harangue pronounced by old Brian Moran of Lagh-buoy, for the purpose of persuading his daughter's sweetheart to waive his pretensions—a piece of diplomacy never very easy to effect, but doubly difficult when the couple so unceremoniously separated have labored under the delusion that they were born for each other, as was the case in the affair of which our story tells; and certainly, whatever Mr. Michael Brennan's other merits may have been, he was very far from exhibiting himself as a pattern of patience on the occasion.

"Why, thin, Brian Moran!" he outrageously exclaimed, "in the name of all that's out of the way, will you give me one reason good, bad, or indifferent, and I'll be satisfied?"

"Och, you unfortunate gossoon, don't be afther axing me," responded Brian dolefully.

"Ah, thin, why wouldn't I?" replied the rejected lover. "Aren't we playing together since she could walk—wasn't she the light of my eyes and the pulse of my heart these six long years—and when did one of ye ever either say or sign that I was to give over until this blessed minute? tell me that."

"Widdy Eelish!" groaned the closely interrogated parent; "'tis true enough for you. Botheration to Peggy, I wish she tould you herself. I knew how it 'ud be; an' sure small blame to you; an' it'll kill Meny out an' out."

"Is it that I amn't rich enough?" he asked impetuously.

"No, avick machree, it isn't; but, sure, can't you wait an' ax Peggy?"

"Is it because there's anything against me?" continued he, without heeding this reference to the mother of his fair one—"Is it because there's anything against me, I say, now or evermore, in the shape of warrant, or summons, or bad word, or anything of the kind?"

"Och, *forrear, forrear !*" answered poor Brian, "but can't you ax Peggy?" and he clasped his hands again and again with bitterness, for the young man's interest had been, from long and constant habit, so interwoven in his mind with those of his darling Meny, that he was utterly unable to check the burst of agony which the question had excited. The old man's evident grief and evasion of the question were not lost upon his companion.

"I'm belied—I know I am—I have it all know," shouted he, utterly losing all command of himself. "Come, Brian Moran, this is no child's play—tell me at once who dared to spake one word against me, an' if I don't drive the lie down his throat, be it man, woman, or child, I'm willing to lose her and everything else I care for!"

"No, then," answered Brian, "the never a one said a word against you—you never left it in their power, avick; an' that's what's breaking my heart. Millia murther, it's all Peggy's own doings."

"What!" he replied—"I'll be bound Peggy had a bad dhrame about the match. Arrah, out with it, an' let us hear what Peggy the Pishogue has to say for herself—out with it, man; I'm asthray for something to laugh at."

"Oh, whist, whist—don't talk that way of Peggy anyhow," exclaimed Brian, offended by this imputation on the unerring wisdom of his helpmate. "Whatever she says, doesn't it come to pass? Didn't it rain on Saturday last, fine as the day looked? Didn't Tim Higgins' cow die? Wasn't Judy Carney married to Tom Knox afther all? Ay, an' as sure as your name is Mickey Brennan, what she says will come true of yourself too. *Forrear, forrear!* that the like should befall one of your decent kin!"

"Why, what's going to happen me?" inquired he, his voice trembling a little in spite of all his assumed carelessness, for contemptuously as he had alluded to the wisdom of his intended mother-in-law, it stood in too high repute not to create in him some dismay at the probability of his figuring unfavorably in any of her prognostications.

"Don't ax me, don't ax me," was the sorrowing answer: "but take your baste out of the stable at once, and go straight to Father Coffey; and who knows but he might put you on some way to escape the bad luck that's afore you."

"Psha! fudge! 'pon my sowl it's a shame for you, Brian Moran."

"Divil a word of lie in it," insisted Brian; "Peggy found it all out last night; an' troth it's troubling her as much as if you were her own flesh and blood. More betoken, haven't you a mole there under your ear?"

"Well, and what if I have?" rejoined he, peevishly, but alarmed all the while by the undisguised pity which his future lot seemed to call forth. "What if I have?—hadn't many a man the same afore me?"

"No doubt, Mickey, agra, and the same bad luck came to them too," replied Brian. "Och, you unfortunate, ignorant crathur, sure you wouldn't have me marry my poor little girl to a man that's sooner or later to end his days on the gallows!"

"The gallows!" he slowly exclaimed. "Holy Virgin! is that what's to become of me after all?" He tried to utter a laugh of derision and defiance, but it would not do; such a vaticination from such a quarter was no laughing matter. So yielding at last to the terror which he had so vainly affected to combat, he buried his face in his hands, and threw himself violently on the ground; while Brian, scarcely less moved by the revelation he had made on the faith of his wife's far-famed sagacity, seated himself compassionately beside him to administer what consolation he could.

Whatever may be the opinion of other and wiser people on the subject, in the parish of Ballycoursey or its vicinity it was rather an ugly joke to be thus devoted to the infernal gods by a prophetess of such unerring sagacity as Peggy Moran, or, as she was sometimes styled with reference to her skill in all supernatural matters, Peggy the Pishogue—that cognomen implying an acquaintance with more things in heaven and earth than are dreamt of in philosophy. Nothing was too great or too small for her all-piercing ken—in every form of augury she was omniscient, from cup-tossing up to necromancy—in vain the mystic dregs of the tea-cup assumed shapes that would have puzzled Doctor Wall himself: with her first glance she detected at once the true meaning of the hieroglyphic symbol, and therefrom dealt out deaths, births and marriages with the infallibility of a newspaper.

The hardest task of all is to describe the feelings of poor Brennan himself on the occasion; for much as he had affected to disparage the sibylline revelations of the weird woman of Ballycoursey, there was no one in the neighborhood who was more disposed to yield them unlimited credence in any case but his own; and even in his own case he was not long enabled to struggle against conviction. How could he be expected to bear up against this terrible denunciation, when all the consolation he could receive from his nearest and dearest was that "it was a good man's death"? Death! poor fellow, he had suffered the pains of a thousand deaths already, in living without the hope of ever being the husband of his Meny. Death, instant and immediate, would have been a relief to him; and it was not long until, by his anxiety to obtain that relief, he afforded an opportunity to Peggy of displaying her own reliance on the correctness of her prognostications. Goaded into madness by his present sufferings and his fears for the future, he made an attempt upon his life by plunging into an adjacent lake when no one, as he thought, was near to interrupt his intentions. It was not so, however—a shepherd had observed him, but at such a distance that before help could be obtained to rescue him he was to all appearance lifeless. The news flew like wildfire: he was dead, stone dead, they said—had lain in the water ten minutes, half an hour, half the day, since last night; but in one point they all concurred—dead he was; dead as St. Dominick.

"Troth, he's not," was Peggy's cool rejoinder. "Be quiet, and I'll engage he'll come to. *Nabocklish*, he that's born to be hanged will never be drowned. Wait awhile an' hould your tongues. *Nabocklish*, I tell you he'll live to spoil a market yet, an' more's the pity."

People shook their heads, and almost began to think their wise woman had made a mistake, and read hemp instead of water. It was no such thing, however: slowly, and beyond all hopes, Brennan recovered the effects of his rash attempt, thereby fulfilling so much of his declared destiny, and raising the reputation of Mrs. Moran to a point that she never had attained before. That very week she discovered no less than six cases of stolen goods, twice detected the good people taking unauthorized liberties with their neighbors' churns, and spaed a score of fortunes, at the very least; and he, poor fellow, satisfied at last that Fortune was not to be bilked so easily, resigned himself to his fate like a man, and began to look about him in earnest for some opportunity of gracing the gallows without disgracing his people.

And Meny—poor, heart-stricken Meny—loving as none but the true and simple-minded can love, the extent of her grief was such as the true and simple-minded only can know; and yet there was worse in store for her. Shortly after this consummation of her mother's fame, a whisper began to creep through the village—a whisper of dire import, portending death and disaster on some luckless wight unknown—"Peggy Moran has something on her mind." What could it be? Silent and mysterious she shook her head when any one ventured to question her; the pipe was never out of her jaw unless when she slept or sat down to her meals; she became as cross as a cat, which, to do her justice, was not her wont, and eschewed all sorts of conversation, which most assuredly was not her wont either. The interest and curiosity of her neighbors were raised to a most agonizing pitch; every one trembled lest the result should be some terrible revelation affecting himself or herself, as the case might be: it was the burden of the first question asked in the morning, the last at night. Every word she uttered during the day was matter of speculation to a hundred anxious inquirers; and there was every danger of the good people of Ballycoursey going absolutely mad with fright if they were kept any longer in the dark on the subject.

At length there was a discovery; but, as is usually the case in all scrutinies into forbidden matters, it was at the cost of the too-daring investigator. Peggy and Brian were sitting one night before the fire, preparing for their retirement, when a notion seized the latter to probe the sorrows of his helpmate.

"'Deed it well becomes you to ax," quoth the weird woman, in answer to his many and urgent inquiries; "for Brian, achorra machree, my poor ould man, there's no use in hiding it—it's all about yourself."

"No, then!" exclaimed the surprised interrogator; "the Lord betune us an' harm, is it?"

"'Deed yes, Brian," responded the sibyl with a melancholy tone, out of the cloud of smoke in which she had sought to hide her troubles. "I'm thinking these last few days you're not yourself at all at all."

"Tare an ounties! maybe I'm not," responded he of the doubtful identity.

"Do you feel nothing on your heart, Brian achree?"

"I do; sure enough I do," gasped poor Brian, ready to believe anything of himself.

"Something like a *plurrisy*, isn't it?" inquired the mourner.

"Ay, sure enough, like a plurrisy for all the world, Lord betune us an' harm!"

"An' you do be very cold, I'll engage, these nights, Brian?" continued she.

"Widdy Eelish! I'm as cowld as ice this minute," answered Brian, and his teeth began to chatter as if he was up to his neck in a mill-pond.

"An' your appetite is gone entirely, achra?" continued his tormentor.

"Sorra a word o' lie in it," answered the newly discovered invalid, forgetful, however, that he had just finished discussing a skib of potatoes and a mug of milk for his supper.

"And the cat, the crathur, looked at you this very night after licking her paw."

"I'll engage she did. Bad luck to her," responded Brian, "I wouldn't put it beyant her."

"Let me feel your pulse, asthore," said Peggy in conclusion; and Brian submitted his trembling wrist to her inspection, anxiously peering into her face all the while to read his doom therein. A long and deep sigh broke from her lips, along with a most voluminous puff of smoke, as she let the limb drop from her hold and commenced rocking herself to and fro, uttering a low and peculiar species of moan, which to her terrified patient sounded as a death summons.

"Murther-an'-ages, Peggy, sure it's not going to die I am!" exclaimed Brian.

"Och, widdy! widdy!" roared the afflicted spouse, now giving full vent to her anguish. "It's little I thought, Brian asthore machree, when I married you in your beauty and your prime, that I'd ever live to cry the keen over you—ochone, ochone! 'tis you was the good ould man in airnest—och! och!"

"Arrah, Peggy!" interposed the object of her rather premature lamentations.

"Oh, don't talk to me—don't talk to me. I'll never hould up my head again, so I won't!" continued the widow that was to be, in a tone that quickly brought all the house about her, and finally all the neighbors. Great was the uproar that ensued, and noisy the explanation, which, however, afforded no small relief to the minds of all persons not immediately concerned in the welfare of the doomed Brian. Peggy was inconsolable at the prospect of such a bereavement. Meny clung in despair to the poor tottering old man, her grief too deep for lamentation, while he hobbled over his prayers as fast and as correctly as his utter dismay would permit him. Next morning he was unable to rise, refused all nourishment, and called vehemently for the priest. Every hour he became worse; he was out of one faint into another; announced symptoms of every complaint that ever vexed mankind, and declared himself affected by a pain in every member, from his toe to his cranium. No wonder it was a case to puzzle the doctor. The man of science could make nothing of it—swore it was the oddest complication of diseases that ever he had heard of—and strongly recommended that the patient be tossed in a blanket, and his wife treated to a taste of the horse-pond. Father Coffey was equally nonplused.

"What ails you, Brian?"

"An all-overness of some kind or other, your reverence," groaned the sufferer in reply, and the priest had to own himself a bothered man. Nothing would induce him to rise—"Where's the use in a man's gettin' up, an' he goin' to die?" was his answer to those who endeavored to rouse him—"isn't it a dale dacinter to die in bed like a Christian?"

"God's good!—maybe you won't die this time, Brian."

"Arrah, don't be talking—doesn't Peggy know best?" And with this undeniable assertion he closed all his arguments, receiving consolation from none, not even his heart-broken Meny. Despite of all his entreaties to be let die in peace, the doctor, who guessed how matters stood, was determined to try the effects of a blister, and accordingly applied one of more than ordinary strength, stoutly affirming that it would have the effect of the patient being up and walking on the morrow. A good many people had gathered into his cabin to witness the cure, as they always do when their presence could be best dispensed with; and to these Peggy, with tears and moans, was declaring her despair in all remedies whatever, and her firm conviction that a widow she'd be before Sunday, when Brian, roused a little by the uneasy stimulant from the lethargy into which they all believed him to be sunk, faintly expressed his wish to be heard.

"Peggy, agra," said he, "there's no denyin' but you're a wonderful woman entirely; an' since I'm goin', it would be a great consolation to me if you'd tell us all how you found out the sickness was on me afore I knew it myself. It's just curiosity, agra—I wouldn't like to die, you see, without knowin' for why an' for what—it 'ud have a foolish look if anybody axed me what I died of, an' me not able to tell them."

Peggy declared her willingness to do him this last favor, and, interrupted by an occasional sob, thus proceeded:

"It was Thursday night week—troth, I'll never forget that night, Brian asthore, if I live to be as ould as Noah—an' it was just after my first sleep that I fell draming. I thought I went down to Dan Keefe's to buy a taste ov mate, for ye all know he killed a *bullsheen* that day for the market ov Moneen; an' I thought when I went into his house, what did I see hangin' up but an ugly *lane* carcass, an' not a bit too fresh neither, an' a strange man dividin' it with a hatchet; an' says he to me with a mighty grum look:

"'Well, honest woman, what do you want?—is it to buy bullsheen?'

"'Yes,' says I, 'but not the likes of that—it's not what we're used to.'

"'Divil may care,' says he; 'I'll make bould to cut out a rib for you.'

"'Oh, don't if you plase,' says I, puttin' out my hand to stop him; an' with that what does he do but he lifts the hatchet an' makes a blow at my hand, an' cuts the weddin' ring in two on my finger!"

"Dth! dth! dth!" was ejaculated on all sides by her wondering auditory, for the application of the dream to Brian was conclusive, according to the popular method of explaining such matters. They looked round to see how he sustained the brunt of such a fatal revelation. There he was sitting bolt upright in the bed, notwithstanding his unpleasant incumbrance, his mouth and eyes wide open.

"Why, thin, blur-an'-ages, Peggy Moran," he slowly exclaimed, when he and they had recovered a little from their surprise, "do you mane to tell me that's all that ailed me?"

Peggy and her coterie started back as he uttered this extraordinary inquiry, there being something in his look that portended his intention to leap out of bed, and probably display his indignation a little too forcibly, for, quiet as he was, his temper wasn't proof against a blister; but his bodily strength failed him in the attempt, and, roaring with pain, he resumed his recumbent position. But Peggy's empire was over—the blister had done its business, and in a few days he was able to stump about as usual, threatening to inflict all sorts of punishment upon any one who dared to laugh at him. A laugh is a thing, however, not easy to be controlled, and finally poor Brian's excellent temper was soured to such a degree by the ridicule which he encountered, that he determined to seek a reconciliation with young Brennan, pitch the decrees of fate to Old Nick, and give Father Coffey a job with the young couple.

To this resolution we are happy to say he adhered: still happier are we to say, that among the county records we have not yet met the name of his son-in-law, and that unless good behavior and industry be declared crimes worthy of bringing their perpetrator to the gallows, there is very little chance indeed of Mickey Brennan fulfilling the prophecy of Peggy the Pishogue.

AN IRISH DANCING-MASTER.

In those racy old times, when the manners and usages of Irishmen were more simple than they are at present, dancing was cultivated as one of the chief amusements of life, and the dancing-master looked upon as a person essentially necessary to the proper enjoyment of our national recreation. He eked out a precarious but generally contented existence by developing in the young those graces of manner, the possession of which was his constant and proudest boast. At one time he led a sort of vagabond life, wandering from house to house; but generally he managed to collect together a number of the youth of both sexes, and, as master of a dancing-school, lorded it over them with all the dignity at his command.

One of the most amusing specimens of the dancing-master that I ever met, was a person who bore the nickname of Buckram-Back.

He was a dapper, light little fellow, with a rich Tipperary brogue, crossed by a lofty strain of illegitimate English, which he picked up whilst in the army. His habiliments sat as tight upon him as he could readily wear them, and were all of the shabby-genteel class. His crimped black coat was a closely worn second-hand, and his crimped face quite as much of a second-hand as the coat. I think I see his little pumps, little white stockings, his coaxed drab breeches, his hat, smart in its cock but brushed to a polish and standing upon three hairs, together with his tight questionably colored gloves, all before me. Certainly he was the jauntiest little cock living—quite a blood, ready to fight any man, and a great defender of the fair sex, whom he never addressed except in that highflown, bombastic style so agreeable to most of them, called by their flatterers the complimentary, and by their friends the fulsome. He was, in fact, a public man, and up to everything. You met him at every fair, where he only had time to give you a wink as he passed, being just then engaged in a very particular affair; but he would tell you again. At cockfights he was a very busy personage, and an angry better from half a crown downwards. At races he was a knowing fellow, always shook hands with the winning jockey, and then looked pompously about, that folks might see that he was hand and glove with those who knew something.

The house where Buckram-Back kept his dancing school, which was open only after the hours of labor, was an uninhabited cabin, the roof of which, at a particular spot, was supported by a post that stood upright from the floor. It was built upon an elevated situation, and commanded a fine view of the whole country for miles about it. A pleasant sight it was to see the modest and pretty girls, dressed in their best frocks and ribbons, radiating in little groups from all directions, accompanied by their partners or lovers, making way through the fragrant summer fields of a calm cloudless evening, to this happy scene of innocent amusement.

And yet what an epitome of general life, with its passions, jealousies, plots, calumnies and contentions, did this little segment of society present! There was the shrew, the slattern, the coquette and the prude as sharply marked within this their humble sphere, as if they appeared on the world's wider stage, with half its wealth and all its temptations to draw forth their prevailing foibles. There, too, was the bully, the rake, the liar, the coxcomb and the coward, each as perfect and distinct in his kind as if he had run through a lengthened course of fashionable dissipation, or spent a fortune in acquiring his particular character. The elements of the human heart, however, and the passions that make up the general business of life, are the same in high and low, and exist with impulses as strong in the cabin as they have in the palace. The only difference is, that they have not equal room to play.

Buckram-Back's system, in originality of design, in comic conception of decorum, and in the easy practical assurance with which he wrought it out, was never equalled, much less surpassed. Had the impudent little rascal confined himself to dancing as usually taught, there would have been nothing so ludicrous or uncommon in it; but no: he was such a stickler for example in everything, that no other mode of instruction would satisfy him. Dancing! Why, it was the least part of what he taught or professed to teach.

In the first place, he undertook to teach every one of us—for I had the honor of being his pupil—how to enter a drawing-room "in the most fashionable manner alive," as he said himself.

Secondly. He was the only man, he said, who could in the most agreeable and polite style taich a gintleman how to salute, or, as he termed it, how to shiloote, a leedy. This he taught, he said, wid great success.

Thirdly. He could taich every leedy and gintleman how to make the most beautiful bow or curchy on airth, by only imitating himself—one that would cause a thousand people, if they were all present, to think that it was particularly intended only for aich o' themselves!

Fourthly. He taught the whole art o' courtship wid all politeness and success, accordin' as it was practiced in Paris durin' the last saison.

Fifthly. He could taich thim how to write love-letthers and valentines, accordin' to the Great Macademetian compliments, which was supposed to be invinted by Bonaparte when he was writing love-letthers to both his wives.

Sixthly. He was the only person who could taich the famous dance called Sir Roger de Coverly, or the Helter-Skelter Drag, which comprehinded widin itself all the advantages and beauties of his whole system—in which every gintleman was at liberty to pull every leedy where he plaised, and every leedy was at liberty to go wherever he pulled her.

With such advantages in prospect, and a method of instruction so agreeable, it is not to be wondered at that his establishment was always in a most flourishing condition. The truth is, he had so contrived that every gentleman should salute his lady as often as possible, and for this purpose actually invented dances, in which not only should every gentleman salute every lady, but every lady, by way of returning the compliment, should render a similar kindness to every gentleman. Nor had his male pupils all his prodigality of salutation to themselves, for the amorous little rascal always commenced first and ended last, in order, he said, that they might *cotch* the manner from himself. "I do this, leedies and gintlemen, as your moral (model), and because it's part o' *my* system—ahem!"

And then he would perk up his little hard face, that was too barren to produce more than an abortive smile, and twirl like a wagtail over the floor, in a manner that he thought irresistible.

Whether Buckram-Back was the only man who tried to reduce kissing to a system of education in this country, I do not know. It is certainly true that many others of his stamp made a knowledge of the arts and modes of courtship, like him, a part of the course. The forms of love-letters, valentines, etc., were taught their pupils of both sexes, with many other polite particulars, which it is to be hoped have disappeared forever.

One thing, however, to the honor of our countrywomen we are bound to observe, which is, that we do not remember a single result incompatible with virtue to follow from the little fellow's system, which by the way was in *this* respect peculiar only to himself, and not the general custom of the country. Several weddings, unquestionably, we had, more than might otherwise have taken place, but in not one instance have we known any case in which a female was brought to unhappiness or shame.

We shall now give a brief sketch of Buckram-Back's manner of tuition, begging our readers at the same time to rest assured that any sketch we could give would fall far short of the original.

"Paddy Corcoran, walk out an' 'inther your drawin'-room;' an' let Miss Judy Hanratty go out along wid you, an' come in as Mrs. Corcoran."

"Faith, I'm afeard, masther, I'll make a bad hand of it; but,

sure, it's something to have Judy here to keep me in countenance."
"Is that by way of compliment, Paddy? Mr. Corcoran, you should ever an' always spaik to a leedy in an alyblasther tone, for that's the cut." [*Paddy and Judy retire.*
"Mickey Scanlan, come up here, now that we're braithin' a little; an' you, Miss Grauna Mulholland, come up along wid him. Miss Mulholland, you are masther of your five positions and your fifteen attitudes, I believe?" "Yes, sir." "Very well, Miss. Mickey Scanlan—ahem!—*Misther* Scanlan, can *you* perfome the positions also, Mickey?"

"Yes, sir; but you remimber I stuck at the eleventh altitude."

"Attitude, sir—no matther. Well, Misther Scanlan, do you know how to shiloote a leedy, Mickey?"

"Faix, it's hard to say, sir, till we thry; but I'm very willin' to larn it. I'll do my best, an' the best can do no more."

"Very well—ahem! Now merk me, Misther Scanlan; you approach your leedy in this style, bowin' politely, as I do. 'Miss Mulholland, will you allow me the honor of a heavenly shiloote?' Don't bow, ma'am; you are to curchy, you know; a little lower eef you plaise. Now you say, 'Wid the greatest pleasure in life, sir, an' many thanks for the feevor.' (*Smack.*) There, now, you are to make another curchy politely, an' say, ' Thank you, kind sir, I owe you one.' Now, Misther Scanlan, proceed."

"I'm to imitate you, masther, as well as I can, sir, I believe?"

"Yes, sir, you are to imiteet *me*. But hould, sir; did you see me lick my lips or pull up my breeches? Be gorra, that's shockin' unswintemintal. First make a curchy, a bow, I mane, to Miss Granna. Stop agin, sir; you are goin' to sthrangle the leedy? Why, one would think that it's about to teek laive of her forever you are. Gently, Misther Scanlan; gently, Mickey. There:—well, that's an improvement. Practice, Misther Scanlan, practice will do all, Mickey; but don't smack so loud, though. Hilloo, gintlemen! where's our drawin'-room folk? Go out, one of you, for Misther an' Mrs. Paddy Corcoran."

Corcoran's face now appears peeping in at the door, lit up with a comic expression of genuine fun, from whatever cause it may have proceeded.

"Aisy, Misther Corcoran; an' where's Mrs. Corcoran, sir?"

"Are we both to come in together, masther?"

"Certainly. Turn out both your toeses—turn them out, I say."

"Faix, sir, it's aisier said than done wid some of us."

"I know that, Misther Corcoran; but practice is everything. The bow legs are strongly against you, I grant. Hut tut, Misther Corcoran—why, if your toes wor where your heels is, you'd be exactly in the first position, Paddy. Well, both of you turn out your toeses; look street forward; clap your caubeen—hem!—your castor undher your ome (arm), an' walk into the middle of the flure, wid your head up. Stop, take care o' the post. Now, take your caubeen, castor, I mane, in your right hand; give it a flourish. Aisy, Mrs. Hanratty—Corcoran I mane—it's not *you* that's to flourish. Well, flourish your castor, Paddy, and thin make a graceful bow to the company. Leedies and gintlemen"—

"Leedies and gintlemen"—

"I'm your most obadient sarvint"—

"I'm your most obadient sarwint."

"Tuts, man alive! that's not a bow. Look at this: *there's* a bow for you. Why, instead of meeking a bow, you appear as if you wor goin' to sit down wid an embargo (lumbago) in your back. Well, practice is everything; and there's luck in leisure."

"Dick Doorish, will you come up, and thry if you can meek anything of that threblin' step. You're a purty lad, Dick; you're a purty lad, Misther Doorish, wid a pair o' left legs an you, to expect to larn to dance; but don't despeer, man alive. I'm not afeard but I'll make a graceful slip o' you yet. Can you meek a curchy?"

"Not right, sir, I doubt."

"Well, sir, I know that; but, Misther Doorish, you ought to know how to meek both a bow an' a curchy. Whin you marry a wife, Misther Doorish, it mightn't come wrong for you to know how to taich her a curchy. Have you the *gad* an' *suggaun* wid you?" "Yes, sir." "Very well, on wid them; the suggaun on the right foot, or what ought to be the right foot, an' the gad upon what ought to be the left. Are you ready?" "Yes, sir." "Come, thin, do as I bid you—rise upon suggaun an' sink upon gad; rise upon suggaun an' sink upon gad; rise upon—— Hould, sir; you're sinkin' upon suggaun an' risin' upon gad, the very thing you ought *not* to do. But, God help you! sure you're left-legged! Ah, Misther Doorish, it 'ud be a long time before you'd be able to dance Jig Polthogue or the College Hornpipe upon a drum-head, as I often did. However, don't despeer, Misther Doorish—if I could only get you to know your right leg —but, God help you! sure you haven't sich a thing—from your left, I'd make something of you yet, Dick."

The Irish dancing-masters were eternally at daggers-drawn among themselves; but as they seldom met, they were forced to abuse each other at a distance, which they did with a virulence and scurrility proportioned to the space between them. Buckram-Back had a rival of this description, who was a sore thorn in his side. His name was Paddy Fitzpatrick, and from having been a horse-jockey, he gave up the turf, and took to the calling of dancing-master. Buckram-Back sent a message to the effect that "if he could not dance Jig Polthogue on the drum-head, he had better hould his tongue forever." To this Paddy replied by asking if he was the man to dance the Connaught Jockey upon the saddle of a blood horse, and the animal at a three-quarter gallop.

At length the friends on each side, from a natural love of fun, prevailed upon them to decide their claims as follows:—Each master, with twelve of his pupils, was to dance against his rival, with twelve of his; the match to come off on the top of Mallybeny Hill, which commanded a view of the whole parish. I have already mentioned that in Buckram-Back's school there stood near the middle of the floor a post, which according to some new manœuvre of his own was very convenient as a guide to the dancers when going through the figure. Now, at the spot where this post stood it was necessary to make a curve, in order to form part of the figure of eight, which they were to follow; but as many of them were rather impenetrable to a due conception of the line of beauty, he forced them to turn round the post rather than make an acute angle of it, which several of them did. Having premised thus much, we proceed with our narrative.

At length they met, and it would have been a matter of much difficulty to determine their relative merits, each was such an admirable match for the other. When Buckram-Back's pupils, however, came to perform, they found that the absence of the post was their ruin. To the post they had been trained—accustomed;—with *it* they could dance; but wanting that, they were like so many ships at sea without rudders or compasses. Of course a scene of ludicrous confusion ensued, which turned the laugh against poor Buckram-Back, who stood likely to explode with shame and venom. In fact he was in an agony.

"Gintlemin, turn the post!" he shouted, stamping upon the ground, and clenching his little hands with fury; "leedies, remimber the post! Oh, for the honor of Kilnahushogue don't be bate. The post! gintlemen; leedies, the post if you love me! Murdher alive, the post!"

"Be gorra, masther, the jockey will distance us," replied Bob Magawly; "it's likely to be the *winnin-post* to him anyhow."

"Any money," shouted the little fellow, "any money for long Sam Sallaghan; he'd do the post to the life. Mind it, boys dear, mind it or we're lost. Divil a bit they heed me; it's a flock o' bees or sheep they're like. Sam Sallaghan, where are you? The post, you blackguards!"

"Oh, masther dear, if we had even a fishin'-rod, or a crowbar, or a poker, we might do yet. But, anyhow, we had better give in, for it's only worse we're gettin'."

At this stage of the proceedings Paddy came over to him, and making a low bow, asked him, "Arra, how do you feel, Misther Dogherty?" for such was Buckram-Back's name.

"Sir," replied Buckram-Back, bowing low, however, in return, "I'll take the shine out o' you yet. Can you shiloote a leedy wid me?—that's the chat! Come, gintlemen, show them what's betther than fifty posts—shiloote your partners like Irishmen. Kilnahushogue forever!"

The scene that ensued baffles all description. The fact is, the little fellow had them trained as it were to kiss in platoons, and the spectators were literally convulsed with laughter at this most novel and ludicrous character which Buckram-Back gave to his defeat, and the ceremony which he introduced. The truth is, he turned the laugh completely against his rival, and swaggered off the ground in high spirits, exclaiming, " He know how to shiloote a leedy ! Why, the poor spalpeen never kissed any woman but his mother, an' her only when she was dyin'. Hurra for Kilnnhushogue !''

Such, reader, is a slight and very imperfect sketch of an Irish dancing-master, which if it possesses any merit at all, is to be ascribed to the circumstance that it is drawn from life, and combines, however faintly, most of the points essential to our conception of the character.

A DANCE AT PAT MALONE'S.

AS RELATED BY ONE OF THE GUESTS.

It was in Tullamore it all took place. It wasn't during the "Rising," so of course there was no blood spilt or landlords popped; it wasn't of a fair day, so of course there was no shillelahs flourished; nor even of a market-day, so of course nobody walked home unsteadily on both sides of the road, murmuring, "Oh! blame not the bard if he fly to the bowers"—and who could blame anybody of a market-day?—but it happened—well, I'll first tell you all how it did happen.

Poor old Father Kinsella, the Lord have mercy on him, that's dead now long years ago, had dispersed a rousing dance, held over at Tim Regan's, about a day or two after Christmas, for he was very strict, Father Kinsella was, and gave it out on the altar that we'd disgrace the holy times we were in, and make a shame of the parish, by holding dances and meetings, and such like foolish observations of the great feasts of the Church, for all the world like Dr. Butler's Catechism, that we all studied when we were little gossoons, and maybe it wouldn't hurt some of you here present to study it too, for all you know about geometry and astronomy, and the likes. Well, as I said, he told us he didn't like dances at that time of the year, and that he'd disperse every one he heard about; so we all inwardly resolved that we couldn't hear a whisper of such a thing as a dance, since his reverence as much as forbade it. Of course that lasted maybe only till the next day, for when we lost his presence among us we forgot all his commands, or, as they say, "Out of sight, out of mind."

At that time I was working for the Widow Walsh, that owned one of the largest farms in the whole country; a good-natured lady she was, too, and the greatest woman for playing tricks that I ever met on either side the Atlantic. Ned Murphy had charge of the cows, the pigs and everything around generally; but I was head master of the horses, and was surgeon, sweeper, stable-boy, coachman, and all rolled into one, and, to tell you the truth, many a time the poor beasts enjoyed the loss of their suppers to give us an evening's sport, but we always made it up to them in the morning by giving them a double breakfast. At the same time Monica Kelly was in the kitchen, and liked her little bit of sport as well as any girl in the parish. She married Ned since, if you remember, and now they have a fine place "out West," I've been told; but in those times it used to be war and contest between Ned and myself to see who'd finish up first to have Monica with him to the dance. Ned was such a schemer that he generally succeeded, and I had to go in company with— myself. At that Christmas, however, no one thought of a dance at all, till at last it leaked out that most probably there'd be a sort of convivial meeting over at Pat Malone's on New Year's night—not a dance, oh no, not at all—but just a sort of social talk over a glass of poteen. The youngsters, however, knew better, for if we once got together it would take something to keep the toes and heels from circumnavigating—ahem. Sure enough, good-natured Pat would have a dance, only it should be kept very quiet—else if it came to Father Kinsella's ears, it's over in the midst of us he'd surely come, and then, indeed, we'd catch it; maybe it's mention us from the altar he would, and, dear knows, that would be a terrible punishment for such a little diversion; but he was strict enough to do it. We were all in great expectation, for a little stolen meeting like that will give more satisfaction than a common one on the green, and twice as much as a set and prepared regular dance; and so, indeed, did this.

Well, the evening came round, and we were all prepared to go, and the Widow Walsh was quite agreeable, only we didn't tell her where we were going—for, though she wouldn't spoil our sport under any consideration, still, she might not let us go, considering what Father Kinsella had said from the altar. So we thought she was blinded entirely, and we were all in the best of spirits, as the story-tellers say. Still, for all that, she knew where we were going, only she wanted the excuse for herself if the priest should ask her about letting us go to the dance. By ill luck it chanced that Tom, her son, and a couple of collegians, came home from Maynooth the same afternoon, and immediately she "sincerely regretted" to us that we'd have to stay for that evening, as she wanted us at home, since Tom had arrived with his college friends. Oh! but we wished Tom and his friends were all ordained and each had the largest parish in Ireland, so they wouldn't come round spoiling all our nicely-contrived plans. But there was Tom, and Peter Kinsella, old Father Kinsella's nephew, and another Maynoothian, and it's home we'd have to stay, and no dance that evening, anyhow. Oh! but Ned was in the doldrums, for he'd thought he'd sport Monica around that evening, and now its *sport* he'd be for all the parish, for deceiving them like that. However, I conceived a mighty nice plan, and when Ned and Monica heard it they thought it would be a queer thing if it didn't succeed. No sooner thought and planned but I went off to put it in execution.

So I called Master Tom one side—for it's great friends I was with him, inasmuch as I took care of all the horses, and especially of his own mare Katey—and says I:

"Master Tom, if you please, wouldn't you ask your mother, and persuade her to let us go to the dance to-night, only she doesn't know it's a dance, and I make bold to ask you, knowing you'd like to see us having a little sport on New Year's night?"

"And where's the dance to be?" says Master Tom.

"Over at Pat Malone's," says I, "and if you'd just put in a good word for us to your mother I know she'll let us go; and it's in fine condition I keep Katey for you now, Master Tom, isn't it?" That about Katey was a kind of stern chaser, as they say in the navy.

"But I thought Father Kinsella forbade all this?"

"Well, it's not exactly a dance, you know, Master Tom, it's a—"

"Yes, I know, a kind of a—"

"Exactly, Master Tom," says I.

"A kind of convivial reception for the devotees of Terpsichore," says he.

"Well, you know best, Master Tom; but ask your mother and get us leave, anyhow, and maybe I don't know where we'd come across some fine jack-hares to-morrow."

"Well," he says, "I'll do my best for you. And so my mother is not to know where you are going—isn't that kind of underhand?"

"Well, sure, Master Tom, you know, out of respect—"

"Out of respect for fear she would refuse, you think it is better she should not know? Well, rest easy. I think I can get you permission, as I have just got home, and mother never refuses me anything then."

"Don't forget, Master Tom," says I.

"Never fear," says he, and so he went off to get us permission immediately, or, perhaps, a little sooner.

Well, when I told Monica and Ned, it's almost smother one with thanks they did, and Ned looked rejoiced, and Monica began to grow saucy again—a sure sign, boys, that a girl is in good humor.

Back came Master Tom and told us it was "all right," as you say in America, and that we needn't be very particular about what time we got back, because he would be answerable for everything to his mother; and sure enough, as we left the house, we heard the greatest laughing up in the parlor, and Father Kinsella's name mentioned once or twice, and then we knew it was all correct and that we had a beautiful night's sport before us. Oh! boys, but it was fine going along the frozen road, the bright stars overhead; a nice, fine, dry, bracing, crackling night, and none of your dirty slush that you have here in New York, when it neither rains, hails or snows, but sends down a kind of mixture and conglomeration of the three. Well, it was fine going along, and we laughed and chatted and talked of past dances, only we passed the priest's house like poachers would crawl by a spring-gun; for Pat Malone's was about a half a mile the other side, and just then Monica nearly choked herself with laughing, and Ned had to slap her on the back to bring her to, while I walked along whistling softly to myself, and murmuring, "I know ye two would like to get rid of me, no doubt; but never fear, I'll stick to you till we get to Pat's anyhow, and then I'll see what I can do for myself."

When we came to Pat's, maybe our hearts didn't jump! There was Pat himself, a good, easy-going sort of an industrious man, that the *vanithee** and the girls could wheedle, coax or scold to do anything that would let them have a dance by all means; but would a good deal rather sit in the back room with a pipe and some old cronies, to talk about "Dan" O'Connell and the Repeal Bill. The *vanithee* herself would sit in the middle of the sport and scold all the boys for being too free with the girls, and then wink at the girls to encourage the boys; tell the girls they were better hands at gallivanting about the country than at spinning their wool, and then tell the boys—in secret, don't you mind—such a lot of good, industrious, merry-hearted girls she never came across as were in the parish then. Ah! but we never have such old men and women here in America as they do home in Ireland; and even when such a jovial old man or woman "comes out," it's change they do entirely, and talk about nothing but what they used to do and see "at home." It's in the air, I think, or maybe the liberty's too strong for them and they can't stand it; for you'll never find such industrious, scolding, laughing, praising, blaming, comfortable and thrifty old men and women, fathers and mothers, out here as at home. We leave them all behind us in the green church-yards or in the thatched cabins when we come out here to America; maybe they're better off where they are, and have almost as much freedom and twice as much comfort as if they did come out. But I'm making a little turn from the railroad, so I'll just come back and tell you all about that night at Pat Malone's, for Pat and his wife were just such a good, hearty old Irish couple.

---

* Woman of the house.

Well, as soon as we opened the door they all trooped up to us, and then such laughing and talking and nudging and scrooging and pinching as you never saw before, except at some other dance.

"Welcome, Monica, and why didn't you come sooner?"

"Is it that good-for-nothing slob, Ned, that's bringing you?"

"Arrah whisht!"

"Don't track the floor, Ned; clean your brogues before you come in!"

"Now stop your impudence, Tim Reilly, or I'll be compelled—"

"Arrah, who touched you? Maybe it's want me you do—"

"You must be cold; come inside and take—"

"The biggest bottle, Nancy, that's on the dresser."

"Is the Widow Walsh better of the '*chronics*' yet, I dunno?"

"Lame-footed and blear-eyed Ned Casey—"

"Flew through the air like a whistle the whole flock, and when—"

"I raised my gun they were all—"

"Having the finest dance ever you saw over at Phil McQuaid's, the whole lot of us."

Well now, boys, you can imagine what a jollification we were all in for; and the fiddler sat at one end of the room, and old Pat and his cronies at the other, and about twenty boys and girls each side crowding on two benches. They were all happy, and the fiddler was just striking up a tune, and the boys and girls were all footing it in high spirits, then comes more arrivals, and the dance stops for them to come in and join us; and so it was for nearly an hour, when at last we got fairly started. And then when we did get started, why, we made Pat and his old cronies give up their seats to come and watch us; they forgot all about "Dan," and only remembered when they were young themselves, and talked of gray Darby Hoolahan, that was at that time almost double, dancing a sling jig with the Widow Meahan, Lord have mercy on her, that died two years ago, with eighty years on her back. The woman of the house moved among us all, and talked like a girl to some, like a mother to others, and like Father Kinsella himself to the wild ones, and there weren't few of them there either. Athanasius Ryan, the schoolmaster, was there, and got out the longest rigmaroles ever you heard ; says he, " But you remind me of Diana ' qualis in Eurotas,' only it's in a farm-house you are; Venus is in the ascendant, I judge; but—" taking a glass of poteen, " I think whisky's in the descendant," and he wasn't far wrong there, either. All the best of the parish was there—that is, all the part that sweetened it, like sugar in the tea; the parish could exist without them, but it wouldn't have the same flavor. Well, the sets were all formed and deformed, and re-formed and re-deformed again; and says Billy Martin:

" But that was a sly trick of Garret Rooney's, on Father Kinsella, last Wednesday."

" Ah ! but it failed," says Thade Hogan; " his reverence was too much for him, and it's a good slash of the whip he got into the bargain."

" What was it ?" " How did it happen ?" " What was it ?" " Tell us all about it."

" Yes, Billy ! tell us all about it," says the *vanithee*.

" Sure it's little I know about it, I only heard it from another. But Moya yonder, blushing in the corner, was present, and can tell you all the ins and outs of it."

" Ah ! how smart you are, Mister Martin."

" What was it, Moya ?" " Yes, Moya, what was it ?"

" Arrah do you think she's at confession to the whole of ye ? Leave her alone," says the *vanithee*.

" Well, what was it, Billy ?"

" Well," says Billy, " I don't want to carry tales, but it was a good trick, anyhow."

" Ah ! can't ye tell us about it, and not keep palavering there ?"

" Well, ye see, Garret, the priest's boy, was on the road in front of the priest's house, carting a few sods in a little barrow, and who should come along but Miss Moya, yonder, and ye all know how the poor boy is gone on her."

"Ah! close your mouth till ye get better manners, Billy Martin, for it's poor ones you have now."

"Arrah whisht, Moya, sure you needn't get vexed, we were all the same way once in our lives," says the *vanithee*. "Go on, Billy, what was the rest of it?"

"Well, what should they do, natural enough, but stop and have a bit of a conflab, and, begorra, nothing would satisfy the boy but he should have one little kiss."

"Oh, shame on you, Billy Martin," cries the girls, and "small blame to him," says the boys.

"And it's little you'd blame him, each of ye, if you were all alone with your own, boys, and nobody near you but the barrow of turf. Well, Moya, of course, wanted to trifle with him."

"I wanted to go home out of that," says Moya.

"To trifle with him before she'd consent—for she would in the end, you know."

"Bad manners to you, Billy."

"Arrah, whisht, Moya, sure we all forgive you. Small blame to you for giving what you were going to take."

"Well, it's scuffling they were on the roadside, and the barrow upset and it's great goin's on they had all to themselves."

"Billy Martin, I'll—"

"When just as they were in the midst of it, who came along on his horse but Father Kinsella as large as life. And says Moya 'Let go your hold! Don't you see the priest?'"

"True for you," says Moya, without thinking, and we all commenced to laugh.

"Ah! you confess, Moya, you confess."

"Well, sure, Garret was in a great way entirely, for the priest seen what he was at; but he was pretty quick, and off he slips his cap and tore it in two halves, and commences to boo-hoo and cry at a great rate.

"'What were you scuffling with that girl for, you young rascal?' says Father Kinsella.

"'Oh! your reverence, boo-hoo, boo-hoo,' sobs Garret, showing his torn hat, 'she tore my new hat, your reverence, that cost me half my week's wages, boo-hoo; and I was just going to—boo-hoo—to—oh, your reverence, she's always up to such tricks, boo-hoo, and I was just going to—boo-hoo—to—to—'

"'To kiss her for doing it, you rascal. Inside, you're a disgrace to the house. If ever I find you attempting that again on the public road I'll horsewhip you soundly.'

"'Then I may in the house, your reverence, boo-hoo.'

"'Inside, you rascal,' and he gives him a slash; but I heard that he was laughing all day in his study, and Garret got a new hat the next day."

"What did you tear the boy's hat for, Moya?" "You'll have to get Garret another hat, Moya." "What'll you tell his reverence about the hat, Moya?" "But that was a queer trick, Moya."

"Oh, leave poor Moya alone," says the *vanithee;* "maybe you don't all wish your hats were torn, and that into smithereens, too."

Well, boys, such was the sport and the stories told at many a dance in Ireland, and told to-day, aye, perhaps this very evening, in your native land. Pretty soon the sport was getting glorious; the fiddle couldn't go fast enough; the boys were all saucy, and the girls were getting high-toned and disdainful, except when a good joke would be told, and then they'd have to laugh; the old men got in the corner again and commenced talking about "Dan" once more, and the whole of us were in the height of our glory, when there came a thundering rap at the door, and we were all as still as mice around a cheese, for there seemed to be throuble and danger in the knock.

"Who's there?" says the *vanithee*.

"Open the door immediately," says the voice.

"Not till I know what you want," says the good woman.

"Open this door, woman," says the one without, and he pushed in an umbrella through the chink, and then indeed we all got sick at heart, for we knew Father Kinsella's umbrella well, every one of us, and felt it, maybe, too; and Malachy Duff peeps out of the window and he cries out:

"Down with the lights, boys, down with them. There's Father Kinsella outside and two curates with him. Oh! what an unlucky night. Down with the lights, or he'll see each of us and we all will be mentioned from the altar."

In a minute the lights were down and out, and we were all in the other room, and under chairs and tables and beds; for every one thought it would be most terrible if his reverence saw *him* above all the others. I was under a table on one side of the room, and Ned Murphy beside me. Monica was in the other room, and dear knows where they all scrooged off to; but there was no one left outside but Malone, his wife and little Athanasius Ryan, the schoolmaster. It was pitch dark, for the lights were all out and the candles made off with. It was a terrible moment, and the *vanithee* was in great distress; you could hear your heart beat, and in the other room they were trying to open the window softly and escape in silence.

"Patrick Malone," says his reverence, "what do you mean by having a dance in your house on New Year's night, and I expressly forbidding it?"

"What dance, your reverence? sure, there's no sign of a dance here anyway."

"Stop! do not attempt to prevaricate and make the matter worse. Light the lights till we see the offenders; I think there must be some of your parish here, too, Father McEvoy," say she to the priest with him.

"I haven't the least doubt," says Father McEvoy and somehow or other the voice seemed very familiar to me.

"Quick, light the lights, Patrick," says Father Kinsella.

"Well, your reverence, you see—" says the *vanithee*.

"Do what I tell you without an instant's delay."

"But, your reverence, they've stole the candles."

"Father McEvoy and I must see the delinquents. Quick, a light;" but he knew he couldn't get one for all the gold in Guinea.

"Quick," says Father McEvoy, "a light, I must look after my parish," and the voice seemed old to me some way. So I waited a minute to make sure.

"Father Kinsella," says he again, "does the woman refuse to obey your commands?"

I was sure. So I caught a little glimpse of the face in a stray bit of moonshine, and I whispers to Ned Murphy:

"Ned! Ned! it's Master Tom. He's got his friends with him playing us a trick; and they've stolen Father Kinsella's clothes."

We were sure in a minute, and Ned had a stray bit of candle he secured in the mess. In a twinkling we lit it and jumped up.

"Ah! Master Tom, we caught you, we caught you. Ah! but you're up to a trick with your cape and hat. Ah! you're caught, for all your umbrella."

"What, man," says he, "do you dare to refuse—" and then he had to laugh; but in a minute he blew out the light in Ned's hand and was just making for the door; but I soon stopped that little game, and then indeed they all trooped from the other room, under tables and beds and chairs, the loft, closets and all over. The candles were soon lit, and there, boys, we had Master Tom and his two friends prisoners in the midst of us, and to tell you the truth they seemed to enjoy the imprisonment too.

Well, then we formed great schemes for their punishment. Everybody had something to say, and each one thought that surely his punishment would be the hardest and most good-natured one that could be devised.

"Make them dance with every girl in the room," says one.

"Make them drink all the poteen," says another; but few favored *that*.

"Put them on the table as kings," says another.

"And tie their hands behind their backs."

"Make Master Tom play the fiddle."

"Oh! by all means." "To be sure." "Certainly." "Why not?"

"Put him on the table."

"Give his friend the rosin, and Peter Kinsella the hat."

"Agreed, agreed." "Up with them." "Put them on the table."

"Now, then, Master Tom, the wind that shakes the 'barley.'"
"The fox-hunter's jig."
"Garryowen."
"Patrick's day."
"Irish washerwoman."
"Arrah, now boys and girls, give him time to draw his breath and he'll give you all the tunes together with one scrape of the bow, won't you, Master Tom?" says the *vanithee*.

"To be sure I will, and half a dozen more for good measure," says Master Tom.

And so, not to keep you waiting any longer, up they put him on the table, and Master Tom took the fiddle, his friend rosined the bow, and they gave the fiddler's hat to Peter Kinsella to gather up the change in. And maybe Master Tom couldn't play —whisht! You'd know how to dance immediately, as soon as you heard him, even if you never saw a jig before in your life; and it would make your heart cry tears of joy and laughter to see Peter Kinsella going round with the hat among us; and maybe it wasn't well filled—because, you see, we were all having such fun on account of our near losing it all, and whenever you're near losing anything that you get a new grasp on, it's twice as sweet as before, as, indeed, I needn't tell you, because you must all know it from experience. Well, of course, there was great talk about the fright we were all in.

"Did you see Darby Duff getting under the *vanithee's* thimble, boys? Sure, if the rest of him got in, the brogues would stick out, anyhow."

"Ay!" says Darby, "but you got into the closet yourself so as to be near your dearest friend, the poteen; but you take it to heart a great deal—almost as much as to stomach."

"How careful you were, Thade," says another, "that Moya wouldn't be seen. Sure, when Garret hears that—"

"Ah! boys, did you see himself?" says Thade; "sure, I thought we'd be all discovered, your lobster nose shone so much in the dark."

Well, such was the talk among us all, and for about ten minutes

we were in great confusion, and there was the greatest hubbub—
every one laughing and talking, blaming others, praising himself, the girls all animation and the boys all spirits, Pat and his cronies laughing and saying that it reminded them of when they were young gaffers themselves. Well, we were all ready just for a renewal of the dance. Master Tom was on the table striking up a tune, and Peter Kinsella was just emptying the hat in the fiddler's lap, when the door, which by ill luck we forgot to bar the second time, was opened, and who stalks in but Father Kinsella himself, as large as life, and his forehead like an August thunder-cloud. There wasn't an instant to blow out a light, or to scrooge away in a corner, but there we stood, looking as dreary and as guilty as a pair of cocks fighting in the rain. Oh! but we were terror-stricken; and when Father Kinsella looked round his eye grew flashy.

"What do you mean," says he, "assembling here on this holy night, and profaning this great feast of God's Church by disturbing the stillness of the night with your drunken revelry?"

"Oh! Father Kinsella! drunk—sorra one of us," we all cried out together.

Well, boys, just then he cast his eyes around, and whom should he see but his own nephew, with the fiddler's hat in his hand, and Master Tom on the table, with the fiddle to his shoulder. Well, the look he put on—Virgil couldn't describe, as Athanasius Ryan said (how could he, sure he never saw Father Kinsella). Well, he wanted to be fiercer than ever, and spite of all he could do he had to smile; and then Master Tom looked at him and laughed, and sure he had to laugh too; and when he saw his own cape, hat and umbrella with Peter Kinsella he burst out into a roar; but, for all that, he remembered his duty, so up he takes his umbrella and told us all to go home. Says he:

"Go home peaceably, now, every one of you, and I'll forgive you all, for sure my own nephew encourages you; but let me never hear of such a thing again. Remember that, and let it sink deep into your hearts."

"Oh, your reverence, never again in all our lives."

"That will do now; go home—no nonsense," for he knew we couldn't keep such a promise if we tried ever so hard.

"Oh, thank you, Father; sure we'll always remember it." "Never fear us, your reverence, sorra dance—" "Never in my house again, your reverence—"

"Home with you all, quick; and as for you three gentlemen, come and walk over a piece with me—"

"Oh! Father, forgive them." "Forgive them, your reverence; sure, 'twas only a little sport on their part—" "Ah, do, Father Kinsella; sure they'll never do it again—"

"Home out of this, every one of you, or this will not be the end of it. Home, quickly, every one of you, or maybe it's mention you I would."

Well, off we went all home, and sure by the time Monica, Ned and myself got back it was very early, and says the Widow Walsh to me:

"And what brought you home so early?"

"Well, ma'am," says I, "you see I forgot to feed Katy when I left, and sure it lay heavy on my mind, and I thought I'd come home and not leave the poor beast without her supper on my account."

"And you, Monica?"

"Well, ma'am, sure I was afraid I hadn't set the dough for the baking, and as James was coming back, I thought I'd come with him and make sure."

"And you, Ned, what brought *you* home so early?"

"Why—because, ma'am, the others came home, and I didn't want to come home alone any later for fear of the fairies, as they do say there's a power of them abroad to-night."

"But sure you're getting very timorous, Ned," says the widow, "and I am very glad to see you other two so tender for the welfare of the house. That will do now; you can go."

A little later the boys came in with Father Kinsella, and such laughing as was in the parlor you never heard the like of before. And sure who was it but the widow who put the boys up to the sport, and then sent word to Father Kinsella of a dance over at

Pat Malone's; and sure didn't she confess, and it was a quāre thing all round, anyhow. When Monica went up with some refreshments, they asked her was "the bread set yet?" and if "Ned saw any fairies by the rath?" but they guessed she was the only one herself. Well, from that day till I left Ireland, five years come next Michaelmas, I never heard Master Tom called anything by his college friends but "Father McEvoy," and, perhaps, occasionally "Fiddler Tom."

MIKE DRISCOLL AND THE FAIRIES.

The picturesque village of Castleconnell lies on the banks of the Shannon, about six miles above Limerick. A lovelier habitation could scarcely be chosen by the most enthusiastic admirer of decaying art and perennial nature. The surrounding district is thickly strewn with the remains of castles, fortresses, and churches, each shrined in the mellow twilight of its own legend; whilst the gently undulating country is belted and darkened with fragments of forest, and overtopped by the bluest of mountains. The noble river itself flows past the village, a quarter mile in breadth, by quaintly-mossed and water-stained weirs, over which the salmon leaps, at times, high in the air, like a sudden gust of jewels; by conical-roofed, old-fashioned mills, whose crooked windows and high gables blend in marvellous harmony with the character of the surrounding landscape; and by pleasant cottages, where peasant girls still sit and sing at the threshold, and the spinning-wheel hums flaxen-toned ditties in the summer weather. Leaving the village, the mighty stream sweeps with a curved rush around the gentle promontory on whose height the castle of the O'Briens still stands in desolate magnificence; and thence, with many a bend, round green elbows of scented woodland and pastoral peninsulas, dotted with dreamy Cuyp-like cattle, towards Doonas. The fall in the bed of the river at this point is considerable. The narrow channel is nearly blocked up by huge boulders, overgrown with citron-colored flora, from whose fissures spring the slender hazel and the flowing elder; and over and around them rushes the great torrent of waters, churning itself into vast cauldrons of boiling foam and clouds of mist; subsiding here and there into weltering pools of flaky emerald. To the right, the bank rises to the height of seventy feet; and viewed from this elevation, the spectacle presented by the falls is one of terrific beauty. Right and left, as far as the eye can penetrate, the river appears to be lashed into a white fury, and sends up a roar which may be heard at a distance of six miles in calm weather. The low shores at the opposite side are buried in the thickest foliage, whilst if the spectator can lean over the cliff on which he stands, he sees but a precipitous wall of rock, which falls with plummet-like sheerness into the raging torrent beneath. The spot has many associations. Some years ago, a lady of high rank attempted to cross the falls at midnight, in order to be present at a ball given at the residence of a gentleman of fortune on the other side. A brave fisherman undertook to convey her across; but he and his fair charge perished in the perilous enterprise. A month after the tragic occurrence, her body was discovered floating some miles further down the river, the bracelets on her wrists and the jewels of her hair matted with water-weeds. The peasantry assert that on the anniversary of her death, wailing voices ascend from the falls, and a spectral lady is seen drifting seaward with the current. On the highest part of the bank are the ruins of a castle, evidently of modern erection. It is stated that the building was burned, by orders of its owner, for the express purpose of heightening the poetical character of the scenery, by adding a picturesque ruin to its other attractions. Then there is an ancient well, enclosed in an oblong of Druidical oaks; and there are raths, and nine-men-morris circles, where the lusmore flourishes, and the genial fairies of the place dance jocund measures in the blinking starlight.

It was the morning of Christmas, 17—. The winter had been unusually clement, for the sycamores still retained a remnant of yellowing foliage, and the frosts were so light that they scarcely crisped the short meadow-grass. The day was brisk and sparkling, and before noon the mists, which had hung over the falls since daylight, were dissipated by the sun and a low breeze from the south. The blackbird felt the time so pleasant that he puffed his golden throat, and whistled the first bars of a spring-tide carol;

the effort naturally provoked the emulative disposition of his rival, the thrush, who, however, broke down in the effort only to hear the crystal twitter of the robin from a neighboring spray of holly. The Driscoll family, as they sat at breakfast, insensible, it must be confessed, to the vocal competition which had just taken place, felt that the season was mild, that the air was delicate, and the oaten bread delicious. So the lightest joke, the most trifling quillet, excited a fit of hearty laughter, with cries of "Tisn't half your best," "Arrah, what'll he say next?" and other complimentary incentives to the rustic humor.

The house occupied by the Driscolls was a large and respectable residence for a middle-class farmer of the period. It had two stories; and, though the walls were seldom whitened, and the sashes and panes exhibited uncomfortable ventilating tendencies, the coat of thick thatch which shielded the roof, and the tufts of smoke which ascended from the chimneys, lent it an air of cozy indolence that was far from being disagreeable. As for its position, it defied criticism. It was a grassy eminence, which sloped to the river edge, and caught the last foam-wreaths that were hurled downward from the falls. From the upper windows of the house one could obtain a good view of the "Jumping Hole," as it is called, and a goodly prospect of the rock-chafed river. Driscoll, senior, whom we do not pretend to quote as an authority on situation, was often heard to declare, that "all Ireland couldn't bate that spot for convanience," and further, that a look at it on a heavy morning was "worth fifty pounds a year to a gauger."

The family group assembled at breakfast on the eventful Christmas morning we write of, consisted of old Denis Driscoll, his wife and his two sons. Of John, the elder son, it would be hard to say much, as his character was of that negative description which offers little to the observer. Shrewd, active and laborious, he was a faithful and valuable helper on the farm on week days, and "an out-and-out buckeen" on Sundays and holidays. Mike was the family genius; he drank more, danced more, and sang more than all his relatives put together. He never missed a fair or a pattern; he was the heavy man at all the local weddings, an indispensable assistant at the wakes, and the very deuce at "a thrial of short-stick." To see Mike was to see the embodiment of humor. When he laughed his guffaw could be heard over a meadow; his mouth would roll back displaying a double line of shining teeth; his black eyes would literally flash with enjoyment, and every muscle of his face contributed some odd wrinkle or cunning fissure to intensify the jollity of his expression. Of Mike's good nature no one was ever known to venture a doubt— his generosity was only limited by his ability; for he was always willing to oblige a friend with the loan of a shilling or the crack of a cudgel, as circumstances required. It is to be deeply regretted, that to all these shining qualities Mike did not unite profound religious principles. Not that his morals were ordinarily lax; but he had a constitutional passion for the open air, which occasionally induced him to neglect the solemn duties of religion. Then, Mike had been inoculated at an early stage of his career with a fancy for card-playing, and was often known to sit up four-and-twenty hours without winking, at his favorite amusement. When the family went to chapel on Sunday, Mike would invariably say, "Go on, father; I'll overtake ye—believe me, I'll overtake ye." But he seldom fulfilled his promise, preferring rather to turn into a deserted lime-kiln, which lay at a stone's throw from the rear of the house, where he met with a group of choice spirits, with whom he gambled till dinner-time.

"What are you dramin' iv, Mike?" asked old Driscoll, eyeing his son, who appeared to have fallen into a brown study. "Eh, what are you dramin' iv? Some misforthunate caper, I'll go bail?"

"Musha, father, as ye're curious to know what, I'll tell you. I'm dramin' of nothin' at all, at all, so I am."

"Wid the blessin' of God," observed Mrs. Driscoll, "he's thinkin' of goin' with us to-day instead of playin' cards. Won't you, Mike?"

"Yes," said Mike. "I'll just go and make myself a thrifle dacent, and then I'll be wid ye."

So saying, Mr. Michael Driscoll rose and climbed the stairs to an upper room for the purpose of refreshing his toilet. His brother, it will be remembered, was a buckeen; but Mike had an intellectual contempt for the proprieties of costume, which no fraternal example, however brilliant, was capable of correcting. He hated shiny hats, despised cravats, repudiated broadcloth, but held buckskin in healthy esteem. Consequently when Mike, "a thrifle dacent," presented himself before his family, and announced himself ready, his attire was more picturesque than elegant. It consisted, if we may descend to details, of buckskin knee-breeches, blue stockings, and brogues; his coat, which was furnished with a cape, descended almost to his heels. On his head he carried a beaver hat, slightly indented about the middle; and the whole was completed by the addition of a coarse shirt, fastened at the throat with a large brass button. In this inventory we have purposely omitted mention of his stick—a short, thick ash cutting, which had performed several curious surgical operations in the hands of its owner, and is therefore entitled to a distinct sentence.

All being in readiness, old Driscoll mounted a favorite gray mare, and his wife was placed on a pillion behind him; the buckeen rode a blood horse borrowed from a neighbor; and poor Mike a one-eyed mule, which he aptly described as "the most cantankerous baste in creation." The little cavalcade set out slowly for the chapel, about three miles distant; and it was evident from the radiant looks of Mrs. Driscoll and the jaunty air of her husband that both were delighted at getting Mike, at long last, on the high road to duty. The road lay in part through a densely-grown shrubbery, whence it turned off, at a sharp angle, and emerged on the open country. As old Driscoll jogged along, a sudden impulse caused him to look in the direction of the farm house. A quick exclamation of surprise passed his lips.

"Mike, avick," he shouted with considerable energy; "ride back as fast as the mule's legs will carry you; the pigs are pullin' the whate in the haggard—bad luck to them, an' the Lord forgive me."

"Bad scannin' to them," said Mrs. Driscoll, "they're the quarest pigs I ever seen. Whate, indeed! 'twould sarve them right if it choked them."

Mike cast a rapid glance at the haggard, and sure enough there were the whole litter, with the sow at their head, poking their noses into the corn-stacks, and munching the precious grain as only pigs and aldermen can munch. To turn back the mule's head and urge her to a canter was the work of a moment. "Don't lose no time, agrah," shouted his mother, as he rode off to arrest the work of demolition.

"Honor bright, mother," replied Mike, and without further parley he provoked the mule into a gallop. On reaching the house he jumped over the haggard fence, and contrived, with the assistance of his stick, to disperse the offending animals. Having secured the gate, he looked around for the mule, but that quadruped, being inclined to excursiveness, had wandered from the road, and was disporting himself in a piece of ploughed land to the north of the farm. To make matters worse, Mike found it impossible to catch him. The cunning beast eluded every attempt which his owner made to capture his reins, and led him such a dance through the soft loam that the latter was obliged to sit down, defeated.

After some time he rose, and was making his way to the road, when the hum of well-known voices from the other side of the ditch reached his ear; and before he could fly, a number of young men, dressed in the provincial holiday gear, leaped into the field, and stood before him.

"Arrah, then, is it yerself? and my Christmas-box on you," said Jerry Toomey. "Is it huntin' the wran all alone you were, and the two best fivers in the country goin' to try it out at the kiln?"

Mike laughed a good-natured laugh, and shook his head.

"Maybe he's goin' coortin'," observed Tom Delany. "See how nate he looks, scooped out to the nines, as the man said to the new piggin. I'd bet ye a fi'penny bit, boys, he'd be ashamed to walk with us—wouldn't he, Tony?"

The individual addressed as Tony, a little fat man, dressed in a faded hunting suit, here walked up to Mike, and, having made a circuit around him, clapped his hands in affected astonishment. "Why thin, Mike," asked the little man, placing his hands on his hips, and throwing back his head with the air of a horse-critic, "you didn't mane to bother us entirely, did you? New buckskins, as my grandfather was a gentleman; new brogues, new coat, new everything—the signs of money flying about him like snuff at a wake. I wonder did he pay the hansel yet?"

"Begor, then, he didn't so," said Tom, "an' more's the shame for him; but we won't forget it if he does. After all, it's raisonable of me thinkin' that Mike was goin' to mass, for he's turnin' pious iv late—a young saint, you know."

The young men laughed simultaneously, much to Mike's chagrin, and with a view to cover his reputation as a good fellow, he said:

"Troth, Tony, if ye'd like to know the ins and outs of it, I was on the look-out for ye, knowin', as I knowed for the last two weeks, that ye'd have a bit of diversion to-day, and now an' iver I'm as good a man as any o' ye."

"More power to your potato cake," cried Tony, slapping Mike encouragingly on the back. "When the Driscolls give up sportin', you may burn all the cards and shoot all the race-horses in the country. Come along, honey, for there's no time to be lost."

When the little party arrived at the kiln, they found it already in the occupation of a dozen of persons, who were disputing loudly over an alleged neglect on the part of some one present.

"Bring us all this way," cried one, "and when we come, there's not a card to play with."

"Dat Ted Nealon," said a sharp, wiry voice, "is de most insonest boy in the barony. He tinks of notin' except atin' and drinkin' and gutlin'. 'Tis neider here nor dere, but 'twas a bleedin' shame to lave de cards to him."

"Howld yer tongue, Tim," said a manly young fellow, who appeared deeply dejected; "ye'd talk from this to Michaelmas, ye would. Look, min, there's only one thing for us. Draw lots to know who'll go to the village to buy a sixpenny pack at Betty Houlihan's."

The proposition was received with delight. A number of straws of various lengths were placed in Tony's hat, and the gamblers drew one each. On comparing them, Mike's was found to be the shortest of the lot. The result startled him not a little, but there was no help for it.

"Dere, you're de lucky man, so you are," said Tim, "and you're well desarvin' of the honor, so you are. Take to your pins, now, and don't cry crack till you're back again wid us. And beware of de Good People."

With many recommendations "not to spare his heels" ringing in his ears, Mike left the kiln. An hour later, with the cards in one of his capacious pockets and a bottle of whiskey in the other, he left the village and bent his steps homewards. He was in the highest spirits, for he anticipated rare sport; nor was his mind troubled by the reflection that he had sacrificed a solemn obligation to human respect for his companions. Whether it was that he had imbibed too much of the contents of the bottle, or that some unusual cause contributed to the elasticity of his temperament, we know not; but it is asserted, that whilst threading his way through Doonas Wood, the gay fellow carolled like a bird, and flourished his stick more than once with playful ingenuity. The extreme beauty of a little lawn, a place known as "The Fairies' Wake," hidden in a verdurous paling of holly trees, arrested his steps as he was about to cross it. The grass seemed to Mike to be grass of a softer and fresher texture than he had ever before seen; the trees, too, were of slenderer trunk and lovelier outline; and the patch of sky overhead was of deeper and richer blue than the sky usually wore at that season. "Surely," thought Mike, "if the Good People—Lord between us and harm—wanted a purty place to foot a double reel, 'tis here they ought to come, and not to the old raths, where two cats couldn't dance comfortably barrin' they held their tails in their mouths. Well, at any rate, though the place is nice, I must say it's cowld; and faith a dhrop would improve a boy's acquaintance with it." Having expressed his opinion, Mike raised the bottle to his lips and swallowed a copious draught of the fiery liquor. At the same time, he became sensible that the cards had fallen from his pocket and were scattered in a brilliant litter on the sward. Placing the bottle in his pocket, he stooped to pick them up, but to his astonishment they wouldn't wait for his fingers; they appeared to be suddenly endowed with life, for they hopped and skipped about in all directions with such liveliness of manner and such variety of motion that it was evident, as Mike subsequently remarked, "The Ould Boy's children had their Daddy's luck."

"Ah, thin, will ye be aisy, will ye, and stop yer capers?" he cried, for the potent spirit had deadened his reverence for the supernatural to a degree bordering on disbelief in its existence. "Say ye'll come if ye'll come, if ye don't, don't, for the deuce a one of me ud be bothered huntin' ye about for tin times yer worth. Knave of spades, bad luck to me, but I'll twist yer neck, you dirty blackamoor, if you go on that way makin' a fool o' me. Queen of Diamonds, there's a darlint—thuck, thuck, thuck—an' she's goin' to let me take her, isn't she? Arrah, only mind how she cuts, head over heels—whoo! will she ever put a stop to her gallop? By dad, she's in debt to her house painter, and takes me for a bailiff. That's a dacent, respectable man, the King of Hearts—a very dacent man. Av coorse he remembers the night when he won me the last thrick of that murtherin' forty-five, when I bate Ned Hegarty to babby-rags. Yerra, look how he comes to me, *faugh-a-balla*, Five of Clubs, you pock-marked thief, and make way for his majesty. Ye're gone agin, King of Hearts. Ye're gone, you shabby desaiver, with your ould petticoats streelin' to your heels. *Farragh-adho*, if you come forninst me now and stood and said, ' Take me, Mick Driscoll, take me,' I'd say, '*Gerout*, you ould bundle of tatters, I'd like to know who'd put you in their pocket?' Musha, Queen o' Spades, 'tis yourself that's a purty colleen, and proud I'll be to take you under my protection, with your nate curls hanging down your rosy cheeks, and the crown o' gold shinin' bright on your head. Whoo! jewel, how she foots it, as if she was dancin' at Billy

Leonard's hop for a wager. Oh, the deeshy dawny little feet of her! and the lily hands, and the white tin fingers, so long and so taper, for all the world like two hanks o' candles! I have you, *achora*, I have you. Arrah, shoot me, but she's gone, like the rest iv 'em—gone clean, as Joe Bolster said, when he polished his brogues and pawned them afterwards. Honest woman, honest woman, I say you don't know me, or you'd behave yourself a thrifle better. I'm Mike Driscoll, o' Doonas, I'd have you know. 'Tisn't myself that would say it, but there's not a girl in the barony that wouldn't cock her cap at me, if she thought 'twas any use for her. Do you hear that, Queen o' Spades! do you? go over to your ould *boccaugh* of a husband, that's makin' a fool iv himself in the bushes, tryin' to coax out the Queen o' Diamonds, iv you please, and tell him I said so. O! thin, murther, what's the matter with them at all at all? There they're flutterin' about, like leaves at harvest time, and all the art o' man couldn't lay hands on one o' their ugly carcasses. Not a hair I care anyhow, for they'll soon get tired in spite iv 'em, and then 'twill be easy enough to go up and talk wid them. Go on, go on, ye varmints, I wouldn't look after ye for the good iv ye. Whoo! that's right; when the somebodies dance *mooneens*, their father, av coorse, pays the piper."

During the delivery of this strange address, the speaker was busily engaged chasing the cards on his hands and knees, from place to place; but his labors proved fruitless. Sometimes a king card would dance within an inch of his hand, but when he stretched forth that member to capture the royal truant, the latter would bound a foot high from the grass, and roll away a dozen feet or more, when it would stand, as if inviting fresh pursuit. The queens insisted on sustaining the reputation of their sex for profound skill in coquetry. They would advance with a winning gait and fascinating air, towards the poor fellow, who used all his eloquence to induce them to return to his custody, and then prostrate themselves on the sward. But, strange to tell, when Mike laid hands on them, they would manage to glide out of his grasp, and go spinning about the lawn like humming tops. The knaves were eminently successful in provoking Mr. Driscoll's indignation. The rogues would stride up to him, with a look which meant to convey—"Can't you put us in your pocket?" then advancing their fat fore-legs, like a row of footmen at a Lord Mayor's dinner, and closing their left eyes, would gaze in his face so imploringly, that Mike was fain to pity them. Still, when he attempted to put them in his pocket, the merry young gentlemen would wheel round on their right heels, shake their wigged heads, and march off towards the trees, the skirts of their coats sticking out, and their swords dangling from their waists. As for the inferior cards they seldom came near him, contenting themselves with executing some mysterious movements under a neighboring holly. Mike was disgusted with the whole business, and he was preparing to retire, when his ear was caught by a strain of unearthly music, which appeared to float up, thin and bodiless as the morning mist, from the falls below; and having hovered overhead for a moment, died out in a chain of bell-like vibrations along the shores of the river. As he turned his eyes in the direction from which the music came, he saw that the sun had long gone down, scarcely a trace of twilight lingered in the skies, but a fragment of the moon had risen to the left, and filled the far-stretching landscape with a tender and melancholy brightness. Only a few stars were visible "in the intense inane;" the roar of the falls was hushed, and a solemn stillness pervaded the air.

The impression which the scene produced on the mind of the bewildered beholder was notably increased by the marvellous change which was taking place in the character and constitution of the cards. Some unseen magician had surely waved his wand above them, and transformed the slips of paper into the fantastic shapes which they were assuming. The four queens were quickly changed into winged fairies, which soared up gracefully from the sward, their airy drapery and wings, spotted with peacocks' eyes, gleaming in the imperfect moonlight. Then the kings were divested of their uncouth robes, and transformed into slender elves, each with a blue bell on his head for a crown. The knaves, by a similarly confounding process, were changed into little old men, with hard, wry, roguish faces, and decrepit bodies. They wore odd little hats, with triangular brims, and such queer jerkins and breeches, that Mike laughed outright as he watched them. As for the common cards, they were transformed into a brood of small fairy-like forms, whose backs and breasts were thickly spotted with clubs, spades, hearts and diamonds. These latter tumbled about on the sward with uproarious merriment, and indulged in the quaintest grimaces and the shrillest laughs. Suddenly a fresh burst of music rose from the falls; this time a gay dancing measure. Directly the card fairies formed sets and chose partners, and fell to tripping one of the gayest double reels which Mike ever witnessed. A couple of elves, mounted on the backs of black-winged bats, sailed about in the air, and eventually ran a race to the corner of the moon for a dewberry handicap. The queen of hearts and diamonds, applying two fox-glove blossoms to their mouths, gave the signal for the start, and away went the jockeys. At the same time, the queen of spades and clubs flew over Mike's head, and dropped golden furze blossoms on his hat, which, as they rolled off the leaf, tickled his ears, and caused him to roar from a sense of exquisite enjoyment. Meanwhile, the elves continued to foot it featly on the delicate tops of the slender brome grass, and with such dexterous energy that Mike felt it impossible to suppress his admiration, and cried out at the top of his voice: "More power to ye, there is not a betther."

The words were scarcely uttered when the king of hearts, a dapper little fellow, who was stretching his legs on a leaf of wild lavender, marched up to him, and, placing his hands behind his back, exclaimed:

"Masha, is that you, Mike Driscoll? Happy Christmas to you, Mick, but arn't you afeard of catchin' cowld on the broad o' yer back, there?"

"Sorra afeard," replied Mike; "the night isn't hot surely, but it isn't cowld, and—"

"Maybe," says the king, "ye'd have no objection, ma bouchal, to a dhrop o' the native. We keep the best you ever clapped eyes on, and betune you and me, it never paid duty aither."

"If it's convanient, I could dispinse with it," said Mike; "but none o' yer thricks, mind. Isn't it the quarest thing on airth," he continued, "that I got the whole lock, stock and barrel o' ye for a few pence from Betty Houlihan this morning, and here ye're caperin' and flutterin' about in such grand style as if yer had the riches of Daymur at yer backs?"

"Keep yer insinivations to yerself," says the king, and his face grew red with anger. "Yer dirty hints won't sarve you here, I can tell you, Mike Driscoll. If you wish to behave dacent, we'll thrate you dacent; and to show you that we mane right, have a dhrop o' comfort afore we go farther." So saying, the king handed Mike a bottle with centuries of cobwebs clogged around its neck and sides.

Before putting the bottle to his mouth, something prompted Mike to look into it. Instead of being full of whiskey it contained a blue vapor, in the middle of which he perceived, floating about, the resemblance of a little girl, who, it was assumed, had been stolen by the fairies from her parents more than six years before. As he was opening his lips to speak to her, she motioned him to keep silent, and then whispered: "Mike, darlint, beware, and don't ate nor dhrink with them." He laid the bottle down in astonishment, and looked at the king.

"Ye're very timperate iv late, Mike," said the king. "Is it because you don't like the color iv it?"

"Troth, and it's not bad at all," replied Mike, "but I'd rather not take it jest now. If yer majesty will lave it to me a while, I promise to finish it before the night is over."

"Faith, an' yer more than welcome to it. Put it in yer pocket, Mike, and step across here till I have the honor and glory of introducing you to the Queen."

Mike followed the King across the grass to where her majesty was rocking herself to sleep on a bit of crowfoot.

"Are you awake, darlint?" said the King; "bekase if you are, I'd like ye'd make the acquaintance of this fine fellow here."

The Queen, who was decidedly handsome, opened her eyes languidly and gazed on Mike. "Would you be after dancin' a double with me, young man?" she asked.

Mike bowed to the ground. "Would a cat drink new milk, ma'am?" was his reply.

"Ye're a flattherer, Mike Driscoll," said the Queen, blushing to the eyebrows. "Faith, ye're great at the blarney, anyhow. Ted," she continued, addressing the King, "will ye put yer finger in yer mouth, and whistle for the prime minister?"

The King smiled and obeyed. In less than a minute the Knave of Hearts made his appearance.

"Ye're not dhrunk yet, are you?" asked the Queen, thoughtfully.

"Dickens a dhrop more than two I tuk," replied the Knave, and as he spoke both his ears shot up like a pair of straight horns at each side of his head.

"Thin as ye're not," said her majesty, "pick out the purtiest pair o' pumps in the chest o' dhrawers, and put them on Mr. Driscoll, for he's condescinded to dance a double with your misthriss."

"Oh, ma'am!" ejaculated Mike, "faith, as for the condescinsion, it's all the other way, indeed."

"Hould your bladdherin'," says the Queen, "hould your bladdherin', will you?"

The Knave, who had disappeared, returned in a moment, and fitted Mike in a pair of beautiful pumps, with green heels and rosettes at the insteps.

"'Tis nate they look, Mr. Driscoll," observed her majesty, "but a plumper pair o' calves than yours I never seed afore. Och, 'tis you must play the dickens intirely with the girls, it is."

"Axin' your ladyship's pardon," exclaimed Mike, "but I'm as innocent as the babe unborn."

"Ha! ha! ha!" roared the Knave, giving, at the same time, a diabolical grin, which distended his mouth almost to his ears. "Ha! ha! ha!"

With a look of supreme contempt at the ugly scoffer, the

Queen gave Mike her hand, and led him to the middle of the lawn, where they mingled with the other royalties, male and female.

"Have a dhrop before you begin, Mike?" said the Queen of Diamonds, who glittered from head to foot with shining jewels, at the same time pointing to the bottle, the neck of which was visible above his pocket.

Mike bowed. "I'm as thankful to you, ma'am, as if I tuk it; but it's nayther here nor there until the blood gets heated; when that biles, I'll cool it."

Diamonds smiled graciously. "May I make bould to ax yer hand for the next set?" she asked.

"Faix, an' you may, and welcome. When the Queen o' Hearts gets wake, I'm yer man, my lady. Whoo! there's the music."

An unseen orchestra struck up a lively tune, and Mike, having led his partner up and down in approved fashion, placed his arms akimbo, and began to foot it with an energy which astonished the denizens of fairy-land around him. Now he flung up his right hand, snapped his fingers with a great thwack, which made the grasses tremble; now he retired, throwing his heels right and left, and making the long tails of his coat fly about distractedly.

"He's a rale jewel," says the Queen of Spades.

"Did you ever see the likes of him?" says her Majesty of Clubs.

"Remember your promise to me, Mike," whispered the Queen of Diamonds.

And the Kings swore he was the best fellow in their dominions, and the Knaves grinned with inextinguishable laughter, whilst the common cards went bobbing up and down, with the most comical gravity imaginable. Suddenly the Queen of Diamonds gave a little shriek, and ran limping to a bed of wild thyme, where she lay down in apparent agony.

"What ails my delight?" screamed her royal consort, rushing to her side; "what's the matter, avourneen?"

"Oh, nothin' at all, at all," says the Queen.

"It's ill said of you," says the King; "and by my twelve retainers, I'll know the ins and outs of it."

"Troth, an' as ye're so curious, I'll tell ye; Mr. Driscoll throd on my corns—there."

"The flamin' blackguard," says the King. "Boys," said he to the Knaves, "take that *boccaugh*, and baste him green with nettles; bad luck to his ugly crubeens to-night."

The other royal personages hastened to interpose in behalf of Mike; and after a great deal of solicitation, backed up by the prayers of the wounded Queen, he was pardoned.

"It'll be all right, darlint," said the Queen of Hearts, bending over the beautiful invalid. "Put a bit o' brown soap to it, and 'twill be well afore ye're twice married."

Kneeling down at the poor Queen's feet, Mike took her foot in his hand and began to chafe it, an operation which appeared to afford the sufferer no small delight. At the same time, a dapper little gentleman, in an oddly-shaped hat, commenced to tickle the left side of his nose, whilst a pair of elves attempted to pull the bottle from his right pocket, and others poured showers of gold doubloons into his bosom.

"Does it pain you much, ma'am?" he asked, with a languishing look at the royal sufferer.

She smiled. "Begor, Mike," she said, "pain from you is a thrate. Are you tired o' dancin'? bekase, if you're not, I'd like to thry a minuet with you."

"You're welcome to it for a whole hour," replied Mr. Driscoll. "What'll be plasin' to you?"

"A minuet, Mike, a minuet."

"Oh, consarnin' the time, I lave that to yourself; but what would ye like? Are you partial to a jig, ma'am?"

The Queen laughed outright.

"We'll dance a min-u-et, Mr. Driscoll, if you plaise. Didn't you ever thry one?" she asked.

"Oh, now I have it. No, thin, I didn't. I contracted with Tim Hinchy for three ha'pence a step, but he chated me out o' that dance, ma'am. Will ye be quiet, there, ye tasin' divils? Ma'am, spake a word or two to Paudheen, and inthrate him to lave off ticklin' my nose. Curse o' Cromwell on ye, and lave the bottle alone—what's it doin' to ye? Can't ye thry and behave like Christhins—eh, can't ye?"

At a wave of the Queen's hand the elves desisted.

"There's the Queen of Hearts," she said; "mind, she'll be jealous o' me, Mike."

"Troth, thin, 'tis ill would become her. Is she spliced yet? I suppose ould Bullock Heart is her husband."

Diamonds was about to reply, when her royal sister seated herself at her side, and thus prevented Mike's curiosity from being gratified. At a signal from the Queen of Clubs, the whole company threw themselves in various positions on the grass; and as the Knave of Diamonds clapped his hands, the ground opened, and a round table, heaped with a sumptuous banquet, rose in their midst. To all solicitations to eat and make merry, Mike, who remembered the warning of the captive in the bottle, gave a firm but respectful refusal.

"Thry some of our blackberry jam?" asked the Queen of Spades.

"Shall I send you a lark's leg, darlint?" said the Queen of Hearts.

"Or a juicy slice from the sirloin of frog?" suggested the King of Clubs.

"I ax your pardons all round," said Mike, "but I couldn't ate another morsel."

As Mike said this, he felt a tiny head laid lovingly on his shoulder, and heard the Queen of Hearts whisper:

"Ah, thin, Mr. Driscoll, were you ever coortin'?"

"Why, thin, not to say much, ma'am. There was a girl o' the Bradys that I had a likin' for, and was goin' to be married to her, till we fell out about a feather-bed and a goat. We wouldn't give, and they wouldn't take, and there was an ind of it."

The Queen sighed. "And did you never love any one since, Mr. Driscoll?"

"Begor, thin, I'm afeard I did," replied Mike; "greatly afeard itself."

"Her name wasn't Brady, Mike—was it?"

"Begor, thin, yer right enough, ma'am, it wasn't Brady; 'twas the—the—"

"The what, darlint?"

"Why, 'twas the Queen o' Hearts, ma'am;" and as Mike made this terrible confession, he wound his arm round the Queen's neck, and imprinted a kiss on her cheek with so much vehemence that the report resounded like a clap of thunder over the locality. Kings, queens, knaves and commoners sprang to their feet. "Treason!" "Revenge!" "Kill him!" "Sting him to death!" were the first cries which arose from the tumult.

"Tie his heels together," cried the Knave of Hearts, "and hang him out o' the moon."

"Give us a garter, Peggy," said the King of Hearts to his wife.

The lady parted with the ligature with evident unwillingness, and Mike's ankles were bound together in a trice. A cold sweat burst out through the pores of his body, and he grew powerless in the presence of the terrible doom which he had earned by his rashness. In vain he remonstrated, pleaded and wept. A power he was unable to resist lifted him on the backs of four gigantic bats, and in three seconds he was being whirled towards the moon, attended by all the fairy company. The planet was reached in less than ten minutes, and Mick felt almost sick to death from the smell of stale cheese that pervaded the atmosphere.

"Hang him to this corner," cried the King of Hearts. "We'll let him see he don't kiss our wife for nothing."

"She can have it back, if 'twill please your majesty," said Mike. "I mint no harm."

"Here's a nice crumbledy corner to tie him to; 'twill break away in an hour, and then he'll be made porridge of," roared the Knave of Hearts.

A suitable spot was at length selected, and Mike, hanging head

downwards between earth and heaven, was left swinging about in
a storm which agitated the lonely lunar regions. Far below he
could see the world, and, when the wind lulled, could catch the
roar of the Falls. His head grew dizzy, his heart sank within
him, and, clasping his hands together, he exclaimed, "May the
Lord have mercy on me." The words had not died on his lips
when the corner of the moon he was hooked to snapped off, and
he fell—down deeper, and deeper, and deeper! The stars shot
past him, as he descended with the velocity of an aerolite; and,
before he had time to bless himself, he alighted, with a great
bound, on the world, narrowly escaping a plunge into the roaring Falls. He started up, he rubbed his eyes—what was this?
Where was the moon? and where were his tormentors? He was
lying in the middle of the "Fairies' Wake," on the identical
spot where he had taken the last draught of whisky on returning homeward. Everything was quiet, not a leaf stirred; it was
long past midnight, and the full, round moon of Christmas had
begun to set. Looking up to the descending planet, he exclaimed, " 'Twas a power of a fall intirely. I wondher was the
bottle broke!" An examination of his pocket convinced him
that it had not sustained a fracture; and, to his astonishment, the
cards were all safe, and tightly packed together. "Afther all,"
he soliloquized, "I was only dhramin'; but old brogues to me,
if I play cards agin in a hurry—Sunday or Monday, or holiday,
aither. What the deuce has got into the bottle?" Holding the
flask between his eyes and the light, he perceived something
moving up and down the inside. For a moment he was convinced that it was the spectral child, who had warned him to reject all offers of food and drink from the fairies, but, breaking the
vessel, he discovered that it was only a field frog. Stiff and sore
in every joint, he rose up and plodded homewards.

"You see, Mike," said his mother, when he had recounted in
detail the experiences of the night, "that there's nayther luck
nor grace in card-playin', for if you had gone where you ought,
the Good People couldn't trouble you."

"Thrue enough, mother," he replied; "but wait till I go

card-playin' agin, and you'll be diggin' the praties on New Year's Day."

"There, go where ye ought to go," he exclaimed, throwing the new cards into the fire. "It's moighty plain that people who ride steeplechases on bats and dine on frog sirloins aren't fit company for honest Christians. And, mother, ye'll never agin have to fall out wid me about my duty; and here, may the Lord send us all A HUNDRED HAPPY CHRISTMASES."

TOM KEARNEY.

Some two score years ago, or over, on the road to Coal Island, in the county of Tyrone, lived Jack McConnaughey, the blacksmith. I remember him well, and his appearance. To the shoulders he was about middle height, but his exceedingly long, thin, scraggy neck, made him fully two or three inches taller.

Jack was a prudent, careful, and extremely frugal soul, who regarded any kind of waste on his premises as an unpardonable sin. Yet he did not stand very high in the esteem of his neighbors; they failed utterly to award him either merit or respect for his saving virtues; on the contrary, they designated him "a miserable old crig." He had a simple simpering manner withal that indicated anything but the skinflint he really was. In the words of Tom Kearney, who was once his journeyman, "Jack was very soft about the mouth till you came to feel his teeth." Tom, however, was somewhat prejudiced in the matter, as the reader most likely will find out.

Jack never married, and there were those who were ill-natured enough to regard the fact as a wise and beneficent stroke of Providence. It was said that he had an old stocking hid away somewhere, and upon it all his affections concentrated and into it went every sovereign, half-crown and shilling his anvil yielded. Even the priest declared he "could not get a rap out of him but the bare dues that he couldn't help." His sister Nancy kept his house, and was said to be the counterpart of Jack himself, but Tom Kearney insisted that, bad as Jack was, Nancy was ten times worse.

Tom was not a native of the place; he was a Leinster man that tramped in there some years before, and got employment from Jack McConnaughey, not knowing anything about him at the time; as he verified afterwards, he "would as soon stay in h—l as wid ould Nancy."

Tom Kearney was a superior workman, deeply versed in the mysterious secrets of his trade; could make a plow or any other mechanism fashioned in a forge, only give him the pattern. At shoeing horses he had no superior, and many believed he had no equal. At periods, ranging from four to six months, Tom would go off on a spree, get gloriously drunk, and keep it up for a week or over. Then came a season of repentance, in which he labored with sickness and headache for several days more. During those special seasons of regret he was invariably the propounder of many wise and moral sayings on the folly of drunkenness, always ending with the most strongly affirmed resolutions and solemn promises to avoid the cursed thing for the time to come. Many farmers and others liked Tom's workmanship so well, that if their horses needed shoeing during his aberrations, they would keep them back until he got sober again. He had not been long in McConnaughey's employment when his talent brought business crowding to Jack's forge, and the latter, though he found him profitable, took advantage of the stranger, paid him as little wages as possible notwithstanding his superior workmanship.

Barney Muldoon was another blacksmith, living at the cross roads, some two miles off, and a generous good fellow, who used to have a good deal of business to do, but Jack's new journeyman took the shine out of them all. Tom in the meantime did not like his quarters, and was saving up what money he could to get away from the place; this was the reason why that for six mortal months he never tasted *barley juice*. He was preparing to leave, when, on a Sunday, he met Barney Muldoon for the first time, and after the usual salutations were over the latter invited Tom to a social drink, and off they went together. Barney was a genial, warm-hearted fellow, and Tom, feeling the influence, could not resist. Hour after hour of cosy enjoyment stole over them, conversing about their trade and other interesting matters, until it was night before they departed. Barney went home and was at his work next day, but Tom went on a spree, and continued at it till all his money was gone.

The time for jollification was over at last, and the time for repentance come; his head ached fearfully, augmented by conjoint lectures from Jack and Nancy for neglecting his work, "and money so hard to be got." Tom walked out to escape the crossfire of tantalizing words and did not return. Jack was soon in the fidgets to know where he went or what had become of him, when sometime during the next week he made the terrible discovery that Tom Kearney was hard at work in Barney Muldoon's forge! This news was very irritating—Barney Muldoon to take away his journeyman! He went there to know how any one dared do it. As he approached the place, however, the thing began to look a little different to his view; he knew it would not be safe to say much to Barney, and so he addressed himself to Tom, who felt little disposed to treat him even civilly. Tom's head was quite recovered now; he was getting better wages, and not at all the meek creature he was when weak, sick and nervous, just after the spree. He ordered McConnaughey to leave, or, if not, he was preparing for hostile demonstrations. Being an active, powerful young man, and looking cross at Jack, the latter took the hint and departed at the same time. Feeling his loss acutely, he judged that as soon as it went forth that Tom had left him, his business, now so flourishing, would soon fall back into the old ruts again, and maybe worse.

His anticipation was not incorrect, for Barney soon got all the horse-shoeing he could do in consequence. Still Jack did not give up hope of coaxing Tom back again, an accession of which he felt the need, for even now that winter was approaching, he had little or nothing to do. He was never done accusing himself for letting Tom go; and was earnestly wishing for an opportunity of talking with him, away from Barney Muldoon's presence. Thus, with his mind tormented in this way, the time was come to lay in his year's stock of coals for the forge, according to his custom. He had got a load or two from the Island, and was going for more, when passing by the public house, a mile or so from his own place, on a fine day, somebody called him from the inside. He went over to see who it was, and had scarcely got in when his attention was directed to a man lying helplessly drunk and asleep, who turned out to be no other than his journeyman, Tom Kearney.

The meeting seemed providential, but how was he going to improve the opportunity, and the fellow so dead drunk? A bright thought occurred to Jack; that he would take Tom along in his cart to the coal pits, and when the latter awoke he might induce him to return and domicile with Nancy again. Full of this promising project, he got more straw into his vehicle, and with the help of some bystanders he succeeded in transferring Tom to it, more like a dead man than a living one. Jack drove on to the pits; though it was a long way, he arrived there at last, and still his charge slept fast as ever. He immediately sought out Bryan Campbell, his first cousin, to whom he communicated all his troubles and desires; how he wished to get Tom back, and the ruse he had practised in order to get him to return.

Now, Bryan Campbell was the wag of the coal mines, an inveterate practical joker. He was a man of considerable intelligence, and though he indulged in the social bowl occasionally, few ever saw him drunk. He was the very centre of all the fun amongst the miners, and when he went on a game of sport, all obeyed him as a commander. Though McConnaughey was his near relative, he had little respect for him, knowing his niggardly disposition well.

"What'll ye give me," said Bryan, "if I git this fellow to go back till you?"

Jack was willing to promise him almost anything if he only effected that. Campbell got Tom carefully into the bucket with himself, and both were lowered down the shaft. The sleeper was conveyed with quiet caution into a coal chamber which has little resemblance to the lady's chamber. There he was peaceably divested of his clothing. An old blanket, procured for the occasion, was wrapped round him, and he was tranquilly placed by his conductor, sitting by a great pillar of coal, just as the inebriate was showing some signs of returning animation.

Tom, at length, had gradually slept off his drunken stupor, and opened his eyes; it was all dark around him. He tried hard to recollect himself, where he went asleep, but his memory was sorely at fault; he could not recall the most distant glimmer. He remembered being at Sam McVicker's public house, where the big picture of King William crossing the Boyne was up; and how Sam saved him from a set of Orangemen, who were about to pound him for cursing King Billy—but where was he now? He felt sick, his throat was dry and husky, and oh, how bitterly he regretted going on that infernal spree, and he doing so well with Barney Muldoon. He soon discovered he was naked, with nothing but an old blanket round him. Where were his clothes, or where did he lose them? He was sensible of a strong odor of brimstone, very ominous; and again the terribly perplexing question smote him—where was he now? He heard the miners picking, but he did not understand it; he had never seen a coal pit in his life, nor had he the remotest notion of what it looked like, and of course the least suspicion of where he was never entered his thoughts.

Poor Tom was thus seriously and sadly ruminating, his usually strong nerves unstrung and his system weakened down, for he had eaten no food for nearly a week—when he saw some strange looking beings approaching, each with a light on his head! They came and ranged silently around him. He could see they were black, and for fear of exposing his nakedness he drew the blanket closer round him. After standing some time in silence, one of these mysterious visitors spoke at last, and he heard in solemn tones: "What is your name?"

"My name," said he, "is Tom Kearney; but tell me, if you please sir, where am I now, or what place is this?"

"Don't you know without asking? Can't you see we're all black? And don't you smell the brimstone?"

"Oh," said Tom, groaning inwardly, "how did I get here, and what's the name of the place?"

"You got here as all like you get. You died drunk, and why need you ask the name of the place?"

"Am I dead?" said Tom, now fairly sobered.

"Of course you're dead."

"And are you the—the imps?" he faintly faltered.

"Yes, we're the imps," was the reply, and they all laughed, which sounded dreadfully hellish in Tom's ears.

"What did you work at in the other world?" resumed the talking imp again.

"I was a blacksmith," said Tom.

"Are you a good blacksmith?"

"I used to be able to forge almost any kind of a job."

"Where did you serve your time?"

"In Dublin, on the mail coach road, with Maguire, that used to be called *The Big Fish*, for a nick-name."

"Can you make chains and bolts?"

"Yes, I can make bolts after a pattern, and I can make chains and close them if I have a good anvil."

"Ye'll have a good anvil, and ye'll be very useful here, for we want a lot o' chains made, and bolts, too, for there's a great deal o' quality coming here just now. There's Lord Castlereagh, that cut his throat the other day; ye've heerd o' him, didn't you?"

"Yes," answered Tom; "but wasn't it in England he did that?"

"Oh, aye, indeed was it, but he must come to the Irish part o' hell for his punishment. He betrayed and robbed Ireland, you know, and it's Irishmen must keep the hot blast till his skin. He is the traitor that sold the country to Billy Pitt, and it's their own fault if they let the fire go down on him—but' there's no danger o' that. We use traitors the worst of all here. The "98" informers are all crammed down very far—Tom Reynolds is undermost,"

Kearney was well pleased at the information the imp gave

him. He thought it was quite right, and said so. His lucid informant asked him if he was not very dry. "Yes, indeed," said Tom, "but sure you have nothing to drink here?"

"Oh, aye have we, troth, for poor fellows like you," and to Tom's astonishment and delight, he was handed a small tin porringer full of pure potteen. He smelled of it and drank it down gratefully, remarking how good it was, and that he never thought they had such good whiskey down here.

"Hut, man," said the imp, "why wouldn't it be good, when it was down in hell whiskey was first made."

Kearney felt much better after this kindness, even if it was in hell, and would have stood up but for shame of his nakedness. Though amongst the devils, he felt shy of appearing with nothing but an old blanket around him. The spokesman fiend, noticing his inclination, told him he must keep sitting until he was called, and continued to enlighten him on the usages of the nether world.

"You see," he resumed, "we do things down here a good deal different to what ye thought. In the other world the rich have it all their own way, and have no marcy on the poor, so we turn the thing right around, when we git them down here, and pay them back in their own coin. All the punishment we give till the poor fellows that come here is to make them keep the fires up till the rich rascals, for all their persecutions on earth, and it's hardly any punishment at all to the poor to do this work, for most o' them take comfort in paying back ould scores to the scoundrels that punished themselves above. That's the way we work down here. Do you see?"

Tom did see and appreciated, too; he listened very attentively, though it was a new system of theology to him; he had never heard it before, but concluded it was about right.

"Yes," rejoined the fiend, "it is right, and many of the tyrants would come off a good deal worse, only the people they injured went up to the other place, and it's drunkards and other poor creatures that didn't know much about them, that must attend to them here; but they keep the fire up to them purty well for all that."

The imp walked off to some other place, leaving Kearney in deep thought; he soon returned, however, and accosted his victim:

"Thomas Kearney, who did you work for last?"

"For Barney Muldoon, at the cross; a very decent man."

"And who did you work for before that?"

"For Jack McConnaughey, God forgive me."

A laugh among the imps followed this remark, and there was a movement behind the great pillar that Tom was sitting against; for Jack himself was there; he came down with a few others who wanted to see the fun, though to him it was no fun at all, but real business. He could not restrain himself, or leave the management of the affair to Bryan; he was so much interested he must come eaves-dropping. It is an old saying that an eaves-dropper seldom hears anything creditable or pleasing to himself. Let us see if Jack's experience was an exception.

"Well," said the fiend, who was no other than Bryan Campbell, "why did you leave Jack McConnaughey?"

"For very good reason," replied Tom, who, by the way, grew quite familiar since he got the drink, "for the very good reason that he was the meanest man I ever knew."

There was a general laugh at this, and Tom was surprised to hear it echoed in different directions away behind him.

"Thomas Kearney," said the dark spokesman again, "if you got a chance to get out o' this place wouldn't you take it?"

"Why, to be sure I would."

"Well, now, Thomas, if you git out of this on conditions of going back to Jack McConnaughey, will you go?—but mind, you can't break any bargain you make here."

This was a terrible and serious dilemma, to which Tom gave the most grave consideration. He thought of Jack's meanness—Nancy's hard visage never appeared more repulsive to him. Feeling that the contract must be binding, he had much difficulty in making up his mind, but notwithstanding this, he arrived at the conclusion finally. McConnaughey, from behind the wall of coal, stretched out his long neck and listened breathlessly, thinking he was to have his journeyman back again.

"Well," said the victim, and all were attentive, "from all you tell me about this place, it's not so bad as I thought. I'd like to scorch ould Castlereagh; and anyhow I'd rather stay here than have to live my life with Jack, and above all with ould Nancy!"

The wild roar of laughter that followed this declaration startled poor Kearney; it reverberated all around through the dark space, where he could not see any one or any thing. The black fiends seemed all merriment, while poor Tom could not understand the cause. Soon the spokesman recovered his equanimity, and he returned to the examination:

"Thomas Kearney, what have you against Jack McConnaughey or his sister Nancy?"

"Well," began Tom, looking at the crowd of imps coming and going with lights on their heads, "I'll tell you as well as I can: Jack is a man I couldn't bear to work for; if he was paying me a shilling I earned from him, he'd squeeze it so hard atween his finger and thumb that you could read the date o' the coin there for hours after—faith, his own neighbors say he'd skin a flea for the hide and fat; and as for ould Nancy—she's ten times worse; she'd starve the divil with her thin stirabout! Gentlemen," he added, looking hard at the infernals, "I don't mean any offence to you; but I think she counts the grains of oatmeal going into the pot."

During the delivery of this speech the imps were in agonies of laughter, screaming in uproarious glee, after which many of them disappeared.

"And so, Tom Kearney," said the familiar fiend, "you'd rather stay here than with old Nancy McConnaughey?"

"Yes," answered Tom, who began to feel rather sick again, "I'd rather stay here than with ould Nancy McConnaughey."

"Well," said the familiar voice, "don't you think you could eat something now?"

"No, I'm too sick; but I'd take another drink of whiskey if you have it."

He got the other drink, and felt but little better when the friendly fiend asked him if he could sleep, but no he could not.

He was now alone, save the one dark habitant who spoke to him all the time, and who now addressed him in a solemn, friendly manner:

"Tom Kearney, ye're too good a fellow to be kept here, so if you let me bandage your eyes and bind your hands, and do everything as I tell you, I think I can lead you out and set you at liberty."

Tom consented, and with his eyes blindfolded, the other led him to where there was some clothing, and told him to dress himself in the dark. He wondered how the clothes fitted him so well; they felt like his own. His hands were then tied securely behind his back, and his companion led him along, until, by his directions, they were seated together in a large tub, and soon they began to ascend up, until at last Tom found himself in the fresh, cool air. He walked a long way with his conductor holding him by the arm, until they entered a house, where he was seated and told to remain very quiet until somebody would come and set him free, which would surely be in a short time. He complied faithfully with the injunction, and after a while some person entered, asking what was the matter with him. But before he could answer the new-comer unbound his hands, and took off the bandage, when Tom found himself in the presence of a stout, good-natured looking man, who eyed him curiously.

Kearney was no less surprised than gratified at his return to daylight again, though not disposed to be very communicative with the stranger about his escape from the lower regions—his train of ideas was sadly confused, and he had too much to think of for talking, just yet. His liberator accompanied him to the turnpike road leading home. Tom was very thoughtful, when his conductor hailed a passing carman, and asked him to give his companion "a lift as far as Barney Muldoon's at the cross."

"Indeed, Bryan Campbell," said the carman, "I'm only too glad to serve a friend of yours."

Tom got home to Barney's house about night-fall, a sadder and perhaps a wiser man than when he left it. Bryan Campbell conceived quite a regard for him after that time, and always said, "Kearney was a man—every inch of him—and never passed the way without calling in."

I forgot to state that Barney Muldoon's daughter, Mary, was the belle of the parish, and in less than a year from that time Tom Kearney led her to the altar, and Bryan Campbell was at the wedding.

These incidents occurred before Father Mathew's time, but Tom took good care ever after not to risk another *descent into the lower regions*. He became a sober, good husband, and in time the father of a fine family of handsome girls and stout boys.

PADDY CORBETT'S FIRST SMUGGLING TRIP.

On a foggy evening in the November of a year of which Irish tradition, not being critically learned in chronology, has not furnished the date, two men pursued their way along a bridle road that led through a wild mountain tract in a remote and far westward district of Kerry. The scene was savage and lonely. Far before them extended the broad Atlantic, upon whose wild and heaving bosom the lowering clouds seemed to settle in fitful repose. Round and beyond on the dark and barren heath, rose picturesque masses of rock—the finger-stones which Nature, it would seem, in some wayward frolic, had tossed into pinnacled heaps of strange and multiform construction. About their base, and in the deep interstices of their sides, grew the holly and the hardy mountain ash, and on their topmost peaks frisked the agile goat in all the pride of unfettered liberty.

These men, each of whom led a Kerry pony that bore an empty sack along the difficult pathway, were as dissimilar in form and appearance as any two of Adam's descendants possibly could be. One was a low-sized, thick-set man; his broad shoulders and muscular limbs gave indication of considerable strength; but the mild expression of his large blue eyes and broad, good-humored countenance, told, as plain as the human face divine could, that the fierce and stormy passions of our kind never exerted the strength of that muscular arm in deeds of violence. A jacket and trousers of brown frieze, and a broad-brimmed hat made of that particular grass named *thraneen*, completed his dress. It would be difficult to conceive a more strange or unseemly figure than the other: he exceeded in height the usual size of men; but his limbs, which hung loosely together, and seemed to accompany his emaciated body with evident reluctance, were literally nothing but skin and bone; his long conical head was thinly strewn with rusty-colored hair that waved in the evening breeze about a haggard face of greasy, sallow hue, where the rheumy, sunken eye, the highly prominent nose, the thin and livid lip, half disclosing a few rotten straggling teeth, significantly seemed to tell how disease and misery can attenuate the human frame. He moved, a living skeleton: yet, strange to say, the smart nag which he led was hardly able to keep pace with the swinging unequal stride of the gaunt pedestrian, though his limbs were so fleshless that his clothes flapped and fluttered around him as he stalked along the chilly moor.

As the travellers proceeded, the road, which had lately been pent within the huge masses of granite, now expanded sufficiently to allow them a little side-by-side discourse; and the first-mentioned person pushed forward to renew a conversation which seemed to have been interrupted by the inequalities of the narrow pathway.

"An' so ye war saying, Shane Glas," he said, advancing in a straight line with his spectre-looking companion, "ye war saying that face of yours would be the means of keeping the gauger from our taste of tibaccy."

"The gauger will never squint at a lafe of it," says Shane Glas, "if I'm in yer road. There was never a cloud over Tim Casey for the twelve months I thravelled with him; and if the foolish man had had me the day his taste o' brandy was taken, he'd have the fat boiling over his pot to-day, 'tisn't that I say it myself."

"The sorrow from me, Shane Glas," returned his friend with a hearty laugh, and a roguish glance of his funny eye at the angular and sallow countenance of the other, "the sorrow be from me if it's much of Tim's *fat* came in your way, at any rate, though I don't say as much for the *graise*."

"It's laughing at the crucked side o' yer mouth ye'd be, I'm thinking, Paddy Corbett," said Shane Glas, "if the thief of a gauger smelt your taste o' tibaccy and I not there to to fricken him off, as I often done afore."

"But couldn't we take our lafe o' tibaccy on our ponies' backs in panniers, and throw a few hake or some oysters over 'em, and let on that we're fish-joulting?"

"Now, mark my words, Paddy Corbett: there's a chap in Killarney as knowledgeable as a jailer; Ould Nick wouldn't bate him in roguery. So put your goods in the thruckle, shake a wisp over 'em, lay me down over that in the fould o' the quilt, and say that I came from Decie's counthry to pay a round at Tubber-na-Treenoda, and that I caught a faver, and that ye're taking me home to die, for the love o' God and yer mother's sowl. Say that Father Darby, who prepared me, said that I had the worst spotted faver that kem to the counthry these seven years. If that doesn't fricken him off, ye're sowld" (betrayed.)

By this time they had reached a deep ravine, through which a narrow stream pursued its murmuring course. Here they left the horses, and, furnished with the empty sacks, pursued their onward route till they reached a steep cliff. Far below in the dark and undefined space sounded the hollow roar of the heaving ocean, as its billowy volume broke upon its granite barrier, and formed along the dark outline a zone of foam, beneath whose snowy crest the ever-impelled and angry wave yielded its last strength in myriad flashes of phosphoric light, that sparkled and danced in arrowy splendor to the wild and sullen music of the dashing sea.

"Paddy Corbett, avick," said Shane Glas, "pull yer legs fair an' aisy afther ye; one inch iv a mistake, achorra, might sind ye a long step of two hundred feet to furnish a could supper for the sharks. The sorrow a many would vinture down here, avourneen, barring the red fox of the hill and the honest smuggler; they are both poor persecuted crathurs, but God has given them *gumpshun* to find a place of shelter for the fruits of their honest industry."

Shane Glas was quite correct in his estimate of the height of this fearful cliff. It overhung the deep Atlantic, and the narrow pathway wound its sinuous way round beneath so many frightful precipices, that had the unpractised feet of Paddy Corbett threaded the mazy declivity in the clear light of day, he would in all probability have performed the saltation, and furnished the banquet of which Shane Glas gave him a passing hint. But ignorance of his fearful situation saved his life. His companion, in addition to his knowledge of this secret route, had a limberness of muscle, and a pliancy of uncouth motion, that enabled him to pursue every winding of the awful slope with all the activity of a weazel. In their descent, the wild sea-fowl, roused by the unusual approach of living things from their couch of repose, swept past on sounding wing into the void and dreary space abroad, uttering discordant cries, which roused the more distant slumberers of the rocks. As they farther descended round the foot of the cliff, where the projecting crags formed the sides of a little cove, a voice, harsh and threatening, demanded "who goes there?" The echo of the questioner's interrogation, reverberating along the receding wall of rocks, would seem to a fanciful ear the challenge of the guardian spirit of the coast pursuing his nightly round. The wild words blended in horrid unison through the mid-air with the sigh of waving wings and discordant screams, which the echoes of the cliffs multiplied a thousand fold, as though all the demons of the viewless world had chosen that hour and place of loneliness to give their baneful pinions and shrieks of terror to the wind.

"Who goes there?" again demanded this strange warder of the savage scene; and again the scream of the sea-bird and the echo of human tones sounded wildly along the sea.

"A friend, avick machree," replied Shane Glas. "Paudh, achorra, what beautiful lungs you have! But keep your voice a thrifle lower, ma bouchal, or the water-guards might be after staling a march on ye, sharp as ye are."

"Shane Glas, ye slinging thief," rejoined the other, "is that yerself? Honest man," addressing the new comer, "take care of that talla-faced schamer. My hand for ye, Shane will see his own funeral yet, for there is not another crathur, barring a fox, could creep down the cliff till the moon rises, anyhow. But I know what saved yer bacon; he that's born to be hanged—you can repate the rest o' the thrue ould saying yerself, ye poor atomy!"

"Whist,"-said Shane Glas, rather chafed by the severe raillery of the other, "is it because ye shoulder an ould gun that an honest man can't tell what a Judy ye make o' yerself, swaggering like a raw Peeler, and frightening every shag on the cliff with yer foolish bull-scuttering! Make way there, or I'll stick that ould barrel in yez—make way there, ye spalpeen!"

"Away to yer masther with ye, ye miserable disciple," returned the unsparing jiber. "Arrah, by the hole o' my coat, afther you have danced yer last jig upon nothing, with yer purty himp cravat on, I'll coax yer miserable carcass from the hangman to frighten the crows with."

When the emaciated man and his companion had proceeded a few paces along the narrow ledge that lay between the steep cliff and the sea, they entered a huge excavation in the rock, which seemed to have been formed by volcanic agency, when the infant world heaved in some dire convulsion of its distempered bowels. The footway of the subterranean vault was strewn with the finest sand, which, hardened by frequent pressure, sent the tramp of the intruder's feet reverberating along the gloomy vacancy. On before gleamed a strong light, which, piercing the surrounding darkness, partially revealed the sides of the cavern, while the far space beneath the lofty roof, impervious to the powerful ray, extended dark and undefined. Then came the sound of human voices mixed in uproarious confusion; and, anon, within a receding angle, a strange scene burst upon their view.

Before a huge fire which lighted all the deep recess of the high over-arching rock that rose sublime as the lofty roof of a Gothic cathedral, sat five wild-looking men of strange semi-nautical raiment. Between them extended a large sea-chest, on which stood an earthen flagon, from which one, who seemed the president of the revel, poured sparkling brandy into a single glass that circled in quick succession, while the jest and laugh and song swelled in mingled confusion, till the dinsome cavern rang again to the roar of the subterranean bacchanals.

"God save all here!" said Shane Glas, approaching the festive group. "Oh, wisha! Misther Cronin, but you and the boys is up to fun. How goes the Colleen Ayrigh, and her Bochal Fadda, that knows how to bark so purty at thim plundering thieves, the wather-guards?"

"Ah! welcome, Shane," replied the person addressed; "the customer you've brought may be depinded on, I hope. Sit down, boys."

"'Tis ourselves that will, and welkim," rejoined Shane. "Depinded on! why, 'scure to the dacenther father's son from this to himself than Paddy Corbett, 'tisn't that he's to the fore."

"Come, taste our brandy, lads, while I help you to some ham," said the smuggler. "Shane, you have the stomach of a shark, and the digestion of an ostrich."

"Be gar ye may say that wid yer own purty mouth, Misther Cronin," responded the garrulous Shane. "Here, gintlemin, here is free thrade to honest min, an' high hangin' to all informers! Oh! murdher maura (smacking his lips), how it tastes! Oh, avirra yealish (laying his bony hand across his shrunken paunch), how it hates the stummuch!"

"You are welcome to our masion, Paddy Corbett," interrupted the hospitable master of the cavern; "the house is covered in, the rent paid, and the cruiskeen of brandy unadulterated; so eat, drink, and be merry. When the moon rises, we can proceed to business."

Paddy Corbett was about to return thanks when the interminable Shane Glas again broke in.

"I never saw a man, beggin' yer pardon, Misther Cronin, lade a finer or rolickinger life than your own four bones—drinking an' coorting on land, and spreading the canvass of the Coolleen Ayrigh over the salt say, for the good o' thrade. If I had Trig Dowl the piper forninst me there, near the cruiskeen, but I'd drink an' dance till morning. But here's God bless us, an' success to our thrip, Paddy, avrahir;" and he drained his glass. Then when many a successive round went past, he called out at the top of his voice, "Silence for a song," and in a tone somewhat between the squeak of a pig and the drone of a bagpipe, poured forth a *comallye*.

Early on a clear sunny morning after this, a man with a horse and truckle car was observed to enter the town of Killarney from the west. He trolled forth before the animal, which, checked by some instinctive dread, with much reluctance allowed himself to be dragged along at the full length of his hair halter. On the rude vehicle was laid what seemed a quantity of straw, upon which was extended a human being, whose greatly attenuated frame appeared fully developed beneath an old flannel quilt. His face, that appeared above its tattered hem, looked the embodiment of disease and famine, which seemed to have gnawed, in horrid union, into his inmost vitals. His distorted features portrayed rending agony; and as the rude vehicle jolted along the rugged pavement, he groaned hideously. This miserable man was our acquaintance Shane Glas, and he that led the strange procession no other than Paddy Corbett, who thus experimented to smuggle his "taste o' tibaccy," which lay concealed in well-packed bales beneath the sick couch of the wretched simulator.

As they proceeded along, Shane Glas uttered a groan, conveying such a feeling of real agony that his startled companion, supposing that he had in verity received the sudden judgment of his deception, rushed back to ascertain whether he had not been suddenly stricken to death.

"Paddy, a chorra-na-nea," he muttered in an undergrowl, "there's the vagabone thief of a gauger down sthreet! Exert yerself, a-lea, to baffle the schamer, an' don't forget 'tis the spotted faver I have."

Sure enough, the gauger did come; and noticing, as he passed along, the confusion and averted features of Paddy Corbett, he immediately drew up.

"Where do you live, honest man, an' how far might you be goin'?" said the keen exciseman.

"O, wisha! may the heavens be yer honor's bed!—ye must be one o' the good ould stock, to ax afther the consarns of a poor angishore like me: but, a yinusal-achree, 'tisn't where I live is worse to me, but where that donan in the thruckle will die with me."

"But how far are you taking him?"

"O, 'tis myself would offer a prayer on my two binded knees for yer honor's soul, if yer honor would tell me that. I forgot to ax the craythur where he *should* be berrid when we kim away, an' now he's speechless out an' out."

"Come, say where is your residence," said the other, whose suspicion was increased by the countryman's prevarication.

"By jamine, yer honor's larnin' bothers me intirely, but if yer honor manes where the woman that owns me and the childre is, 'tis that way, west at Tubber-na-Treenoda; yer honor has heard tell o' Tubber-na-Treenoda, by coorse?"

"Never, indeed."

"O, wisha! don't let yer honor be a day longer that way. If the sickness, God betune us an' harum, kim an ye, 'twould be betther for yer honor give a testher to the durhogh there, to offer up a rosary for ye, than to *shell out* three pounds to Doctor Crump."

"Perhaps you have some *soft goods* concealed under the sick man," said the ganger, approaching the car. "I frequently find smuggled wares in such situations."

"Sorra a taste *good* or *saft* under him, sir dear, but the could sop from the top o' the stack. *Ketch!* why, not a haporth ye'll *ketch* here but the spotted faver."

"Fever!" repeated the startled exciseman, retiring a step or two.

"Yes, faver, yer honor; what else? Didn't Father Darby that prepared him, say that he had spotted faver enough for a thousand min! Do, yer honor, come look in his face, an' thin throw the poor dying craythur, that kem all the way from Decie's counthry, by raisin' of a dhream, to pay a round for his wife's sowl at Tubber-na-Treenoda: yes, throw him out an the road an' let his blood, the blood o' the stranger, be on yer soul an' his faver in yer body."

Paddy Corbett's eloquence operating on the exciseman's dread of contagion, saved the tobacco.

Our adventurers considering it rather dangerous to seek a buyer in Killarney, directed their course eastward to Kanturk. The hour of evening was rather advanced as they entered the town; and Shane, who could spell his way without much difficulty through the letters of a sign-board, seeing "entertainment for man and horse" over the door, said they would put up there for the night, and then directed Paddy to the shop of the only tobacconist in town, whither for some private motive he declined to attend him. Mr. Pigtail was after dispatching a batch of customers when Paddy entered, who, seeing the coast clear, gave him the "God save all here," which is the usual phrase of greeting in the kingdom of Kerry. Mr. Pigtail was startled at the rude salutation, which, though a beautiful benediction, and characteristic of a highly religious people, is yet too uncouth for modern "ears polite," and has, excepting among the lowest class of peasants, entirely given way to that very sincere and expressive phrase of address, "your servant."

Now, Mr. Pigtail, who meted out the length of his replies in exact proportion to the several ranks and degrees of his querists, upon hearing the vulgar voice that uttered the more vulgar salute hesitated to deign the slightest notice, but, measuring with a glance the outward man of the saluter, he gave a slight nod of acknowledgment, and the dissyllabic response "servant;" but seeing Paddy Corbett with gaping mouth about to open his embassy, and that, like Burns's Death,

> "He seemed to make a kind o' stan',
> But naething spak,"

he immediately added, "Honest man, you came from the west, I believe?"

"Thrue enough for yer honor," said Pat; "my next door

neighbors at that side are the wild Ingins of Immeriky. A wet and could foot an' a dry heart I had coming to ye; but welkim be the gifts o' God, sure poor people should make out an honest bit an' sup for the weeny crathurs at home; an' I have thirteen o' thim, all thackeens."

"And I dare say you have brought a trifle in my line of business in your road?"

"Faith, 'tis yerself may book it; I have the natest lafe o' tibaccy that ever left Connor Cro-ab-a-bo. I was going to *skin* an honest man—Lord betune us and harum, I'd be the first informer of my name, anyhow. But, talking o' the tibaccy, the man that giv it said a sweeter taste never left the hould of his ship, and that's a great word. I'll give it dog chape, by raison o' the long road it thravelled to your honor."

" You don't seem to be long in this business," said Mr. Pigtail.

"Thrue for you there agin, a-yinusal; 'tis yourself may say so."

Now Mr. Pigtail supposed from the man's seeming simplicity, and his inexperience in running smuggled goods, that he should drive a very profitable adventure with him. He ordered him to bring the goods privately to the back way that led to his premises; and Paddy, who had the fear of the gauger vividly before him, lost no time in obeying the mandate. But when Mr. Pigtail examined the several packages, he turns round upon poor Paddy with a look of disapprobation, and exclaims, "This article will not suit, good man—entirely damaged by sea water—never do."

"*See* wather, anagh!" returns Paddy Corbett; "bad luck to the dhrop o' water, salt or fresh, did my taste o' tibaccy ever *see*. The Colleen Ayrigh that brought it could dip an' skim along the waves like a sea-gull. There are two things she never yet let in, Mr. Pigtail, avourneen—wather nor wather guards; the one ships off her, all as one as a duck; and the Boochal Fadda on her deck keeps t'other a good mile off, more spunk to him." This piece of nautical information Paddy had ventured from gleanings collected from the rich stores which the conversation of Shane Glas presented along the road and in the smugglers' cave,

"But, my good man, you cannot instruct me in the way of my business. Take it away—no man in the trade would venture an article like it. But I shall make a sacrifice, rather than let a poor ignorant man fall into the hands of the gauger. I shall give you five pounds for the lot."

Paddy Corbett, who had been buoyed up by the hope of making two hundred per cent. of his lading, now seeing all his gainful views vanish into thin air, was loud and impassioned in the expression of his disappointment. "Oh, Jillian Dawly!" he cried, swinging himself to and fro, "Jillian, aroon manima, what'll ye say to yer man, afther throwing out of his hand the half year's rint that he had to give the agint? Oh, what'll ye say, aveen, but that I med a purty padder-napeka of myself, listening to Shane Glas, the yellow schamer; or what'll Sheelabeg, the crathur, say, whin Tim Murphy won't take her without the cows that I won't have to give her? Oh, Misther Pigtail, avourneen, be marciful to an honest father's son; don't take me short, avourneen, an' that God might take you short. Give me the tin pounds it cost me, an' I'll pray for yer sowl, both now an' in the world to come. Oh, Jillian, Jillian, I'll never face ye, nor Sheelabeg, nor any o' the crathur's agin, without the tin pound, anyhow."

"Well, if you don't give the tobacco to me for less than that, you can call on one Mr. Prywell, at the other side of the bridge; he deals in such articles, too. You see I cannot do more for you, but you may go farther and fare worse," said the perfidious tobacconist, as he directed the unfortunate man to the residence of Mr. Paul Prywell, the officer of excise.

With heavy heart, and anxious eye peering in every direction beneath his broad-leafed hat, Paddy Corbett proceeded till he reached a private residence having a green door and a brass knocker. He hesitated, seeing no shop nor appearance of business there; but, on being assured that this was indeed the house of Mr. Paul Prywell, he approached, and gave the door three thundering knocks with the butt end of his holly-handled whip. The owner of the domicile, roused by this very unceremonious mode of announcement, came forth to demand the intruder's business, and to wonder that he would not prefer giving a single rap with the brass knocker, as was the wont of persons in his grade of society, instead of sledging away at the door like a "peep-o'-day boy."

"Yer honor will excuse my bouldness," said Paddy, taking off his hat, and scraping the mud before and behind him a full yard; "excuse my bouldness, for I never seed such things on a dure afore, an' I wouldn't throuble yer honor's house at all at all, only in regard of a taste of goods that I was tould would *shoot* yer honor. Ye can have it, a-yinusal, for less than nothing, 'case I don't find myself in heart to push on farther; for the baste is slow, the crathur, an' myself that's saying it, making buttons for fear o' the gauger."

"Who, might I ask," said the astonished officer of excise, "directed you here to sell smuggled tobacco?"

"A very honest gintleman, but a bad buyer, over the bridge, sir. He'd give but five pound for what cost myself tin—foreer dhota, that I had ever had a hand in it! I put the half year's rint in it, yer honor; and my thirteen femul grawls an' their mother, God help 'em, will be soon on the sachrawn. I'll never go home without the tin pound, anyhow. High hanging to ye, Shane Glas, ye tallow-faced thief, that sint me smuggling. Oh, Jillian, 'tis sogering I'll soon be, with a gun an my shoulder!"

"Shane Glas!" said the exciseman; "do you know Shane Glas? I'd give ten pounds to see the villain."

"'Tis myself does, yer honor, an' could put yer finger an him, if I had ye at Tubber-na-Treenoda, saving yer presence; but as I was setting away, he was lying undher an old quilt, an' I heard him telling that the priest said he had spotted fever enough for a thousand min."

"That villain will never die of spotted fever, in my humble opinion," said the exciseman.

"A good judgment in yer mouth, sir, achree. I heard the rogue himself say, 'Bad cess to the thief! that a cup-tosser tould him he'd die of stoppage of breath.' But won't yer honor allow me to turn in the lafe o' tibaccy?"

The officer of excise was struck with deep indignation at the villainy of him who would ruin a comparatively innocent man when he failed in circumventing him, and was resolved to punish his treachery. "My good fellow," said he, "you are now before the gauger you dread so much, and I must do my duty, and seize upon the tobacco. However, it is but common justice to punish the false-hearted traitor that sent you hither. Go back quickly, and say that he can have the lot at his own terms; I shall follow close, and yield him the reward of his treachery. Act discreetly in this good work of biting the biter, and on the word of a gentleman I shall give you ten pounds more."

Paddy rapidly retraced his steps, ejaculating as he went along, "Oh, the noble gintleman, may the Lord make a bed in Heaven for his sowl in glory! Oh, that chating imposthor, 'twas sinding the fox to mind the hins, sure enough. Oh, high hanging to him of a windy day! the informer o' the world, I'll make him sup sorrow."

"Have you seen the gentleman I directed you to?" said Mr. Pigtail.

"Arrah, sir, dear, whin I came to the bridge an' looked about me, I thought that every roguish-looking fellow I met was the thief of a gauger, an' thin afther standing a while, quite amplushed with the botheration and the dread upon me, I forgot yer friend's name, an' so kim back agin to ax it, if ye plase."

"You had better take the five pounds than venture again; there's a gauger in town, and your situation is somewhat dangerous."

"A gauger in town!" cried Paddy Corbett, with well-affected surprise. "What'll I do at all at all? now I'm a gone man all out. Take it for anything ye like, sir, dear, an' if any throuble like this should ever come down an ye, it will be a comfort and a raycreation to yer heart to know that ye had a poor man's blessing, *avick deelish machree*, an' I give it to ye on the knees of my heart, as ye desarved it, an' that it may go in yer road, an' yer childre's road, late an' early, eating an' dhrinking, lying an' rising, buying an' selling."

Our story has approached its close: the tobacco was safely stowed inside, in order to be consigned to Mr. Pigtail's private receptacle for such contraband articles. Paddy had just pocketed his five pounds, and at that moment in burst Mr. Prywell. The execration which ever after pursued the tobacconist for his treacherous conduct, and the heavy fine in which he was amerced, so wrought upon his health and circumstances, that in a short time he died in extreme poverty, and it is upon record, among the brave and high-minded men of Duhallow, that Jeffrey Pigtail of Kanturk was the only betrayer that ever disgraced the barony.

HANNABERRY THE PIPER.

The County Wexford, of all parts of Ireland, is peculiarly rich in legends, traditions and fairy tales. In former days, before the advent of the newspaper press and the national schoolmaster, there was not a district, town or village within its borders but boasted of its story-teller, who was generally the depository of all the marvellous and uncanny events that had taken place in the neighborhood for ages past. But in these days of railroads, telegraphs, schools and cheap literature, the long-honored tribe of story-tellers is disappearing, even in the County of Wexford. A few remain, however, to this day, but their occupation has fearfully fallen into desuetude. Some of them may still be found lingering around their old haunts at the glowing firesides of comfortable farmers, but many of them were swallowed up in that great stream of immigration that poor old Erin has been pouring on our American shores for the last half century. Of the latter was Jimmy Chili, who, though he bore a name that savored of South America, was as true a Wexfordian as ever danced a jig in New Ross, from which good old town he hailed. I first became acquainted with Jimmy when he was a "youngster" in the ancient colony of Newfoundland. Like myself, he was then employed in the dangerous but profitable occupation of seal hunting. In the intervals of the hunt, and in the long winter nights, seated around the forecastle fire, he often beguiled the tedium of the slow passing hours with story, jest and song. Jimmy was a firm believer in witchcraft, ghosts, fairies, warnings, second sight, and all the mysteries which are supposed to hedge in the supernatural order. Whether he believed in his own tales or not I cannot say; but certain he always delivered himself of them, particularly when they related to ghosts and fairies in such a solemn, oracular way, as to carry conviction to his hearers among the simple fishermen and seal hunters of Newfoundland. I well remember one night, after having made everything snug on deck, we were seated at the forecastle fire. After Jimmy had drank his tea, filled his pipe and smoked it, he was called upon for a story.

"Be gob, boys," said he in response, "I'll tell you the story of Hannaberry the Piper and the Marquis of Waterford. Hannaberry was the greatest piper in all the country around New Ross. Divil a marriage, christening, fair or wake widin' miles but he would be at wid his pipes, and thim were the pipes, don't be talking."

I will not attempt, however, to give the story verbatim in Jimmy's vernacular, but that was the opening sentence. What follows I shall relate as concisely as possible, and keeping as near the original text as I can.

"One night," Jimmy went on, "Hannaberry, who had been to the fair of Taghmon, which is situated between New Ross and Wexford town, was returning home, with his pipes, as usual, under his arm. He had passed a merry day of it, and, as a consequence, felt pretty much as Tam O'Shanter, of Scottish memory, felt when he pronounced himself victorious over all the ills of life. Down came Hannaberry, in this jolly mood, along the road to New Ross. From Taghmon to his home it was a goodly walk, and after the fatigues of the day it was only natural that he should feel a trifle tired. When he came to the old lime-kiln, that is exactly four miles from Ross bridge, he thought he would rest himself and have a pull at his old *dudheen;* 'twould refresh him and waken up his faculties, which were, in a manner, becoming oblivious. He had no sooner conceived the idea than he proceeded to carry it into execution by seating himself on the sloping ground that led to the top of the lime-kiln, lighting his pipe and commencing to smoke. Before seating himself he laid his beloved pipes carefully away in a nook of the kiln. He had not smoked long before a dreamy, drowsy, undefinable sensation crept over him. The smoke from his pipe appeared to resolve itself into a mysterious halo of light, which gradually began to enshroud him. Suddenly he heard the most delicious strains of music proceeding from a short distance behind where he was seated. Never had such strains been produced on Irish pipes as Hannaberry now listened to, and turning, he beheld a sight which struck him with awe and astonishment. Coming towards him, with the pipes under his arm, was a little, a very little, old man, nattily dressed in green. The little old man handled the pipes with the most consummate skill and grace, and, standing before the astonished Hannaberry, he played twelve of the most delightful and patriotic airs in a style the most lovely and bewitching. When he had ceased playing he laid down the pipes, and, fixing a pair of piercing black eyes on the bewildered piper, addressed him thus:

"'Why, then, Mick Hannaberry, it's yourself that's a brave man, by daring to sit down so comfortably in a fairy *rath*. I have been here now bordering on five hundred years, and you are the first man that has had the courage to cross the magic ring and rest himself in my domains. And now, me man, let me tell you that you have conferred a favor on me that shall not go unrewarded.'

"When the little old man in green had stopped speaking, he lifted the pipes from the ground, and placing them under Hannaberry's arm, he ordered the now fairly bewildered piper to strike up a tune. Hannaberry at first was very timid and bashful, particularly after hearing such beautiful music from the fairy, as he now fully knew him to be. He pleaded weariness and inability, but the little old man with a quiet dignity awed, while at the same time he reassured, the piper into a compliance with his demand, and Mick Hannaberry struck up a jig so lively and soul-stirring, that the performer himself was completely surprised at the delicacy and proficiency with which he handled the keys of his instrument. Tune after tune, to the number of twelve, was rattled off on the pipes, by the now thoroughly delighted piper, who already began to congratulate himself on the great advantage his increased proficiency in his art would give him over his less fortunate rivals, who had never stumbled into a fairy *rath* to become acquainted with its occult mysteries. The little man in green eyed the piper all the while with the keenest and shrewdest glances, apparently reading the thoughts that were uppermost in his mind.

"'Be aisy, now, Mick,' said he, 'and lay down the pipes till I explain. As I said afore, yours is the first mortyal face of a piper that I have set eyes on in this sacred ring for five hundred years.'

"'Be gorra, then, that's a long time, your honor,' said Mick in reply, looking out curiously from under the rim of his old hat at the little old man in green, and wondering all the while what was coming next.

"'Yes, five hundred weary years have I been imprisoned here, till this blessed night, when some good chance has sent you to my relief. And Mick, me man, I'll forever bless the day you came to relieve me, besides assisting you to make your fortune.'

"'It's thankful I am to your honor,' replied Mick, still feeling not quite at ease, and wishing in his heart that he was safely at home with the old woman and children.

"'There is a condition, however,' said the little old man in green, 'and, unfortunately, one that cannot be dispensed with. It is inseparable from my unfortunate position, and in many respects will counterbalance the great benefit conferred upon you. When you leave here to-night your fame will be abroad through all the country; indeed, it will not be confined to poor old Ireland, but will be spread throughout the whole of the three kingdoms. Your services will be in great request. Your pipes, by merely placing them on a table, will be operated upon by an unseen agency, and the most delicious music will be produced; but,' and here the little old man's face assumed a grave aspect, '*every time the pipes are played you will lose a near relative by death.* This is the inevitable condition, which you must either accept or remain with me until another piper comes to your relief and mine. Five hundred years ago, when in the flesh, like you, I was a piper. I wasted my days in mirth, joviality and song. I was idle and encouraged idleness in others, and as a punishment for my thoughtless conduct, I was condemned to pass ages in the narrow confines of this *rath*. I was to be freed, however, when a man of my own profession would voluntarily come within the magic circle which surrounds my limited domains. It has been your fortune to be the man, and whether that fortune is to be good or evil for you your future conduct will tell. Take your pipes, you are now at liberty to go; but do not forget the penalty that is attached to your music, and remember, also, you must never refuse a reasonable request for your services as a piper.'

"The halo of light gradually faded away, and the dazed Hannaberry found himself cold, benumbed and damp, his pipes beside him, and still seated on the side of the little mound that led to the top of the lime kilns. He rubbed his eyes and wondered if it was not all a dream, and if he had not taken too much whisky, and whether the little old man in green and the music was not a phantom of a disordered brain. But no, it must have been a reality; for there, sure enough, was the fairy ring all around him, and no true Irish piper could ever doubt the evidence of his senses, when he was environed by so palpable a fact as that.

"With many misgivings and doubts he got up and started for his home, and the way he put himself over the ground between the old lime kiln and Ross bridge was wonderful to behold. The next morning, bright and early, before Hannaberry was awake, a well-to-do farmer from a neighboring district was after him to come and play at his daughter's wedding, which was about to take place. With the recollection of the scenes of last night still fresh in his mind, the poor piper faltered and hesitated for some time. The farmer wondered at his reluctance, and at his mysterious and absent manner. Such conduct was unusual in Hannaberry, and the farmer thought he would try what effect a glass or two would have upon him. In Hannaberry's depressed condition the whisky worked a magic charm. After imbibing he at once recovered his assurance and old sprightliness and promised to attend the wedding of the farmer's daughter on the following night. And sure enough, when the guests assembled at the farmer's at the appointed time, there was the piper with his pipes promptly on hand. When he made his appearance in the dancing-room, he placed his pipes on the table, and went to congratulate the new-married pair. In the mean time the lads and lasses had ranged themselves on the floor in sets for the dance, and the word went around, 'Strike up the music, Hannaberry!' No sooner had the request been made, than the pipes on the table commenced to play the most beautiful dancing tunes that had ever been heard in those parts. Hannaberry was as much astonished at first as any of the company; but by a powerful effort of the will he controlled his emotions, muttering only to himself, 'Be gorra, I am an enchanted man, surely.' The dancers turned to the piper for an explanation, charging him with witchcraft, the black art, and all other kinds of magic. Determined to make the best of a bad job, and now perfectly self-possessed, Hannaberry replied, 'Be aisy now, boys; sure it's only a new invention of me own in the the musical line. Sarra a thing yez need do but dance, and I'll furnish the music. Dance away, and never a hair of yer head will be hurt.' His coolness reassured them, his advice was good, the music was better, the guests in good humor, and so on the light fantastic toe they tripped the merry hours away until the dawning of another day. When poor Hannaberry returned home in the morning, a new and sad revelation broke in upon him. His mother-in-law, stark and stiff, lay dead in the house. His wife informed him that about midnight the family Banshee had set up the death-cry in the garden behind the house; that shortly after her mother was taken suddenly faint, and gave up the ghost in a short time, before a doctor or any other person could be called to her assistance. This was a stunning blow to the piper. Of what use was the great gift of musical proficiency, if, on every occasion it was exercised, he was to lose a near and dear relative? For, strange as it may appear, he really loved his mother-in-law. But as the little old man in green had predicted, Hannaberry's fame spread over all Ireland. It was the theme of conversation in all circles, high and low. At last it came to the ears of the Marquis of Waterford, who was at that time the leading sporting man in all Ireland. The marquis was well known as the greatest betting man of his day, and on a certain evening after dinner, in conversation with his guests, English and Scotch noblemen, he boldly asserted that Mick Hannaberry was the greatest piper in all the three kingdoms. Of course no patriotic English or Scotch nobleman could admit this. The marquis, however, insisted on the truth of his assertion, and offered to back it up by staking the whole of his immense estates on the issue of a contest with the pipes between Hannaberry and any other piper that England or Scotland could produce. His challenge was instantly accepted by an English nobleman, who stipulated that the trial of skill should come off in London, before the Court and all the nobility. The next day the marquis sought out Hannaberry, and told him what he had done. The poor piper had not yet forgotten the mysterious death of his mother-in-law, and in consequence received the proposal of the marquis to go to London to play rather coolly. 'Hannaberry,' said the marquis, 'the best farm on my estate shall be given to you and yours while grass grows and water runs, if you come with me to London ; and besides, man, isn't my whole estate bet upon you, and for the honor of old Ireland, surely, you would not see me deprived of my estates by the bluff of any Englishman that ever lived?'

"This fervent appeal settled the question, and Harnaberry agreed to accompany the marquis to London to test the skill of the best English and Scotch pipers. The next day the marquis, with the piper and a large retinue, set out for London, where they arrived in due time. The scene of the trial of skill was to be in the palace court-yard, before the Queen and all the highest nobility of the land. When the great day arrived, pipers from England and Scotland, including the Duke of Argyle's own piper, were on hand to contest the marquis' claim for the championship of Hannaberry. The poor fellow himself felt somewhat abashed when he stepped into the arena with his pipes, but the recollection of the little old man in green cheered him up. Seated around in a vast amphitheatre was the Queen, Prince Albert, the Duke of Wellington, and all the other great nobles of the land, arrayed in the most dazzling uniforms it was possible to imagine. Out from the gaily-dressed crowd stepped the Marquis of Waterford, and called for a table. It was brought instantly, and Hannaberry placed the pipes upon it. Moved by the unseen agency of the fairies, the pipes struck up and produced the most ravishing music, to the astonishment and delight of the vast audience. After the twelve tunes were played in grand style, the marquis stepped out and said: 'Show me the man in England or Scotland that can bate that.'

"'The divil a man in England or Scotland either,' said the Duke of Wellington, 'that can bate that, and its proud I am this day—yis, as proud as I was the day I bate the Frinch at Waterloo—that a countryman of mine can take the shine out of the whole world on the pipes. Be off home with you now, Hannaberry, and good luck to you; and, marquis, mind you treat him well.'

"'Be dad, I'll do that same,' replied the marquis. And he did; for on their return to Ireland he settled, as he had promised, the finest farm on his estate on the victorious piper, whose good fortune was rather dampened, however, when he was told that his uncle and his aunt, too, had died at the very time the shouts of victory were going up for him from the aristocracy in London.

"He never played the pipes after that, and, for all I know, he still lives on the same farm," said Jimmy Chili, as he lit his pipe and went on deck to take his trick at the wheel.

THE IRISH FIDDLER.

In my native parish there were four or five fiddlers—all good in their way; but the Paganini of the district was the far-famed Mickey M'Rorey. Where Mickey properly lived I never could actually discover, and for the best reason in the world—he was not at home once in twelve months. As Colley Cibber says in the play, he was "a kind of a here-and-thereian—a stranger nowhere." This, however, mattered little; for though perpetually shifting day after day from place to place, yet it somehow happened that nobody ever was at a loss where to find him. The truth is, he never felt disposed to travel *incog.*, because he knew that his interest must suffer by doing so; the consequence was, that wherever he went, a little nucleus of local fame always attended him, which rendered it an easy matter to find his whereabouts.

Mickey was blind from his infancy, and, as usual, owed to the small-pox the loss of his eyesight. He was about the middle size, of rather a slender make, and possessed an intelligent countenance, on which beamed that singular expression of inward serenity so peculiar to the blind. His temper was sweet and even, but capable of rising through the buoyancy of his own humor to a high pitch of exhilaration and enjoyment. The dress he wore, as far as I can remember, was always the same in color and fabric—to wit, a brown coat, a sober-tinted cotton waistcoat, grey stockings, and black corduroys. Poor Mickey! I think I see him before me, his head erect, as the heads of all blind men are, the fiddle-case under his left arm, and his hazel staff held out like a feeler, exploring with experimental pokes the nature of the ground before him, even although some happy urchin leads him onward with an exulting eye ; an honor which he will boast to his companions for many a mortal month to come.

The first time I ever heard Mickey play was also the first I ever heard a fiddle. Well and distinctly do I remember the occasion. The season was summer—but summer *was* summer then—and a new house belonging to Frank Thomas had been finished, and was just ready to receive him and his family. The floors of Irish houses in the country generally consist at first of wet clay ; and when this is sufficiently well smoothed and hardened, a dance is known to be an excellent thing to bind and prevent them from cracking. On this occasion the evening had been appointed, and the day was nearly half advanced, but no appearance of the fiddler. The state of excitement in which I found myself could not be described. The name of Mickey M'Rorey had been ringing in my ears for I don't know how long, but I had never seen him, or even heard his fiddle. Every two minutes I was on the top of a little eminence looking out for him, my eyes straining out of their sockets, and my head dizzy with the prophetic expectation of rapture and delight. Human patience, however, could bear this painful suspense no longer, and I privately resolved to find Mickey or perish. I accordingly proceeded across the hills, a distance of about three miles, to a place called Kilnahushogue, where I found him waiting for a guide. At this time I could not have been more than seven years of age ; and how I wrought out my way over the lonely hills, or through what mysterious instinct I was led to him, and that by a path, too, over which I had never travelled before, must be left unrevealed, until it shall please that Power which guides the bee to its home, and the bird for thousands of miles through the air, to disclose the principle upon which it is accomplished.

On our return home I could see the young persons of both sexes flying out to the little eminence I spoke of, looking eagerly towards the point we travelled from, and immediately scampering in again, clapping their hands, and shouting with delight.

Instantly the whole village was out, young and old, standing for a moment to satisfy themselves that the intelligence was correct; after which, about a dozen of the youngsters sprang forward, with the speed of so many antelopes, to meet us, whilst the elders returned with a soberer but not less satisfied manner into the houses. Then commenced the usual battle, as to who should be honored by permission to carry the fiddle-case. Oh, that fiddle-case! For seven long years it was an honor exclusively allowed to myself, whenever Mickey attended a dance anywhere at all near us; and never was the Lord Chancellor's mace—to which, by the way, with great respect for his lordship, it bore a considerable resemblance—carried with a prouder heart or a more exulting eye. But so it is—

"These little things are great to *little men*."

"Blood alive, Mickey, you're welcome!" "How is every bone of you, Mickey? Bedad we gev ye up." "No, we didn't give you up, Mickey; never heed him; sure we knew very well you'd not desart the Towny boys—whoo!—Fol de rol lol!" "Ah, Mickey, won't you sing 'There was a wee devil come over the wall?'" "To be sure he will, but wait till he comes home and gets his dinner first. Is't off an empty stomach you'd have him to sing?" "Mickey, give me the fiddle-case, won't you, Mickey!" "No, to *me*, Mickey." "Never heed them, Mickey; you promised it to me at the dance in Carntaul."

"Aisy, boys, aisy. The truth is, none of yez can get the fiddle-case. Shibby, my fiddle, hasn't been well for the last day or two, and can't bear to be carried by any one barrin' meself."

"Blood alive! sick, is it, Mickey?—and what ails her?"

"Why, some o' the doctors says there's a frog in her, and others that she has colic; but I'm going to give her a dose of Balgriffauns when I get up to the house above."

As we went along, Mickey, with his usual tact, got out of us all the information respecting the several courtships of the neighborhood that had reached us, and as much, too, of the village gossip and scandal as we knew.

Nothing can exceed the overflowing kindness and affection

with which the Irish fiddler is received on the occasion of a dance
or merry-making; and to do him justice he loses no opportunity
of exaggerating his own importance. From habit, and his position among the people, his wit and power of repartee are necessarily cultivated and sharpened. Not one of his jokes ever fails
—a circumstance which improves his humor mightily; for nothing on earth sustains it so much as knowing that, whether good
or bad, it will be laughed at. Mickey, by the way, was a
bachelor, and, though blind, was able, as he himself used to say,
to see through his ears better than another could through the
eyes. He knew every voice at once, and every boy and girl in
the parish by name, the moment he heard them speak.

On reaching the house he is bound for, he either partakes of,
or at least is offered, refreshment, after which comes the ecstatic
moment to the youngsters; but all this is done by due and solemn
preparation. First he calls for a pair of scissors, with which he
pares or seems to pare his nails; then asks for a piece of rosin,
and in an instant half a dozen boys are off at a break-neck pace,
to the next shoemaker's, to procure it; whilst in the meantime he
deliberately pulls a piece out of his pocket and rosins his bow.
But, heavens! what a ceremony the opening of that fiddle-case
is! The manipulation of the blind man as he runs his hand
down to the key-hole—the turning of the key—the taking out of
the fiddle—the twang twang—and then the first ecstatic sound,
as the bow is drawn across the strings; then comes a screwing;
then a delicious saw or two; again another screwing—twang
twang—and away he goes with the favorite tune of the good
woman, for such is the etiquette upon these occasions. The house
is immediately thronged with the neighbors, and a preliminary
dance is taken, in which the old folks, with good humored violence, are literally dragged out, and forced to join. Then come
the congratulations—"Ah, Jack, you could do it wanst," says
Mickey, "an' can still; you have a kick in you yet." "Why,
Mickey, I seen dancin' in my time," the old man will reply, his
brow relaxed by a remnant of his former pride, and the hilarity
of the moment, "but you see the breath isn't what it used to be

wid me, when I could dance the *Balleorum Jig* on the bottom of a ten-gallon cask. Heigho!—well, well—I'm sure I thought *my* dancin' days wor over"

"Bedad an' you wor matched anyhow," rejoined the fiddler. "Molshy carried as light a heel as ever you did; sorra a woman of her years ever I seen could cut the buckle wid her. You would know the tune on her feet still."

"Ah, Mickey, the thruth is," the good woman would say, "we have no sich dancin' now as there was in my days."

"But as good fiddlers, Molshy, eh? Come now, sit down, Jack, till I give you your ould favorite, '*Cannie Soogah.*'"

These were happy moments and happy times, which might well be looked upon as picturing the simple manners of country life with very little of moral shadow to obscure the cheerfulness which lit up the Irish heart and hearth into humble happiness. Mickey, with his usual good nature, never forgot the younger portion of the audience. After entertaining the old and full-grown, he would call for a key, one end of which he placed in his mouth, in order to make the fiddle sing for the children their favorite song, beginning with

"Oh! grandmamma, will you squeeze my wig?"

This he did in such a manner, through the medium of the key, that the words seemed to be spoken by the instrument, and not by himself. After this was over, he would sing us, to his own accompaniment, another favorite. "There was a wee devil looked over the wall," which generally closed that portion of the entertainment so kindly designed for *us*.

Upon those moments I have often witnessed marks of deep and pious feeling, occasioned by some memory of the absent or the dead, that were as beautiful as they were affecting. If, for instance, a favorite son or daughter happened to be removed by death, the father or mother, remembering the air which was loved best by the departed, would pause a moment, and with a voice full of sorrow, say, "Mickey, there is *one tune* that I would like to hear; I love to think of it, and to hear it; I do for the sake of them that's gone—my darlin' son that's lyin' low;

it was he that loved it. His ear is closed against it now; but for *his* sake—aye, for your sake, avourneen machree—we will hear it wanst more."

Mickey always played such tunes in his best style, and amidst a silence that was only broken by sobs, suppressed moanings, and the other tokens of profound sorrow. These gushes, however, of natural feeling soon passed away. In a few minutes the smiles returned, the mirth broke out again, and the lively dance went on as if their hearts had been incapable of such affection for the dead—affection at once so deep and tender. But many a time the light of cheerfulness plays along the stream of Irish feeling, when cherished sorrow lies removed from the human eye far down from the surface.

These preliminary amusements being now over, Mickey is conducted to the dance-house, where he is carefully installed in the best chair, and immediately the dancing commences. It is not my purpose to describe an Irish dance here, having done it more than once elsewhere. It is enough to say that Mickey is now in his glory; and proud may the young man be who fills the honorable post of his companion, and sits next him. He is a living storehouse of intelligence, a travelling directory for the parish—the lover's text-book—the young woman's best companion; for where is the courtship going on of which he is not cognizant? where is there a marriage on the tapis, with the particulars of which he is not acquainted? He is an authority whom nobody would think of questioning. It is now, too, that he scatters his jokes about; and so correct and well trained is his ear, that he can frequently name the young man who dances, by the peculiarity of his step.

"Ah ha! Paddy Brien, you're there? Sure I'd know the sound of your smoothin'-irons anywhere. Is it thrue, Paddy, that you wor sint for down to Errigle Keerogue, to kill the clocks for Dan M'Mahon? But, nabuklish! Paddy, what'll you have?

" Is that Grace Reilly on the flure? Faix, avourneen, you can do it; devil o' your likes I *see* anywhere. I'll lay Shibby to a penny trump that you could dance your own namesake—the *Calleen dhas dhun*, the bonny brown girl—upon a spider's cobweb, widout breakin' it. Don't be in a hurry, Grace, dear, to tie the knot; *I'll* wait for you."

Several times in the course of the night a plate is brought round, and a collection made for the fiddler; this was the moment when Mickey used to let the jokes fly in every direction. The timid he shamed into liberality, the vain he praised; and the niggardly he assailed by open hardy satire; all managed, however, with such an under-current of good humor, that no one could take offense. No joke ever told better than that of the broken string. Whenever this happened at night, Mickey would call out to some soft fellow, "Blood alive, Ned Martin, will you bring me a candle?—I've broken a string." The unthinking young man, forgetting that he was blind, would take the candle in a hurry, and fetch it to him.

"Faix, Ned, I knew you wor jist fit for't; houldin' a candle to a dark man! Isn't he a beauty, boys?—look at him, girls—as cute as a pancake."

It is unnecessary to say that the mirth on such occasions was convulsive. Another similar joke was also played off by him against such as he knew to be ungenerous at the collection.

"Paddy Smith, I want a word wid you. I'm goin' across the countlhry as far as Ned Donnelly's, and I wan't you to help me along the road, as the night is dark."

"To be sure, Mickey. I'll bring you over as snug as if you were on a clane plate, man alive!"

"Thank you, Paddy; throth, you've the dacency in you; an' kind father for you, Paddy. Maybe I'll do as much for you some other time."

Mickey never spoke of this until the trick was played off, after which he published it to the whole parish; and Paddy of course was made a standing jest for being so silly as to think that night or day had any difference to a man who could not see.

Thus passed the life of Mickey M'Rorey, and thus pass the lives of most of his class, serenely and happily. As the sailor to his ship, the sportsman to his gun, so is the fiddler attached to his fiddle. His hopes and pleasures, though limited, are full. His heart is necessarily light, for he comes in contact with the best and brightest side of life and nature; and the consequence is that their mild and mellow lights are reflected on and from himself. I am ignorant whether poor Mickey is dead or not; but I dare say he forgets the boy to whose young spirit he communicated so much delight, and who often danced with a buoyant and careless heart to the pleasant notes of his fiddle. Mickey M'Rorey, farewell! Whether living or dead, peace be with you.

BARNY O'GRADY.

Behold me safely landed at Philadelphia, with one hundred pounds in my pocket—a small sum of money, but many, from yet more trifling beginnings, have grown rich in America. Many passengers who came over in the same ship with me had not half so much. Several of them were indeed wretchedly poor. Among others there was an Irishman, who was known by the name of Barny—a contraction, I believe, for Barnaby. As to his surname, he could not undertake to spell it, but he assured me there was no better. This man, with many of his relatives, had come to England, according to their custom, during harvest time, to assist in reaping, because they gain higher wages than in their own country. Barny had heard that he could get still higher wages for labor in America, and accordingly he and his two sons, lads of eighteen and twenty, took their passage for Philadelphia. A merrier mortal I never saw. We used to hear him upon deck, continually singing or whistling his Irish tunes; and I should never have guessed that this man's life had been a series of hardships and misfortunes.

When we were leaving the ship, I saw him, to my great surprise, crying bitterly; and upon inquiring what was the matter, he answered that it was not for himself, but for his two sons, he was grieving; because they were to be made *redemption men*, that is, they were to be bound to work, during a certain time, for the captain, or for whomsoever he pleased, till the money due for their passage should be paid. Although I was somewhat surprised at any one's thinking of coming on board a vessel without having one farthing in his pocket, yet I could not forbear paying the money for this poor fellow. He dropped down

on the deck upon both his knees, as suddenly as if he had been
shot, and holding up his hands to heaven, prayed, first in Irish,
and then in English, with fervent fluency, that "I and mine
might never want; that I might live long and happy; that
success might attend my honor wherever I went, and that I
might enjoy for evermore all sorts of blessings and crowns of
glory." As I had an English prejudice in favor of silent grati-
tude, I was rather disgusted by all this eloquence; I turned away
abruptly, and got into the boat which waited to carry me to
shore.

* * * * * * * *

I had now passed three years in Philadelphia, and was not a
farthing the richer, but, alas, a great deal poorer. My inveterate habit of procrastination—of delaying everything till to-
morrow, always stood betwixt me and prosperity. I at last resolved upon leaving the land of the star-spangled banner; but
when I came to reckon up my resources, I found that I could not
do so, unless I disposed of my watch and my wife's trinkets. I
was not accustomed to such things, and I was ashamed to go to
the pawnbroker's, lest I should be met and recognized by some
of my friends. I wrapped myself up in an old surtout, and
slouched my hat over my face. As I was crossing the quay, I
met a party of gentlemen walking arm in arm. I squeezed past
them, but one stopped and looked after me; and though I
turned down another street to escape him, he dodged me unper-
ceived. Just as I came out of the pawnbroker's shop I saw him
posted opposite me; I brushed by; I could with pleasure have
knocked him down for his impertinence. By the time that I had
reached the corner of the street I heard a child calling after me;
I stopped, and a little boy put into my hand my watch, saying,
"Sir, the gentleman says you left your watch and these thingum-
bobs by mistake."

"What gentleman?"

"I don't know, but he was one that said I looked like an
honest chap, and he'd trust me to run and give you the watch.
He is dressed in a blue coat, and went towards the quay. That's
all I know."

On opening the paper of trinkets, I found a card with these words:—"*Barny*—with kind thanks."

"Barny! poor Barny! An Irishman whose passage I paid coming to America three years ago. Is it possible?"

I ran after him the way which the child directed, and was so fortunate as just to catch a glimpse of the skirt of his coat as he went into a neat, good-looking house. I walked up and down for some time, expecting him to come out again; for I could not suppose that it belonged to Barny. I asked a grocer who was leaning over his hatch-door if he knew who lived in the next house?

"An Irish gentleman of the name of O'Grady."

"And his Christian name?"

"Here it is in my books, sir—Barnaby O'Grady."

I knocked at Mr. O'Grady's door and made my way into the parlor, where I found him, his two sons, and his wife, sitting very sociably at tea. He and the two young men rose immediately, to set me a chair.

"You are welcome, kindly welcome, sir," said he. "This is an honor I never expected, any way. Be pleased to take the seat next the fire. 'Twould be hard, indeed, if you should not have the best seat that's to be had in this house, where we none of us ever should have sat, nor had seats to sit upon, but for you."

The sons pulled off my shabby greatcoat and took away my hat, and Mrs. O'Grady made up the fire. There was something in their manner, altogether, which touched me so much that it was with difficulty I could keep myself from bursting into tears. They saw this, and Barny (for I shall never call him anything else), as he thought that I should like better to hear of public affairs than to speak of my own, began to ask his sons if they had seen the day's paper, and what news there were.

As soon as I could command my voice, I congratulated this family upon the happy situation in which I found them, and asked by what lucky accident they had succeeded so well.

"The luckiest accident ever *happened me* before or since I came to America," said Barny, " was being on board the same vessel with such a man as you. If you had not given me the first lift, I had been down for good and all, and trampled under foot, long and long ago. But after that first lift, all was as easy as life. My two sons here were not taken from me—God bless you; for I never can bless you enough for that. The lads were left to work for me and with me; and we never parted, hand or heart, but just kept working on together, and put all our earnings, as fast as we got them, into the hands of that good woman, and lived hard at first, as we were born and bred to do, thanks be to heaven. Then we swore against all sorts of drink entirely. And as I had occasionally served the masons when I lived a laboring man in the county of Dublin, and knew something of that business, why, whatever I knew I made the most of it, and a trowel felt noways strange to me, so I went to work, and had higher wages at first than I deserved. The same with the two boys: one was as much of a blacksmith as would shoe a horse, and the other a bit of a carpenter; so the one got plenty of work in the forges, and the other in the dock-yards as a ship-carpenter. So, early and late, morning and evening, we were all at the work, and just went this way struggling on even for a twelvemonth, and found, with the high wages and constant employ we had met, that we were getting greatly better in the world. Besides, my wife was not idle. When a girl, she had seen baking, and had always a good notion of it, and just tried her hand upon it now, and found the loaves went down with the customers, who came faster and faster for them; and this was a great help. Then I turned master mason, and had my men under me, and took a house to build by the job, and that did; and then on to another; and after building many for the neighbors, 'twas fit and my turn, I thought, to build one for myself, which I did out of theirs, without wronging them of a penny. In short," continued Barny, if you were to question me how I have got on so well in the world, upon my conscience, I should answer, we never made Saint Monday, and never put off till to-morrow what we could do to-day."

I believe I sighed deeply at this observation of Barny's, notwithstanding the comic phraseology in which it was expressed.

"And would it be too much liberty to ask you," said Barny, "to drink a cup of tea, and to taste a slice of my good woman's bread and butter? And happy the day we see you eating it, and only wish we could serve you in any way whatsoever."

I verily believe the generous fellow forgot at this instant that he had redeemed my watch and wife's trinkets. He would not let me thank him as much as I wished, but kept pressing upon me fresh offers of service. When he found I was going to leave America, he asked what vessel we should go in. I was really afraid to tell him, lest he should attempt to pay for my passage. But for this he had, as I afterwards found, too much delicacy of sentiment. He discovered, by questioning the captains, in what ship we were to sail; and when we went on board, we found him and his sons there to take leave of us, which they did in the most affectionate manner; and after they were gone, we found in the state cabin, directed to me, everything that could be useful or agreeable to us, as sea stores for a long voyage.

OROHOO, THE FAIRY MAN.

At one time I resided in the neighborhood of the "plains of Boyle," a celebrated pasture country, and was the possessor of a cow whose milk and butter were plentiful in quantity and excellent in quality, and materially contributed to the comforts of my family. She was a beautiful and a gentle creature, and I flattered myself that in her I possessed the foundress of a numerous herd, and the germ of a profitable and extensive dairy.

The idea was very prevalent there that it was in the power of evil-disposed persons to deprive you of your milk and butter, and I heard many complaints of the kind; the general voice fastened the imputation on a woman who lived in the vicinity, who was locally termed "the Hawk," and certainly the fire of her eye and the sharpness of her beak justified the appellation: she was a comely middle-aged person, in rather easy circumstances, her husband being a small farmer; but he lay under the suspicion of being concerned in a murder some time before. She was a reputed witch, and the entire family were disliked and avoided.

One morning in the month of January I was informed that a woman had come into my kitchen, who occupied herself in watching the motions of the family, without stating her business. On going down, I found her well dressed and well looking, but with a very sinister cast of countenance. On asking if she wanted me, she said she had heard I was in want of some geese, and that she had a few to dispose of. "How many?" said I. "A goose and a gander," she replied. "How much do you want for them?" "Seven-and-sixpence!" I exclaimed in surprise, as the usual price then was from one shilling to one-and-sixpence each. "Why, how many have you?" as I really thought I had made a mistake in the number. "A goose and a gander," said she. "And do you suppose me to be a goose, to give such a price as that?" said I. "Oh," said she, "they are good geese, and only I wish to serve you, I would not offer them at all." "Indeed! I am much obliged by your good wishes," said I; "but as I think you want to impose upon me, you must take your geese to another market, for I will not have them at any price, and the sooner you take yourself off the better." She got higly offended, muttered something about my being sorry for refusing them, and went away in high dudgeon; and after she was gone I found it was "the Hawk" who had favored me with the visit.

On the same morning a gang of strollers, consisting of tinkers, chimney-sweeps, a brace or two of beggars, and a piper, had pitched their tent on the roadside, a short distance from my residence; the members of the party had distributed themselves over the surrounding district in pursuit of their various avocations; it also happened to be churning day, and my wife having set her vessels in order, was proceeding with her lacteal operations favorably—the milk had cracked, the butter was expected—when the sound of music was heard; the piper attached to the party had come to give us a specimen of his skill; he favored us with a few Connaught planxties, was duly rewarded, and departed. Shortly after he was gone, two buxom baggages, brown and bare-legged, with cans in their hands, kerchiefs on their heads, and huge massive rings on their fingers, came and demanded an alms. They were told there was nothing then ready, on which one of them asked a drink. "I have nothing to offer you but water," said my wife, "until the churning's done." "Well, water itself," said she; on getting which, she took a sup or two, put the remainder in her can, and went off; and, strange as it may seem, my butter went too. And from that day in January until May eve following, not a morsel had we from our beautiful Brownie.

As I did not put faith in witchcraft, I was willing to attribute this to some natural cause affecting the cow, though the milk showed no perceptible change in either quantity or quality;

neither did she exhibit any symptoms of ailment or disorder, except that she began to cast her hair. She was well supplied with good fodder, comfortably lodged and well attended, and every possible care taken of the milk, but all to no purpose; the butter was not forthcoming; and for my incredulity I was laughed at by my neighbors. "Your cow is bewitched," cried they; "and you may as well throw chaff against the wind as think you will get your butter back till you get the charm." Some said "the Hawk" had it, some that the gypsy took it away in her can, and others that it followed the piper. Be that as it may, I had to eat my bread butterless, and brood over my loss, without even the comfort of common condolence.

Various were the counter-charms recommended for my adoption. "Send for Fraser the Scotchman from beyond the Lough," said one; "he fears neither man nor fiend, and he will surely get it." "Send for 'the Hawk,' and clip a bit off her ear," said another. "Let them keep their mouths full of water, and never speak while they are churning," said a third. In short, I found there were as many ways of getting it back as there were of losing it—all equally simple, and probably as efficacious.

Thus matters continued until the early part of the month of April, when one morning a man called, who desired to see me. I found him a light, active, 'cute-looking fellow, low in stature and spare in habit, but sinewy, well set and well knit, and regularly smoke-dried. He was pretty well clad in frieze, cord breeches, and yard stockings and pumps; his caubeen on one side, a cutty in his mouth, and a certain jauntiness in his air, and crafty audacity in his look, which seemed to say, "I'd have you to know I'm a clever fellow."

"So," said he at once without preamble, "so you've lost your butter."

"Yes," said I, "'tis certainly gone."

"Well, if you like, I'll get it for you. My name is OROHOO (O'Hara); I live at Sliev Bawn—the people call me the Fairy man—I can find things that's stole—and I keep the *garvally*."

"Indeed!" said I; "why, you must be a clever fellow; but can you get my butter?"

"Not a doubt of it," said he, "if it is in the country."

I had heard of the garvally before, which was described as "a crooked thing like the handle of an umbrella, covered with green baize." It was formerly in much repute for swearing on; "and a terrible thing it was, for if you swore falsely and it round your neck, your mouth would turn to the back of your head, or you'd get such a throttling as you'd never get the better of." It had latterly, however, lost much of its virtue, or rather of its fame, by an unbelieving vagabond yoking it on and swearing to a manifest falsehood, without suffering any visible inconvenience. But to return to Orohoo.

He made no stipulation; but requiring a deep plate, some water and salt, with a little of the cow's milk, he commenced by desiring my wife and me to stand forward. He then asked our names, if I was the owner of the cow, how long I had had her, if that woman was my wife when we had lost our butter, and if we suspected any person for taking it. To these queries I answered as was necessary; but to the last I replied, I did not believe in witchcraft.

"Don't you believe in fairies?" he asked.

"Scarcely," said I.

"No matter," said he; "maybe before I'm done you will believe in them."

He then, in a very solemn manner, poured some water into the plate at three several times. He added the milk in the same manner, and then sprinkled in the salt, using the same formula. He now stirred round the mixture three times with his finger, repeating the words as before, and desired us to do the same. To this I demurred, for I did not wish to evince any faith in the proceeding by taking an active part; but he combated my scruples by asking " was it not done in a good name?" Certainly for so far I saw nothing very objectionable, and my wife feeling no scruple on the subject, at their joint persuasion I did as directed.

He next made the sign of the cross over the plate with his hands, and, waving them over his head, cut several curious figures in the air, at the same time muttering an unintelligible jargon

I could not understand, but which, as I could catch a sound or syllable, bore a close affinity to what is called bog Latin. Gradually he became much excited; he raved like a demon, stamped with his feet, and threatened with his fists: now his tones were those of supplication or entreaty, anon of abjuration or command; while his eye seemed fixed upon and to follow the motions of some, to us invisible, being, with which he appeared to hold converse. Suddenly he gave an unearthly scream, as if in an agony of terror and perturbation, and, holding up his hands as in the act of warding off a threatened danger, he retreated backwards round the room, pursued, as it seemed, by an implacable enemy. Gradually he regained the spot he had left, turned himself to the four cardinal points, making the sign of the cross at each turn, dipped his fingers in the mixture, devoutly blessed himself, anointing his forehead, shoulders, and breast, regained his self-possession, raised his hands and eyes in an attitude of fervent thankfulness to heaven, wiped the perspiration which profusely streamed from his brow with the cuff of his coat, gradually recovered his breath, and from a state of the greatest possible excitement became calm and collected.

Now, this was all acting, to be sure, but it was inimitably done, and I confess, even armed as I was with unbelief, it made a powerful impression on me. I acknowledge I did not feel at all comfortable. I did not like the idea of being in the same room with the evil one, who to all appearance was chasing my friend the conjuror round and round it. I felt an indescribable sensation of dread creeping over me, and, if I mistake not, there were a few drops of perspiration on my brow; and my hair, of which I have not a superabundance, to my apprehension began to get stiff and wiry. My wife, too, clung closely to my side for protection, and the agitation of her mind was evident by the audible action of her heart, which in that case beat only responsive to my own.

Having taken breath, he asked for a ribbon, which he passed over his forehead and round his head, and, bringing the ends in front, knotted it over his nose; then twining it round his fingers in the manner children call a cat's cradle, he knelt down and peered through it attentively into the mixture, which I imagined fermented and sent up a blue vapor. After gazing a few seconds in this manner,

"Aha!" said he, "she is not far off that has your butter; bring me a lighted candle," which on being brought he placed in the plate. "Now," said he, "both of you kneel down; do as I do, and say as I say, and we'll have her here directly."

"No," said I decidedly, "we will not."

I thought we had gone far enough, and was convinced that if what we were engaged in was not an unholy act, it was at least a piece of gross deception, and I would not countenance it by any farther participation.

"Why," exclaimed he, "don't you want to get your butter?"

"Yes," said I, "I would like to have my butter, but I don't choose to resort to a charm to obtain it."

"No doubt this is a charm," said he, "but it is done in a good name; and I have done it before for as good as ever you were."

"So much the worse," I replied; "the holy name should never be profaned in such a manner, and I am sorry any person would be so wicked or so foolish as to encourage you in your tricks. I neither like you nor your proceedings, and the sooner you go about your business the better."

He started to his feet in a passion, blew out the candle, seized the plate, and attempted to throw the contents into the fireplace; but my wife, who did not wish her hearth to be wet, took it from him and laid it past. He fumed and stormed, said I let him take a great deal of trouble on my account, and insisted on proceeding; but I was determined, and, being considerably chafed and annoyed by the transaction, I again ordered him off and left him.

In a few moments I heard the noise of a violent altercation and scuffle, and I was loudly called on. I hastened to the scene of contention, and found my wife holding Orohoo by the neck, and preventing his departure.

"What's all this?" I exclaimed.

"This fellow," said she, "when he was going, took a live coal out of the grate, and told me to take care of my children."

This he stiffly denied, until confronted by the servant, and I threatened to give him up to the police as an impostor, when he quailed, and acknowledged that he had said so, but that he meant no harm by it.

"And sure," said he, "there's no harm in bidding you mind them; for if your cow was hurt, so may your childre. You're not treating me right," he continued; "I came at the bidding of a friend to do you a good turn, and asked nothing for it, and now you're putting me out; you'll be glad to see me yet, though. But take my advice; never throw out your Sunday's ashes until Tuesday morning, and always sweep your floor in from the door to the hearth." And away he went.

My heart now beat easy, for I thought we had fairly got rid of the fairy man; but I was to be still further mystified and bewildered. On examining the plate over which he had held his incantations, we found the contents to be thick, yellow and slimy with a red sediment like globules of blood at the bottom. This seemed extraordinary, as I certainly watched him closely, and did not see him put anything into the plate but milk, water and salt.

The month now drew near a close, and our bread was still butterless. This often caused the morsel to stick in the throat of my poor dear partner, who felt none of the scruples of conscience with which I was affected, and firmly believed her cow was bewitched.

"Here we are, day after day, losing our substance, and might have it only for your squeamishness in not letting the fairy man finish his job."

Thus she would argue, and hesitated not to call me a fool, nay, a downright ass; and indeed my neighbors were much of the same opinion; one of them, a respectable farmer's wife, was particularly pertinacious. "My Robin," said she one evening, as they were harping on the old string, "my Robin was down in Sligo, and he heard that if you got the coulter of a plough, and made it red-hot in the fire while you were churning the butter it would come back; or if you chose to churn on Sunday morning before the lark sings, you will surely get it."

"Tempt me no more with your spells or Sabbath-breaking; I will have none of them," said I, impatiently; "I will never barter my peace of mind for a pound of butter, if I should never eat a morsel."

But, in truth, my peace of mind was gone, for the continual urging and yammering I was subjected to made me heartily sick, and I inwardly resolved to sell the cow the first opportunity, and so end the matter.

On May eve, in the afternoon, I had occasion to leave home for a short time, and on my return was rather surprised to find all the windows closed and the door locked against me. I knocked and called for admittance but received no answer; and hearing the noise of churning going on within, "fast and furious," the truth flashed across my mind, and, lamenting my wife's credulity, I retired to the garden to await the result. In a short time she came running out like one demented, clapping her hands and screaming, "Oh! we've got the butter, we've got the butter!" and on going in I found a coulter phizzing and sparkling at a white heat in the fire, an ass's shoe (which had been found a few days previously) under the churn, my worthy neighbor aforesaid standing over it, panting and blowing from the exertions she had made on my behoof, and wiping the dew-drops from her really comely countenance, and in the churn, floating like lumps of gold in a sea of silver, as fine a churning of butter as ever we were blessed with.

Well, I own I was staggered, and being triumphantly asked, "Now, is there no witchcraft or virtue in a red-hot coulter?" I could scarcely muster up courage to utter "No." In vain I protested the butter came back because "Brownie" got back to her pasture, in consequence of the change in her feeding, from dry fodder to the mellow and genial produce of spring, as the loss at first was owing to the transition from grass to hay. 'Twas to no purpose to argue thus: all else were positive it was otherwise; but whether the virtue was in Orohoo's incantations, the efficacy of the red-hot coulter, the influence of the ass's shoe, or the tremendous pommelling the milk was subjected to on the occasion, no one could exactly say.

A few days after, I conversed on the subject with an intelligent person, a herd in charge of an extensive stock farm. After hearing my story to an end, he indulged in a hearty laugh at my expense. "Faith," said he, "I took you for a sensible man, and did not suppose you would credit such folly." "I'd as soon believe my mother was a bishop," said I, "as put any faith in it some time ago. But how can I get over the chain of circumstantial evidence?—not a link of it wanting. First, 'the Hawk' coming with her seven-and-sixpenny geese, then the gypsies and the piper, and losing my butter just then." "'Tis very easy," said he, "to account for it. In the first place, you took your cow from grass and fed her on hay." "Yes, but she had plenty of winter cabbage, and we gave her boiled potatoes." "Just the thing; cabbage is good for plenty of milk, but not for butter. I'll engage you gave her the potatoes warm." "Yes." "And she got a scour?" "Indeed she did, and her hair fell off." "So I thought. And afterwards she got in good condition?" "Yes." "Oh! ay, she put her butter on her ribs. Did you kill a pig at Christmas?" "I did." "Where did you put your bacon in press?" "Why, under the shelf in the dairy." "Now the murder is out! Never as long as you live put meat, either fresh or salt, near your milk-vessels; if you do, you will surely spoil your milk and lose your butter." "This may account for my loss, but what have you to say to its coming back?" "Why, what's to hinder it, when your bacon is in the chimney and your cow at grass?" "But the red blobs in the plate, and Orohoo fighting the devil for me, what do you say to that?" Here he gave way to such a violent fit of laughter that I really thought he would burst the waistband of his doe-skins. "Orohoo! ha! ha!—Orohoo! ha! ha! ha!—the greatest villain that ever breathed He came to me one time that I had a cow sick, and said she was fairy-smitten, and that he would cure her. He began with his tricks with the milk and water, just the same as he did with you; but I watched him closer; and when I saw the smoke rising out of the plate, I got him by the neck, shook a little bottle of vitriol out of the cuff of his coat, and took a paper of red earthy powder out of his waistcoat pocket." I looked aghast and confounded. Was I, then, the dupe of the fairy man? The thought was humiliating, and I even wished that I had remained in ignorance, but on reflection had reason to congratulate myself that it was only a temporary lapse, and that I was right in my original opinion, that, except the witchery of a pair of blue languishers, or the fairy spell of a silver-tongued siren, there is now no evil of the kind to be apprehended.

A TALE OF OTHER DAYS.

Finn MacCool, we all know, was a great fellow. From licking a dozen of his enemies with his own two hands, to building a castle, nothing came wrong to him. He built Dunluce Castle* beyond, out on the rock, as you may see, without any help at all.

The ould chief that he built it for, when he got the promise to build it from Finn, promised that no help that men could give him should be wanting, and he had at his orders men enough, but they were of no use to Finn. He made a great hand-barrow for them, and threw great stones into the water, from the shore to the rock, for them to step on and carry the stones across to where he wanted them. But the sarra a stone could they bring to him. The first attempt was made by four of the stoutest of them, but before they were half-way from the shore to the rock every mother's son of them was as dizzy as a duck, and all they could do was to scrame at Finn to save them. They could neither go to the rock or to the shore, and but for Finn's immediate help their time was come. What they complained of was the depth of the water, twenty feet or so. Finn tould them he didn't want them to walk on the water, but on the stones he had thrown in for them to step on, and they were firm enough. He bade them step on them where they had dry footing, and think none about the depth of the water between the stepping-stones.

"That," as a timid Scotchman said, that happened to be among them, "was jeest the deeficulty. It makes a body seek tae think o't, and wha, a wunner, could help thinking o't, after

---

*The ruins of Dunluce Castle are still of deep interest to the antiquarian.

seeing the great waves rowling and roaring under yer very nose, and when ane kent it was sae far to the bottom."

Finn told him if it was far to bottom it was not necessary to go to the bottom, and its being far to it need not be regarded as an objection.

Sawney said: "This was Eerish fun, and it would take a heap o' that to make up the loss to his payer wife at hame if he wur drooned at Dunluce."

At that time there were a great many Scotchmen in Ireland that tried to pass for Irish, and as they could all speak Irish (which they called Gaelic in Scotland) it was not easy to find them out at all times, but whenever the rale true courage was wanted, it was easy enough to see they weren't true sons of the sod.

When Sawney M'Wha had said his say, it became clear to Finn that in the gang sent to help him there were a great many Sawney M'Whas. Finn was every inch an Irishman. He lost all patience with the cowardly budaghs, and without losing time he began at wanst and gave them such a licking, that, as he said, "would do them good to the end of their days;" and which the Scotchmen said "was het and heavy, but better nor being drooned!"

Finn's first idea after beating the Scotchmen—which seemed to do him a great deal of good—was to get as many Irishmen to help him; but somehow, from a late harvest or something, he could not find so many as he wanted. What did he do, do you think? He had his foundations cut in the rock, and all was ready but the building stones which were lying on the dry land, squared, dressed and ready, if they were only on the rock. To wait long for the help of others was not in Finn's line. He commenced at once to carry them stone by stone to the rock, throwing them each as he raised them on his shoulder, just as you or me would do a dry sod of turf. In a short time he had all on the rock, and in a shorter he had every stone in its place, and the castle was built, and the prettiest too that ever was seen in that country, or anywhere, I might say, and the strongest—aye, so strong as to defy the strongest blast and biggest wave that ever blew or dashed against it—and you all know these were no trifles.

It would be a long story to tell all that he done besides building Dunluce Castle and the Causey—the greatest of all his works. As I said before, there was nothing he could not do, and he must be busy. Making things pleased him best, unless he had a great job of fighting to do—for that he would leave anything else undone; and he never had to fight on his own account, for he never had an enemy. When he felt called upon to thrash a set of fellows for bad manners, or cruelty to any of the ould stock, when he'd see them sprawling, bleeding and screaming, his big heart was so tender that he would run to their relief, raise them up, bring them water, and handle them as tenderly as a mother would her infant. Who could be the enemy of such a man? If anybody could, he must be a budagh, heart and sowl, every inch of him.

Like every other Irishman, Finn would go courting every purty girl he met; and then, as well as now, wherever you turned there they were—God bless them—like daisies in spring, blushing before you. Of course this was dangerous ground for Finn. The wise old people would often say to him, " Take care of your heart, Finn." " Arrah, be aisy," he would reply, "sure I have it in a strong box!" If he had, the key was found, and quickly too. Wan beautiful summer day, a holiday it was, Finn met the " flower of the glen," as she was called, Shelah O'Donnell, coming from Mass. Maybe he had forgot the strong box that morning; anyway his heart was lost, and found by Shelah O'Donnell, and not being accustomed to live without his heart, he kept as near it as possible, till Shelah consented, you know, and the soggarth made the two into wan.

And Shelah made a man of him all out. There was no more fighting for fun with Finn, and games that used to take up half his time. Everything he did now must have Shelah's approval; and her approval, he had good sense to see, was the best security he could have for the thing being right. It was not by scolding or growling she made this impression on Finn; her loud word was never heard, outside or inside. Shelah was a pattern for her countrywomen, or women anywhere. All Finn's time was employed doing good, in improving the condition of his countrymen in every way. Sure it was he that first showed them how to weave and to play all sorts of music. He showed them how to make looms, and left for a pattern a loom set up at the end of the Causey if they should forget the best shapes of a first-rate one. But his teaching in this way 'ill never be forgotten. He showed his friends—and all were his friends—how everything should be done with the linen, for it grew on the field till it appeared on the green whiter than the new-fallen snow. If you look round you anywhere in Ulster, you will see proof galore that his teaching has been well-remembered. He could play, as I have said, all sorts of instruments. When he took up the fiddle, all for miles round found life and action in their heels, and the boys and girls in Argyleshire might be seen, of a clear evening, footing it away like fun, so loud and clear were the tones of his fiddle; and there was no instrument he couldn't make, from a plow to an organ, and for that the way to make this grand instrument ; and fearing it should be forgotten when he was gone, he built a pattern of his new improved one near the end of the Causey, as well as of his loom, as may be seen to this hour.*

Well, of course his biggest job of all was the Causey. But I must tell you how he came to make it. There was a giant on the other side of the water, a great bare-leggit Heelin-man, that had a great loud voice, that used to shout across at Finn: "If I was ower there, I would take the cruceness out you. I would gie ye sich a lickin' as you would ne'er forget." Many a time he tould Shelah about this. But her advice was to him: "Finn, agrah, never mind the budagh. Of course you know you could lick him in ten minutes any day of the week. You can afford to let the cock crow on his own dung hill." Finn saw the truth of all she said. He, as he said himself, had nothing to gain by lickin' a Scotchman.

---

* Few, we should say, of those who visit the Giant's "Causey" are allowed by the guide to pass unnoticed "the giant's loom" or "the giant's organ."

However, as I have said before, Finn was every inch an Irishman; and one day the Heelin-man shouted so long and so loud that Finn lost all patience, and before he let the sun go down he commenced to build the Causey, to let the Scotchman across, that he might give him a useful lesson, just to improve his manners—a service he had done a few other Scotchmen, as I have already tould ye. Whether they were thankful I won't tell you. Anyway, it seemed from the improvement in their manners to have done them a power of good; and one thing is quite certain, it did Finn himself a great deal of good. Often he was heard to say that of all the refreshments he ever tried, the real mountain dew was the best; and that to this he made only one exception, and that was, when the chance came his way, the pleasure of lickin' a Scotchman. He felt the benefit, he said, of that for months.

Well, as I have already tould you, he commenced the Causey, to let this bad-mannered Scotchman get across. Well, the day after it was finished Finn was on the look-out for the Heelin-man's movements, and he was not long looking when he saw the bould fellow fairly started, with his kilt above his knee; for the Scotch end of the Causey was not above the surface, like the Irish end— which was intended for ornament, or to show his countrymen what good or everlasting work should be—and there it's for a pattern till this day. Well, between the depth of the water—over mid-leg—and the caution required to keep on the Causey, Finn was able to see the shape and size of the fellow without being seen himself. When he saw of him all he wanted to see just then, he went to have a talk with Shelah, to tell her the Scotchman was coming across.

"What do you think of him?" said Shelah.

"Faith," said Finn, "Shelah agra, I don't like his looks at all at all. He's a terrible baste of a fellow. In all my born days I'never saw such a busthoge of a Scotchman. If I hadn't better work to do, I might make a small fortune, after thrashing him, by making a show of him from town to town in his tartans. But I mustn't—for the credit of the ould country I can't do this. I must only lick him and send him home again, as soon as he is able to go. So, Shelah, I have no choice as to what I'm to do with this Sawney More (or big Alick), as they call him at home in his own country. Thrashing him 'ill no be a small job. Of course I can do 't; but it would be as easy to thrash all the corn from Dunluce to Ballycastle."

After thinking in her own cool, aisy way, Shelah said: "Couldn't he be sent back without taking all that trouble with him? If you lave it to me I think I can manage it for you. Go you out and see if he's coming and near, and come in and tell me, and I'll tell what to do."

"In troth and I will," said Finn, "for I never yet was sorry for doing what ye tould me."

Finn went out, and behold ye, the Scotchman was on the Irish shore, wringing some of the water out of his tartans, to be as daicent looking as he could before he would go up to Finn's house before the quality, he said. Finn went back to hear what Shelah had to say, and her directions to Finn were to lie down in a big cradle he had made years before for twins that at their birth promised that they would be bigger than ever their father was. Finn was determined, as he said, to give them room enough to grow, and he made it so large that he could himself lie in it full stretch, just as Shelah tould him to do now, and when he was in it she tould him what to do when Sawney More would come.

Finn was not long in the cradle when Sawney arrived, and he walked in saying, "Gude e'en be here." Of course Shelah bade him sit down, and treated him to the best in the house for the honor of the ould country. Well, when he had Shelah's bread, butter, and eggs before him, he set to as if he had been fasting a fortnight or so for good of his sowl, but he kept packing away so long and so determinedly that she began to fear he wouldn't be able to get away without help. However, there is a limit to all things, even to the cravings of the maw of a Scotchman. Sawney, as he said, "fun himself at length well-crammed." Then he turned to the fire and brought out his dudheen for a smoke; and then, too, Finn raised his great head of hair and beard, such as Sawney never saw before. Finn called out in his loudest voice, "Mother, I want something to ate, and I am sure that great baste of a Scotchman has aten up all the ready mate in the house. I watched him, bad luck to the baste; but wait to my father comes in, and I'll tell him all about it."

As soon as Sawney found breath to speak, he shouted, "Gude save us, is that the bairn? And sick a bairn!"

"Indeed it's my youngest, and a troublesome bouchal he is." Then she said, "Whisht avic, and I'll get you plenty very soon. Bedehust and sleep." But Sawney could think of nothing but the "awfau bairn." At length he said, "The father o' that ane's nae chicken."

"Indeed an' you may say so," said Shelah. "You are considered a big fellow, and no doubt you are, among your aen folk, as you say, but when I saw you coming in the door there, you come in with your big Highland bonnet on, and you might have had a man standing on your shoulders and walked in without any difficulty. I thought of Finn, who always has to take his hat off, and stoop, too, before he can come in."

"Well, well," said Sawney, "he maun', frae a' I hae heard and seen, be nane of the chiels o' last year's growth, but a wanted to see him jest in a freendly way, ye ken. A like to make freens where'er a gang, and a see, clear enough, it would be better to be your gude man's freen nor his enemy; but ony wiy, I maun be gangin. Tell the gude man a'll come to visit him some other day."

"Well, I'm sorry," said Shelah, "in one way, you're going so soon, but in another I'm not sorry. That child," she said, pointing to the cradle, "is very hard to manage, and the worst of it is, his father will hear no complaint against him; but he listens to all his, as if it was the priest at the altar, and when he thinks the bouchal has been wronged in any way, he's neither to howld nor to bind. Whoever he believes has wronged him suffers, I can tell you. I could not tell you what complaint he mightn't make against you for eating all the bread and butter and lavin' him to starve; and, though no Irishman was ever civiler or kinder to strangers than Finn, if a complaint came from his pet—the bouchal there—he'd forget all his other good, kind feelings for a good long hour anyway, and by that time there would be few whole bones in your body."

"Gude preserve us," said Sawney More, "I'm glad you toul' me in time. I hope he'll not be here soon."

"I'll take care," said Shelah, "that you'll get off safely. I'll keep a look-out for his coming. I know the way he'll come, and, when I see him, I'll go to meet him. On the way to the house he'll have a great deal to tell me that will take time; anyway, I'll take care to delay him long enough to let you get safe off."

By this time Sawney was ready for the road—ready to make the best use of his long legs. He was soon outside the door, where, for a wonder, he took the time to say, "Gude e'en. A'll aye be thankfou to you, gude wife, when I'm far awa. Ye hae been a true freen tae me."

What was the story he tould when he got back again I cannot tell you, but he was the first and the last Scotchman that ever ventured on the Causey.

WHAT MR. MAGUIRE SAW IN THE KITCHEN.

Mrs. Maguire, wife of Denny Maguire, of the Kilshane Arms, had retired to rest. The church bell was tolling eleven when she took a last look at the room and quenched the candle. It was Saturday night, and Denis, according to immemorial custom, had remained in the parlor to contribute his wit and jocularity to the conversation of a few friends who had returned from a christening, and slipped into the Arms to spend an hour until midnight. The courtesy of her husband was but ill-approved by Mrs. Maguire, who entertained a vague suspicion that the house was haunted by the fairies, or descendants of fairies, who formerly occupied the rath on which the Kilshane Arms was built. Her fears, it is only just to admit, had some foundation. Night after night, when every one was in bed, and only Bill, the watch-dog, was up and abroad, supernatural noises proceeded from the kitchen. Now there came a sharp clatter, as if jugs, and plates, and delft tea-pots had come to grief in a simultaneous collision; and anon a jingling which foreboded destruction to every wine-glass, tumbler and decanter on the dresser. Denis had repeatedly listened with eyes a-stare, and mouth open, to those supernatural manifestations, but, however alarmed he felt, he always contrived to allay his wife's apprehensions by such exclamations as—" Musha, the dickens take that cat!" or, "Will them mice never be aisy?" Consoled by the practical philosophy of such words, Mrs. Maguire would draw a long sigh, insinuate, in her blandest tones, that "luck never came of meddling with the good people," and so commit herself to the heaven of sleep.

The church clock struck three, and Mrs. Maguire awoke.

"Much she marvelled," as the old ballad has it, that Denis should have prolonged his carousals to so unseasonable an hour. Her astonishment was increased when, on listening attentively, till the silence tingled in her ears, she could not catch the sound of a single voice or the jingle of a solitary glass from the room in which she had left the revellers. To arise, to light a candle, and descend the stairs in search of Denis, was but the work of a few moments. On reaching the ground floor, what was her surprise to find that individual, with his back propped up against the kitchen door, his head sunken on his chest, and a broken pipe scattered in fragments by his side, seated fast asleep on the ground.

"Dinis," she exclaimed, "Dinis, get up iv ye've any shame left, ye flamin' drunkard;" and with these words she seized him by the collar, and gave him one of those shakes with which a mastiff sometimes honors a spaniel.

Denis lazily opened his eyes, and rapidly reclosed them. "I consint," he muttered, "I consint, though it goes hard aginst me, mind yez."

"Musha, alanna, do ye hear him? the unforthinate man that has no more business takin' a dhrop than an omadhaun! Consint, yerra! come, come, ye'll get yer death o' could, sittin' here, you foolish crathur."

Denis received a duplicate of the first shrug, and again unclosed his eyes. "Didn't I tell yez," he exclaimed, with no small show of bitterness—"didn't I tell yez that I consinted? And what more does yez want. Ai! ai! gour that, you desaver," he continued, addressing his wife, who was suddenly startled by his altered manner. "Be off wid yer, ould man—do; have yer choice, an' more luck to yez. Arrah, what kem acrass yez, that yez didn't fut it to the North Pole, ai?"

"Oh, then, what is he dhramin' of?" asked Mrs. Maguire, in a voice of tremulous expostulation, "who is the ould man, and what is he sayin'? Lord betune us an' harm iv the North Pole! He's crackt, crackt entirely, so he is," and she raised her hastily-donned gown to her eyes, and began crying.

"I'll bell it all over the parish," groaned Denis, who now sat more upright, and was, to all appearances, rational enough. "Show yer nose at the cross if yez dare, and there's not a girl from the post-office to the tay-shop, but'll pin a tin kittle to yer tail, da-a-rlint!"

"Oh, thin, Dinis, Dinis, alanna."

"None o' yer Dinises to me," screamed Mr. Maguire. "Hould yer tongue, yeh, yeh—gour that, I tell yez," and he shot his fist fiercely at his wife.

"Come out iv this, Dinis, dear, and don't be ravin' like a madman—come."

"Yis, av coorse; cock yez up, ai! Arrah, then, maybe I be bowld to ask yez where's the little lord, ai?—the nate little lord, with the hump betune his shoulders, and the hape of a pimple on his nose? Be the mortial frost, but yez was a purty pair, wasn't yez? Lave the house this minit, and be off wid 'im; lave the house, and never darken the doore again."

"Dinis, darlint, ah, thin, what's comin' over yez, to thrate me in this way," sobbed Mrs. Maguire, as she retreated from her husband, who compelled her, with repeated threats, in the direction of the door.

"Will yez be off, or say yez won't; will yez?"

"I'll do anything, Dinis, to plaze yez."

"Thin show us your back, and keep yer face to yerself till 'tis wanted. Out wid yez—out wid yez," and so saying, Mr. Maguire ejected his wife over the threshold into the village street.

"Ye'll be sorry for this, Dinis," exclaimed Mrs. Maguire, turning back for a moment.

"Will yez take yerself to the lordheen?" replied Dinis; "shure, he'll want some one to straighten his hump for him, and who'd do it better nor his wife, ai, my jewel?"

"The Lord forgive yez, Dinis."

"That's more than yez desarve yerself, at any rate. Top o' the mornin' to yez," and, with this polite wish, Mr. Maguire closed the door and disappeared.

Mrs. Maguire, completely mystified by her husband's conduct, and wondering what serious change could have deprived her in one night of the burthen of his affections, turned into the house of a neighbor, and seated herself dejectedly on a three-legged stool, or "creepeen," by the side of the turf fire. She was rocking herself to and fro uneasily, whilst her tears came thick and fast and her sobs almost choked her, when the mistress of the house, Mrs. O'Shaughnessy, returned from the bawn and discovered her.

"Why, thin, Mrs. Maguire, is it yourself's afore me? Oh! the poor woman cryin', I declare cryin'! Why, thin, is there anything gone wrong over the way?"

"Himself—'tis himself!" groaned Mrs. Maguire.

"Himself, jewel! Arrah, thim min are always crazy when they take a drop or two over night, and 'tis a fool ud mind 'em. My jintleman 'll miss you afore 'tis dark, believe me. He didn't bate yez, did he?"

"No, Mistress Shaughnessy, I'll be bowld, he didn't. He sez to me, sez he, go off wid your lordheen, for a bite or sup ye'll never take agin wid me, sez he."

"A lordheen, inagh. Gondoutha, what put that in his head, I wondher?"

"Thim faries, the sarra shoot thim," replied Mrs. Maguire. "Shure I often said, if he had luck or grace he'd lave 'em alone, and not be meddlin' or makin' with thim that didn't consarn him."

Mrs. O'Shaughnessy looked mysterious, and shook her head in token of assent. "Thim ould places doesn't answer Christians, anyhow. I wouldn't sod a lark out iv 'em if there wasn't another green spot in the barony. Here, lave off now, for there's the min comin' to breakfast, and we'll have our tay when they shows their backs, so we will."

Somewhat cheered by the prospect of the non-inebriating cup, Mrs. Maguire hastened to indulge her sorrows in the privacy of an inner room. The laborers soon arrived, and she listened intently to their conversation, in order to satisfy herself that the scandal of which she was the victim had not spread through the village. Nothing occurred to alarm her, however, until one of the men, whose mouth, judging from the thickness of his articulation, was embarrassed by the presence of a lumper, exclaimed:

"Dick Boulster was done out of his sudden death,* this mornin', sure, and sorra the one could spake to him, he was so down in the mouth."

"Begor," remarked another voice, "he must be goin' to the wall entirely, when he'd pass by Dinny Maguire's without paying his respects to the native."

"Faith its toight enough wid him," observed a man with a north Tipperary accent. "Didn't we see him on Friday, standing on one fut at Mick Lalor's bulk, whilst he was gettin' a thievcent† on the other?"

"He has a great back in America, dough," said a man, with an exceedingly weak organ. "De girls send home hapes o' money—I wish he was tirty pounds in my books dis morning."

"Musha, talk sinse," exclaimed the first speaker, "an don't be runnin away wed yourselves, like goms;‡ I tell yez that the raisin he hadn't his dhrop is bekase he couldn't get it, and the raisin he couldn't get it is, bekase Dinny wouldn't open the doore, he's getting so holy, *gondoutha!*"

A roar of laughter succeeded the sarcastic comment implied in the last observation. The men soon afterwards rose and left the house, and Mrs. Maguire was preparing to emerge from her hiding, when Mrs. O'Shaughnessy exclaimed, in a half whisper:

"Be as mute as a mouse, for himself is comin' up the paddock."

"For the love of God don't say I'm here, or there'll be ructions till Michaelmas!"

"Aisy, now be aisy, till we hears what he sez for himself. Be quiet, alanna, and who knows but it's all for the best."

So saying, Mrs. O'Shaughnessy threw herself into a posture of affected inattention, and was merrily humming a milking song, when Dennis Maguire entered the house, looking pale and haggard.

---

* Glass of raw whisky. † Patch of leather. ‡ Fools.

"God bless all here!" he said, with a slight quaver in his voice.

"And you too, Dinis. How's all at home wid yez?"

"Purty middlin', begor; we can't complain, ma'am."

"Won't yez sit down and rest yerself, Dinis?" said the lady, driving the cat from a hay-bottomed chair, and handing it to the visitor. "Is herself fine and strongly?"

Dennis groaned. "Consarnin' *her*, Mrs. O'Shaughnessy, I'm afeerd I've put my fut in it."

"Fut, agra! that's a quare thing!"

"Mortial quare, ma'am, intirely. Mrs. O'Shaughnessy, I'm the manest, ungratefulest baste in crayation."

"Is the man dhramin' wid his eyes open?" asked the good woman, suspending the operation of washing a butter tub, and looking at the speaker.

"Faith, they're open wide enough now, ma'am. If you saw thim this mornin' airly, 'tisn't that ye'd say, I be bail."

"Cobwebs, after the night, yez mane?"

"Dust, ma'am—fairy dust that tuk away my five sinses to the other world, and put me beyant meself, and made me turn Biddy out o' doors—made a pote—a rale, live pote o' me intirely, ma'am!"

"The dickens take it, sure yez wasn't as bad as all that, Dinis? Pote, inagh. Shure thim niver has wives or houses, and yez has both, God bless 'em!"

"And I don't desarve 'em, Mrs. O'Shaughnessy, for I'm a baste, and no mistake, to turn out that kind-hearted crathur on the cowld world, without a bit o' breakfast or a tester in her pocket, av a mornin' airly;" and so affected was the speaker by the pathos of his own discourse, that he buried his face between his hands and wept audibly. Mrs. Maguire, who was a breathless listener to all that passed, in the next room, imitated his example with that rare facility for which the female eye-ducts are celebrated; but she took care to drown her sobs in the folds of her cloak, lest her grief should betray her.

"Tut, tut, man, come, don't be killin' yerself that way," insisted Mrs. O'Shaughnessy, in a voice of the kindest sympathy. "The thruest couple on the face iv the earth will have their thrials and fallin'-outs. But, Dinis, I'm complately bothered to make out the raisin that came over yez, all of a hape, to malthreat poor Biddy. Was she throublesome?"

"Herself throublesome! An angel playin' on a harp o' goold isn't her aiquil for civility, ma'am. Oh, that dhrame, that dhrame!"

"What dhrame?" asked Mrs. O'Shaughnessy.

"Musha, sit down, and ye'll hear the whole of it."

Mrs. O'Shaughnessy followed the direction, and, after many introductory "hems" and "haws," and several apparently ineffectual efforts to clear his throat, Dennis began:

"You must know, ma'am, that last night, it being Sathurday, two o' the boys dropped in, betther nor an hour afore midnight, to have a weeny dhrop afore they should lave for home. My mimory may disave me (that's an ould thrick wid it), but I'd be afeered to say that I tuk more nor six or seven glasses with a dash o' spring water in each iv 'em, to cool them a bit, you know. Howsomever, the boys went, and I barred the doore, and I tuk the candle from the hob, and, just as I put my foot on the first step, what do you consave I should hear but the rattlin' and tearin' of spoons, the new spoons we bought at the pattern iv Bruff, and the greatest divarsion of cut glass in the kitchen! Well, my hair stood on an end, like a shafe of bulrushes, and my knees knocked together for all the world like a pair o' dale clappers. 'What does that mean, at all, at all?' sez I, to meself. Nobody answered, av coorse, but, instead o' that, the glasses, man alive, fell to rattlin' agin and agin, and the spoons fell to kicking up the most unmarciful ructions. As I was sayin', I cocked my ear like a hare, and hearkened to the fun that was goin' on inside, and all at wanst I heard an ould man coughin' and crowin', and three or four more ould men, too, I be bail, laughin' as if they'd split their sides with the divarsion. I tuk my fut off the stairs, and the kitchen door bein' a taste open, I clapped my eye to it and looked in. Holy jewel, if you saw thim ! A lump of mate, with a double hedge of yellow fat—a hump you couldn't cram into a *skiagh*, was on the table ; one ould man stood forninst me, dressed in blue knee-breeches, and whited darned stockings, and a rale swallow-tail wid goold buttons, shinin' like a clane candlestick, and a hat for all the world like Tom Lacy's caubogue, only it was turned up at the sides; his white hair was all rolled up in a ball with a skiver stuck behind in it ; and he had a bottle of the best Jameson's (two shillings, and every farthen iv it, a pint) to his mouth, guttlin' away, ma'am, as iv he'd swallow Poul-a-phouca, the Lord save us! Betune him and I there was a laddo upon one knee, decantin' a bottle iv somethin' or another, like the big bottle in Dr. Sloane's window ; this laddo wore boots up to his knees, and such a cambric handkercher ondernathe his ould chin ! The fire was blazin' betune the hobs, as if they were bint on manufactherin' an anvil, and forninst it was sated an ould codger, wid a jug of hot punch in his hand, and snappin' away wid his fingers, like wildfire, to the chune o' the 'Limerick Lasses.' The flure was all a spread of rale chainey, and lashins o' feedin', ham, and pork, and beef, and cabbage, and mate o' that sort. But what opened my eyes, intirely, intirely, was a murtherin' queer thing betune a frog and a buttherfly, fluttherin' and flying around the room, and divartin' himself, wid his legs up to the ceilin', as if he was a rale fly. Some o' the min were cuttin' capers in the dancin' way, wid the wimen. Arrah, to see thim—such dandies as thim was, wid wings, *moryagh*, stuck out o' their shoulders, and castles iv cock's feathers growin' out iv the tops o' their heads. But 'twas the coortin' and *collogueing** that put me pipe out complately, for there was sated forninst me an ould buckeen wid a hump as big as a churn on his back, and his old arm, if yez plaze, around a young lady in a high-cauled cap and a turkey-red handkercher. 'Faith,' sez I to myself, 'I'll have an eye to yez, my darlint,' and so I kept it on 'em, until the lady turned round her purty head, and, Mrs. O'Shaughnessy, I'll take my book-oath on't, the lady

---

*Whispering.

—the lady, mind yez, was (here the narrator spread out his legs, twirled his thumbs rapidly, and continued in a hoarse whisper,) the wife! When I saw her, sated on the barrel, *collogueing* wid the ould Cromwellian of a villyan, I tried to make a haul at the pair, and twist his head off iv him, but the dickens resave the step the legs would go, and I had to stand there in the cowld like a pilgarlic, seein' Biddy divartin' herself wid the good people. All at once the music caysed, and the laddo with the skiver in his head sez, sez he :

"'That Maguire is the scum of a vagabond—he's the sworn inimy of the ould stock,' sez he, 'an', if I had my own way, I'd open his eye whilst ye'd be sayin' Jack Robinson.'

"'Thrue for yez, Harelip, avic,' says the man that was bottlin' the medicine, 'thrue for yez,' sez he, 'and the pookah take him an' his breed, an' every stick and stone belongin' to thim.'

"The laddo that was dancin' wid the paycock lady here opened his mouth, and sez he, 'Teranages, but his wife's a gim, a rale gim, and its the dickens iv a shame that she should be livin' wid that monstherosity. Min,' sez he, to the fellows that might wear a tailor's thimble for a waist-band—'min,' sez he, 'I moves we whips her off and marry her to Lord Plumtop.'

"'Right,' sez Skiver, 'right. I was pondherin over that meself, and sorra' betther way I sees,' sez he, 'of punishin' the spalpeen.'

"Before that boy's tongue had time to get into his cheek, the humpy back, that was sittin' alongside Biddy, turns about, and immegiately I got a sight of a pimple as red as a bantam's comb, perched atop of his nose. 'Have I always thrated yez da cently ?' sez he.

"'Iss, my lord,' says the whole o' the pinkeens, bowin' and scrapin' until they'd pick a pin off the flure with their eye-lashers—'Iss, my lord,' sez they.

"'Thin,' sez he, 'by the honor and glory of the Plumtops, I swear on the top and bottom iv the griddle to have the gim for myself—I'm king o' the castle,' sez he, and the pimple grew reddher and reddher, 'and who dare rassle ?'

"'Be the hokey,' says the Skiver, 'my lord is gettin' as stiff as Bill Haly's dog, that swallowed a stone of starch, and a blue-bag, into the bargin. Yez may lead me, if it plazes yez,' sez Skiver, bouldly, 'but I'd see the whole stock of yez hanged, dhrawn and quarthered, before I'm dhruv.'

"The ould man that was engravin' his shins afore the fire, here got up, and sez he, takin' out his handkercher, 'I blush for yez, Skiver, I blush for yez. If yez have any rimnint of dacency in yez, go down on yer binded knees, and beg his lordship's pardinN.'

"Arrah, woman alive, to hear Skiver laughin' at that would do you good for a Shrovetide. He cocked his head, he cocked his eye, 'One man is as good as another,' sez he, 'barrin' he's a lord or a duke—begor, barrin' he's an earl, for all that. And if his lordship,' sez he, standin' on his toes, and lookin' down on Plumtop, 'sez to the conthrary, let him keep on his jacket and I'll dust it for him.'

"Plumtop, heerin' iv the discoorse, tuk a pinch o' Cork snuff, and when the sneezin' was ever, he sez, 'Skiver, are yez bint (*ash-thee*, the sneezin' wasn't over), are yez bint on kickin' up a rucshin in my dominions? Yer pinance is,' sez he, 'to go down on yer (*ash-thee*, *ash-thee*)—that snuff is murtherin' strong—yer four ugly bones, and all the min and wimen in the rath walk over yer ugly carcass.'

"Up jumps Biddy, as live as a lark, my dear, and sez she, 'If thrubble's about me, put an ind to it, for I'm promised to Lord Plumtop here, an' I wouldn't change my mind for the best grocery in Caherconlish,' and sayin' this, she turned up her mouth and kissed the pimple on the lord's nose, begor—may I never see another Sunday, but she did.

"'Stand out,' sez Skiver, squarin' his fists for the divarshin. "If I'm to be thrated like a baste, I'll be a baste,' and wid that he up wid his fist and knocked down the lordheen. There was the hape of a pillilu on the head of this, the scrawlin* became

---

*Fighting.

WHAT MR. MAGUIRE SAW IN THE KITCHEN. 255

gineral, but faith, my bowld Skiver flaked them right and left, min, wimen and childrin, as they was, until the physic man came up wid a decanter and laid him as flat as a pancake. In the meantime I looked around for Biddy, and, shure enough, there she was, sittin' on the barrel, breakin' her heart cryin', and tyin' up the lordheen's head with a shally shawl I bought her the Sathurday night afore. The physic man kum up to feel his pulse.

"'Only wan thing 'll cure him,' sez he, takin' out a watch as big as a pot-lid, and cockin' it to his ear. 'He'll be as stiff as a herrin' afore five minutes if it's not administhered.' 'And what's that?' sez Biddy, in a heart-broken voice. 'Ai, what is it?' 'A weddin'-ring,' sez the docthor, 'boiled down in a pot of goat's milk. Haven't yez a ring yerself, my lady?'

"'Begor, thin, I have,' sez she, 'an' here it's for him, if 'twas goold tin times over.'

"So she whipped off the ring, ma'am, and then Physic sez, 'What'll Dinis think o' this whin it kums to his ears?' sez he.

"'Will you hould your jaw, and don't be botherin' me about the spalpeen. I've somethin' else to consarn me.'

"Well, the milk was boiled, and no sooner did the lordheen swallow it, than he got up and marched about the room as grand as a paycock.

"'Does yez love me, Biddy?' sez he.

"'I dotes on you,' sez Biddy; 'shure,' sez she, 'a nater pimple was never seen than that on your lordship's nose.'

"'What 'ud Maguire give for such a lump of grandher?' sez the lordheen.

"'The two eyes out iv his head,' sez Biddy.

"'When will we be married, Biddy?' sez he.

"'Faith, as soon as it's convaynant,' sez she.

"'Where'll we be married, jewel?' sez he.

"'Why, thin, where but at the North Pole?' sez she.

"'We must have Dinis' consint, Biddy,' sez the ould scoun. drel. 'Will it be aisy to find him?'

"'There he's behind the doore,' sez she. 'Hurrah, hurrah,' sez the lordheen, wheeling his stick around his head. 'Min,' sez he, 'drag in that quadruped, and ask him if he consints to my marrying Biddy?' and, sure enough, before I could lift a leg they had me off my pins and planted in the middle iv the flure.

"'Biddy,' sez I, 'Biddy, the Lord forgive yez!'

"'Musha, hould your ugly mouth,' sez she, 'and don't be cacklin' like a gandher.'

"'Does yer consint?' sez the lordheen, with a scrame like a wild crane; 'does yer consint to separate from yer wife and give her to them that can support her dacently?'

"'No,' sez I.

"'Pull off his hair, one by one, min,' sez the lordheen, 'we'll taich him manners afore he's much ouldher.'

"So the pinkeens kem around me and they pulled away until I put my hand on the top of my head, roarin' all the time wid pain, and saw I had only three hairs remainin'. Begor I was frightened to think of wearin' a wig, and as all the hair was goin' I thought best to keep the seed of a new crop, so sez I, 'I consint,' and hardly were the words out o' my mouth when I sits up and sees Biddy afore me. 'Get out iv the house this minute,' sez I, and wid that I planted her in the middle iv the pavement, for I couldn't consaive I had been dhramin'. Arrah isn't that her cryin' away in the room there?" said Denis, suspending the story and listening.

"'Tis herself, then, poor woman," said Mrs. O'Shaughnessy; "here, go in an' make friends with her."

Denis went, and returned in a few minutes, holding his wife by the hand.

"'Twas all a dhrame, ma'am, an' she forgives me, an' I'm going to take the pledge to-morrow."

"An' when you do," said his wife, laughing, "I'll run off with the lordheen."

"Are yez at it again?" said Denis, catching and kissing her, "the dickens take him for a lordheen, anyhow!"

THE WILL.

It was a little after midnight that a knock came to the door of our cabin. I heard it first, for I used to sleep in a little snug basket near the fire; but I didn't speak, for I was frightened. It was still repeated louder, and then came a cry—"Con. Cregan; Con. I say, open the door! I want you." I knew the voice well; it was Peter McCabe's; but I pretended to be fast asleep, and snored loudly. At last my father unbolted the door, and I heard him say, "Oh, Mr. Peter, what's the matter? is the ould man worse?"

"Faix that's what he is, for he's dead!"

"Glory be his bed! when did it happen?"

"About an hour ago," said Peter, in a voice that even I, from my corner, could perceive greatly agitated. "He died like an ould hathen, Con., and never made a will!"

"That's bad," says my father, for he was always a polite man, and said whatever was pleasing to the company.

"It is bad," said Peter; "but it would be worse if he couldn't help it. Listen to me now, Corney; I want ye to help me in this business; and here are five guineas in gold if ye do what I bid ye. You know that ye were always reckoned the image of my father, and before he took ill ye were mistaken for each other every day of the week."

"Anan!" said my father, for he was getting frightened at the notion, without well knowing why.

"Well, what I want is for ye to come over into the house and get into the bed."

"Not beside the corpse?" said my father, trembling.

"By no means, but by yourself; and you're to pretend to be my father, and that ye want to make yer will before ye die; and then I'll send for the neighbors, and Billy Scanlan, the schoolmaster, and ye'll tell him what to write, leaving all the farm and everything to me—ye understand. And as the neighbors will see ye and hear yer voice, it will never be believed but it was himself that did it."

"The room must be very dark," says my father.

"To be sure it will; but have no fear! Nobody will dare to come nigh the bed; and ye'll only have to make a cross with yer pen under the name. Come along, now—quick—for we've no time to lose; it must be all finished before the day breaks."

My father did not lose much time at his toilet, for he just wrapped his big coat round him, and, slipping on the brogues, left the house. I sat up in the basket, and listened till they were gone some minutes; and then, in a costume as light as my parent's, set out after them to watch the course of the adventure. I thought to take a short cut, and be before them; but by bad luck I fell into a bog-hole, and only escaped drowning by a chance. As it was, when I reached the house the performance had already begun.

I think I see the whole scene this instant before my eyes, as I sat on a little window with one pane, and that a broken one, and surveyed the proceeding. It was a large room, at one end of which was a bed, and beside it was a table with physic bottles and spoons and tea-cups; a little further off was another table, at which sat Billy Scanlan, with all manner of writing materials before him.

The country people sat two and sometimes three deep around the walls, all intently eager and anxious for the coming event; Peter himself went from place to place, trying to smother his grief, and occasionally helping the company to something, which was supplied with more than accustomed liberality.

All my consciousness of the deceit and trickery could not deprive the scene of a certain solemnity. The misty distance of the half-lighted room; the highly-wrought expression of the country people's faces, never more intensely excited than at some moment of this kind; the low, deep-drawn breathing, unbroken save by a sigh or a sob—the tribute of affectionate sorrow to some lost friend, whose memory was thus forcibly brought back; these were all so real, that, as I looked, a thrilling sense of awe stole over me, and I actually shook with fear.

A low, faint cough from the dark corner where the bed stood seemed to cause even a deeper stillness; and then, in a silence where the buzzing of a fly would have been heard, my father said:

"Where's Billy Scanlan? I want to make my will!"

"He's here, father," said Peter, taking Billy by the hand and leading him to the bed-side.

"Write what I bid ye, Billy, and be quick; for I haven't a long time afore me here; I die a good Catholic, though Father O'Rafferty won't give me the rites!"

A general chorus of muttered "Oh! musha, musha!" was now heard through the room; but whether in grief over the sad fate of the dying man, or the unflinching justice of the priest, is hard to say.

"I die in peace with all my neighbors and all mankind."

Another chorus of the company seemed to approve these charitable expressions.

"I bequeath unto my son Peter—and never was there a better son or a decenter boy!—have you that down? I bequeath unto my son Peter the whole of my two farms of Killimundoonery and Knocksheboora, with the fallow meadows behind Lynch's house, the forge and right of turf on the Dooran bog. I give him—and much good may it do him—Lanty Cassarn's acre, and the Luary field with the lime-kiln; and that reminds me that my mouth is just as dry. Let me taste what ye have in the jug." Here the dying man took a very hearty pull, and seemed considerably refreshed by it.

"Where was I, Billy Scanlan?" says he; "oh, I remember, at the lime-kiln. I leave him—that's Peter, I mean—the two potato gardens at Noonan's Well; and it is the elegant, fine crops grows there."

"Ain't you gettin' wake, father darlin'?" says Peter, who began to be afraid of my father's loquaciousness; for, to say the truth, the punch got into his head, and he was greatly disposed to talk.

"I am, Peter, my son," says he; "I am getting wake; just touch my lips again with the jug. Ah! Peter, Peter, you watered the drink."

"No, indeed, father, but it's the taste is leavin' you," says Peter, and again a low chorus of compassionate pity murmured through the cabin.

"Well, I'm nearly done now," says my father; "there's only one little plot of ground remaining, and I put it on you, Peter— as ye wish to live a good man, and die with the same easy heart as I do now—that ye mind my last words to ye here. Are ye listening? Are the neighbors listening? Is Billy Scanlan listening?"

"Yes, sir; yes, father, we're all minding," chorused the audience.

"Well, then, it's my last will and testament, and may—give me over the jug"—here he took a long drink—"and may that blessed liquor be poison to me if I'm not as eager about this as every other part of the will; I say, then, I bequeath the little plot at the cross roads to poor Con. Cregan, for he has a heavy charge, and is as honest and as hard-working a man as ever I knew. Be a friend to him, Peter, dear; never let him want while ye have it yourself—think of me on my death-bed whenever he asks ye for any trifle. Is it down, Billy Scanlan?—the two acres at the cross to Con. Cregan, and his heirs in *secla seclorum?* Ah, blessed be the saints! but I feel my heart lighter after that," says he—"a good work makes an easy conscience. And now I'll drink all the company's good health, and many happy returns—"

What he was going to add there's no saying; but Peter, who was now terribly frightened at the lively tone the sick man was assuming, hurried all the people into another room, to let his father die in peace.

When they were all gone, Peter slipped back to my father, who was putting on his brogues in a corner : "Con.," says he, "ye did it all well; but sure that was a joke about the two acres at the cross."

"Of course it was, Peter!" says he; "sure it was all a joke, for the matter of that; won't I make the neighbors laugh hearty to-morrow when I tell them all about it!"

"You wouldn't be mean enough to betray me!" says Peter, trembling with fright.

"Sure you wouldn't be mean enough to go against your father's dying words!" says my father; "the last sentence ever he spoke;" and here he gave a low, wicked laugh, that made myself shake with fear.

"Very well, Con.!" says Peter, holding out his hand; "a bargain's a bargain; yer a deep fellow, that's all." And so it ended, and my father slipped quietly over the bog, mighty well satisfied with the legacy he left himself.

And thus we became the owners of the little spot known to this day as Con.'s Acre.

SERVING A WRIT.

My father, who, for reasons registered in the King's Bench, spent a great many years of his life in that part of Ireland geographically known as lying west of the law, was obliged, for certain reasons of family, to come up to Dublin. This he proceeded to do with due caution: two trusty servants formed an advance guard, and patrolled the country for at least five miles in advance; after them came a skirmishing body of a few tenants, who, for the consideration of never paying rent, would have charged the whole Court of Chancery, if needful. My father himself, in an old chaise victualled like a fortress, brought up the rear; and, as I said before, he was a bold man who would have attempted to have laid siege to him. As the column advanced into the enemy's country, they assumed a closer order, the patrol and the picket falling back upon the main body; and in this way they reached that most interesting city called Kilbeggan. What a fortunate thing it is for us in Ireland that we can see so much of the world without foreign travel, and that any gentleman, for six and eightpence, can leave Dublin in the morning and visit Timbuctoo against dinner-time! Don't stare! it's truth I'm telling; for dirt, misery, smoke, unaffected behavior and black faces, I'll back Kilbeggan against all Africa. Free-and-easy, pleasant people they are, with a skin as begrimed and as rugged as their own potatoes! But to resume: the sun was just rising in a delicious morning of June, when my father—whose loyal antipathies I have mentioned made him also an earlier riser—was preparing for the road. A stout escort of his followers were, as usual, under arms to see him safe in the chaise, the passage to and from which every day being the critical moment of my father's life.

"It's all right, your honor," said his own man, as, armed with a blunderbuss, he opened the bed-room door.

"Time enough, Tim," said my father; "close the door, for I haven't finished my breakfast."

Now the real truth was, that my father's attention was at that moment withdrawn from his own concerns by a scene which was taking place in a field beneath his window.

But a few minutes before a hack-chaise had stopped upon the road-side, out of which sprang three gentlemen, who, proceeding to the field, seemed bent upon something which, whether a survey or a duel, my father could not make out. He was not long, however, to remain in ignorance. One with an easy, lounging gait strode towards a distant corner; another took an opposite direction; while the third, a short, pursy gentleman, in a red handkerchief and a rabbit-skin waistcoat, proceeded to open a mahogany box, which, to the critical eyes of my respected father, was agreeably suggestive of bloodshed and murder.

"A duel, by Jupiter!" said my father, rubbing his hands. "What a heavenly morning the scoundrels have—not a leaf stirring, and a sod like a billiard-table."

Meanwhile the little man who officiated as second, it would appear, to *both* parties, bustled about with activity little congenial to his shape; and, what between snapping the pistols, examining the flints and ramming down the charges, had got himself into a sufficient prespiration before he commenced to measure off the ground.

"Short distance and no quarter!" shouted one of the combatants from the corner of the field.

"Across a handkerchief if you like!" roared the other.

"Gentlemen, every inch of them!" responded my father.

"Twelve paces!" cried the little man. "No more and no less. Don't forget that I'm alone in this business."

"A very true remark!" observed my father; "and an awkward predicament yours will be, if they are both shot!"

By this time the combatants had taken their places, and the little man, having delivered the pistols, was leisurely retiring to give the word. My father, however, whose critical eye was never at fault, detected a circumstance which promised an immense advantage to one at the expense of the other; in fact, one of the parties was so placed with his back to the sun, that his shadow extended in a straight line to the very foot of his antagonist.

"Unfair! unfair!" cried my father, opening the window as he spoke, and addressing himself to him of the rabbit-skin. "I crave your pardon for the interruption," said he; "but I feel bound to observe that that gentleman's shadow is likely to be made a shade of him."

"And so it is," observed the short man: "a thousand thanks for your kindness; but the truth is, I am totally unaccustomed to this kind of thing, and the affair will not admit of delay."

"Not an hour!" said one.

"Not five minutes!" growled the other of the combatants.

"Put them up north and south!" said my father.

"Is it thus?"

"Exactly so; but now again the gentleman in the brown coat is covered with the ash tree."

"And so he is!" said rabbit-skin, wiping his forehead with agitation.

"Move them a little to the left," said he.

"That brings me upon an eminence," said the gentleman in blue; "I'll not be made a cock shot of."

"What an awkward little thing it is in the hairy waistcoat!" said my father; "he's lucky if he don't get shot himself."

"May I never! if I'm not sick of you both!" ejaculated rabbit-skin, in a passion. "I've moved you round every point of the compass, and the sorrow a nearer we are than ever."

"Give us the word," said one.

"The word!"

"Downright murder," said my father.

"I don't care," said the little man; "we shall be here till doomsday."

"I can't permit this," said my father. "Allow me—" so saying, he stepped upon the window-sill and leaped down into the field.

"Before I can accept of your politeness," said he of the rabbit-skin, "may I beg to know your name and position in society?"

"Nothing more reasonable," said my father. "I'm Miles O'Shaughnessy, Colonel of the Royal Raspers; here is my card."

The piece of pasteboard was complacently handed from one to the other of the party, who saluted my father with a smile of most courteous benignity.

"Colonel O'Shaughnessy," said one.

"Miles O'Shaughnessy," said another.

"Of Killinahoula Castle," said the third.

"At your service," said my father, bowing as he presented his snuff-box: "and now to business, if you please; for my time also is limited."

"Very true," observed he of the rabbit-skin, "and, as you observe, now to business; in virtue of which, Colonel Miles O'Shaughnessy, I hereby arrest you in the king's name. Here is the writ: it's at the suit of Barnaby Kelly, of Loughrea, for the sum of £1,583 19s. 7½d., which—"

Before he could conclude the sentence, my father discharged one obligation by implanting his closed knuckles in his face. The blow, well-aimed and well-intentioned, sent the little fellow somersetting like a sugar hogshead. But, alas! it was of no use; the others, strong and able-bodied, fell both upon him, and after a desperate struggle succeeded in getting him down. To tie his hands and convey him to the chaise was the work of a few moments, and as my father drove by the inn, the last object which caught his view was a bloody encounter between his own people and the myrmidons of the law, who in great numbers had laid siege to the house during his capture. Thus was my father taken, and thus, in reward for yielding to a virtuous weakness in his character, was he consigned to the ignominious durance of a prison.

THE GAUGER OUTWITTED.

Young Condy Cullen was descended from a long line of private distillers, and, of course, exhibited in his own person all the practical wit, sagacity, cunning and fertility of invention, which the natural genius of the family, sharpened by long experience, had created from generation to generation, as a standing capital to be handed down from father to son. There was scarcely a trick, evasion, plot, scheme or manœuvre that had ever been resorted to by his ancestors, that Condy had not at his fingers' ends, and though but a lad of sixteen at the time we present him to the reader, yet be it observed, that he had his mind, even at that age, admirably trained by four or five years of keen, vigorous practice, in all the resources needed to meet the subtle vigilance and stealthy circumvention of that prowling animal—the gauger. In fact, Condy's talents did not merely consist in an acquaintance with the hereditary tricks of his family. These of themselves would prove but a miserable defense against the ever-varying ingenuity with which the progressive skill of the still-hunter masks his approaches and conducts his designs. On the contrary, every new plan of the gauger must be met and defeated by a counter-plan equally novel, but with this difference in the character of both, that whereas the excise-man's devices are the result of mature deliberation—Paddy's, from the very nature of the circumstances, must be necessarily extemporaneous and rapid. The hostility between the parties being, as it is, carried on through such varied stratagem on both sides, and characterized by such adroit and able duplicity, by so many quick and unexpected turns of incident—it would be utter fatuity in either, to rely upon obsolete tricks and stale manœuvres. Their relative position and occupation do not, therefore, merely exhibit a contest between Law and that mountain nymph, Liberty, or between the Excise Board and the Smuggler—it presents a more interesting point for observation—namely, the struggle between wit and wit—between roguery and knavery.

It might be very amusing to detail, from time to time, a few of those keen encounters of practical cunning which take place between the potheen distiller and his lynx-eyed foe, the gauger. They are curious as throwing light upon the national character of our people, and as evidences of the surprising readiness of wit, fertility of invention and irresistible humor which they mix up with almost every actual concern of life, no matter how difficult or critical it may be. Nay, it mostly happens that the character of the peasant, in all its fullness, rises in proportion to what he is called upon to encounter, and that the laugh at, or the hoax upon the gauger, keeps pace with the difficulty that is overcome. But now to our short story.

Two men in the garb of gentlemen were riding along a remote by-road, one morning in the month of October, about the year 1827, or '28, I am not certain which. The air was remarkably clear, keen and bracing; a hoar frost for the few preceding nights had set in, and then lay upon the fields about them, melting gradually, however, as the sun got strength, with the exception of the sides of such hills and valleys as his beams could not reach, until evening chilled their influence too much to absorb the feathery whiteness which covered them. Our equestrians had nearly reached a turn in the way, which, we should observe in this place, skirted the brow of a small declivity that lay on the right. In point of fact, it was a moderately inclined plane or slope rather than a declivity; but be this as it may, the flat at its foot was studded over with furze bushes, which grew so close and level, that a person might almost imagine it possible to walk upon their surface.

On coming within about two hundred and fifty yards of this angle, the riders noticed a lad, not more than sixteen, jogging on towards them, with a keg upon his back. The eye of one of them was immediately lit with that vivacious sparkling of habitual sagacity which marks the practiced gauger among ten thousand. For a single moment he drew up his horse—an action which, however slight in itself, intimated more plainly than he could have wished the obvious interest which had just been excited in him. Short as was the pause, it betrayed him, for no sooner had the lad noticed it, than he crossed the ditch and disappeared round the angle we have mentioned, and upon the side of the declivity. To gallop to the spot, dismount, cross the ditch also, and pursue him, was only the work of a few minutes.

"We have him," said the gauger, "we have him. One thing is clear, he cannot escape us."

"Speak for yourself, Stinton," replied his companion "As for me, not being an officer of his Majesty's Excise, I decline taking any part in the pursuit. It is a fair battle; so fight it out between you; I am with you now only through curiosity." He had scarcely concluded, when they heard a voice singing the following lines, in a spirit of that hearty hilarity which betokens a cheerful contempt of care, and an utter absence of all apprehension:

> "Oh! Jemmy, she sez, you are my true lover,
> You are all the riches that I do adore;
> I solemnly sware now I'll ne'er have another,
> My heart it is fixed to never love more."

The music then changed into a joyous whistle, and immediately they were confronted by a lad, dressed in an old red coat, patched with gray frieze, who, on seeing them, exhibited in his features a most ingenious air of natural surprise He immediately ceased to whistle, and with every mark of respect, putting his hand to his hat, said in a voice, the tones of which spoke of kindness and deference:

"God save ye, gintlemen."

"I say, my lad," said the gauger, "where is that customer with the keg on his back?—he crossed over there this moment."

"Where, when, sir?" said the lad, with a stare of surprise.

"Where? when? why, this minute, and in this place."

"And was it a whiskey keg, sir?"

"Sir, I am not here to be examined by you," replied Stinton; "confound me if the conniving young rascal is not striking me into a cross-examination already—I say, redcoat, where is the boy with the keg, sir?"

"As for a boy, I did see a boy, sir; but the never a keg he had—hadn't he a gray frieze coat, sir?"

"He had."

"And wasn't it a dauny bit short about the skirts, please your honor?"

"Again he's at me. Sirra, unless you tell me where he is in a half second, I shall lay my whip to your shoulders."

"The sorra a keg I seen then, sir—the last keg I seen was—"

"Did you see a boy without the keg, answering to the description I gave you?"

"You gave me no description of it, sir—but even if you did—when I didn't see it, how could I tell your honor anything about it?"

"Where is the fellow, you villain?" exclaimed the gauger in a fury, "where is he gone to? You admit you saw him; as for the keg, it cannot be far from us—but where is he?"

"By dad, I saw a boy wid a short frieze coat upon him, crossing the road there below and runnin' down the other side of that ditch."

This was too palpable a lie to stand the test even of a glance at the ditch in question, which was nothing more than a slight mound that ran down a long lea field, on which there was not the appearance of a shrub.

The gauger looked at his companion, then turning to the boy, "Come, come my lad," said he, " you know that lie is rather cool. Don't you feel in your soul that a rat could not have gone in that direction without our seeing it?"

"Bedad an' I saw him," returned the lad, "wid a gray coat upon him, that was a little too short in the tail—it's better than half an hour agone."

"The boy I speak of, you must have met," said Stinton; "it's not five minutes—no, not more than three, since he came inside the field."

"That my feet may grow to the ground, then, if I seen a boy in or about this place, widin the time, barrin' myself."

The gauger eyed him closely for a short space, and pulling out half a crown, said—"Harkee, my lad, a word with you in private."

The fact is, that during the latter part of this dialogue the worthy exciseman observed the cautious distance at which the boy kept himself from the grasp of him and his companion. A suspicion consequently began to dawn upon him that in defiance of appearances, the lad himself might be the actual smuggler. On reconsidering the matter, this suspicion almost amounted to certainty; the time was too short to permit even the most ingenious cheat to render himself and his keg invisible in a manner so utterly unaccountable. On the other hand, when he reflected on the open, artless character of the boy's song; the capricious change to a light-hearted whistle; the surprise so naturally and the respect so deferentially expressed, joined to the dissimilarity of dress, he was confounded again, and scarcely knew on which side to determine. Even the lad's reluctance to approach him might proceed from fear of the whip. He felt resolved, however, to ascertain this point, and with the view of getting the lad into his hands, he showed him half a crown and addressed him as already stated.

The lad, on seeing the money, appeared to be instantly caught by it, and approached him as if it had been a bait he could not resist—a circumstance which again staggered the gauger. In a moment, however, he had seized him.

"Come, now," said he, unbuttoning his coat, "you will oblige me by stripping."

"And why so?" said the lad, with a face that might have furnished a painter or sculptor with a perfect notion of curiosity, perplexity and wonder.

"Why so?" replied Stinson; "we shall see—we shall soon see."

"Surely you don't think I've hid the keg about me," said the other, his features now relaxing into such an appearance of utter simplicity as would have certainly made any other man but a gauger give up the examination as hopeless and exonerate the boy from any participation whatsoever in the transaction.

"No, no," replied the gauger, "by no means, you young rascal. "See here, Cartwright," he continued, addressing his companion—"the keg, my precious;" again turning to the lad— "Oh! no, no; it would be cruel to suspect you of anything but the purest of simplicity."

"Look here, Cartwright," having stripped the boy of his coat and turned it inside out, "there's a coat—there's thrift—there's economy for you. Come, sir, tuck on, tuck on instantly; here, I shall assist you—up with your arms—straighten your neck; it will be both straightened and stretched yet, my cherub. What think you now, Cartwright? Did you ever see a metamorphosis in your life so quick, complete and unexpected?"

His companion was certainly astonished in no small degree, on seeing the red coat, when turned, become a comfortable gray freize; one precisely such as he who bore the keg had on. Nay, after surveying his person and dress a second time, he instantly recognized him as the same.

The only interest, we should observe, which this gentleman had in the transaction, arose from the mere gratification which a keen observer of character, gifted with a strong relish for humor, might be supposed to feel. The gauger, in sifting the matter, and scenting the trail of the keg, was now in his glory, and certainly, when met by so able an opponent as our friend Condy, for it was indeed himself, furnished a very rich treat to his friend.

"Now," he continued, addressing the boy again—"lose not a moment in letting us know where you've hid the keg."

"The sorra bit of it I hid—it fell off o' me an' I lost it; sure I'm lookin' after it myself, so I am," and he moved off while speaking, as if pretending to search for it in a thin hedge, which could by no means conceal it.

"Cartwright," said the gauger, "did you ever see anything so perfect as this, so ripe a rascal—you don't understand him now. Here, you simpleton; harkee, sirra, there must be no playing the lapwing with me; back here to the same point. We may lay it down as a sure thing that whatever direction he takes from this spot is the wrong one; so back here, you sir, till we survey the premises about us for your traces."

The boy walked sheepishly back, and appeared to look about him for the keg with a kind of earnest stupidity, which was altogether inimitable.

"I say, my boy," asked Stinton, ironically, "don't you look rather foolish now? Can you tell your right hand from your left?"

"I can," replied Condy, holding up his left, "there's my right hand."

"And what do you call the other?" said Cartwright.

"My left, bedad, anyhow, an' that's true enough."

Both gentlemen laughed heartily.

"But it's carrying the thing a little too far," said the gauger; "in the mean time let us hear how you prove it."

"Aisy enough, sir," replied Condy, "bekase I am left-handed—this," holding up the left, "is the right hand to me, whatever you may say to the contrary."

Condy's countenance expanded, after he had spoken, into a grin so broad and full of grotesque sarcasm, that Stinton and his companion both found their faces, in spite of them, get rather blank under its influence.

"What the deuce!" exclaimed the gauger, "are we to be here all day? Come, sir, bring us at once to the keg."

He was here interrupted by a laugh from Cartwright, so vociferous, loud and hearty, that he looked at him with amazement.

"Hey, day," he exclaimed, "what's the matter, what new joke is this?"

For some minutes, however, he could not get a word from the other, whose laughter appeared as if never to end; he walked to and fro in absolute convulsions, bending his body and clapping his hands together, with a vehemence quite unintelligible.

"What is it, man?" cried the other, "confound you, what is it?"

"Oh!" replied Cartwright, "I am sick, perfectly feeble."

"You have it to yourself, at all events," observed Stinton.

"And shall keep it to myself," said Cartwright; "your sagacity is overreached; you must be contented to sit down under defeat. I won't interfere."

Now, in this contest between the gauger and Condy, even so slight a thing as one glance of the eye by the latter might have given a proper cue to an opponent so sharp as Stinton. Condy during the whole dialogue, consequently, preserved the most vague and undefinable visage imaginable except in the matter of his distinction between "right" and "left," and Stinton, who watched his eyes with the shrewdest vigilance, could make nothing of it. Not so was it between him and Cartwright; for during the closing paroxysms of his mirth, Stinton caught his eye fixed upon a certain mark barely visible upon the hoar frost, which mark extended down to the furze bushes that grew at the foot of the slope where they then stood.

As a staunch old hound lays his nose to the trail of a hare or fox, so did the gauger pursue the trace of the keg, down the little hill; for the fact was, that Condy, having no other resource, tumbled it off toward the furze, into which it settled perfectly to his satisfaction; and with all the quickness of youth and practice, instantly turned his coat, which had been made purposely for such encounters. This accomplished, he had barely time to advance a few yards round the angle of the hedge, and changing his whole manner as well as his appearance, acquitted himself as the reader has already seen. That he could have carried the keg down to the cover, then conceal it, and return to the spot where they met him, was utterly beyond the reach of human exertion, so that in point of fact they never could have suspected that the whiskey lay in such a place.

The triumph of the gauger was now complete, and a complacent sense of his own sagacity sat visible on his features. Condy's face, on the other hand, became considerably lengthened, and appeared quite as rueful and mortified as the other's was joyous and confident.

"Who's the sharpest now, my knowing one?" said he, "who is the laugh against, as matters stand between us?"

"The sorra give you good of it," said Condy sulkily.

"What is your name?" inquired Stinton.

"Barney Keerigan's my name," replied the other indignantly; "an' I'm not ashamed of it, nor afraid to tell it to you or any other man."

"What, of the Keerigans of Killogan?"

"Ay jist, of the Keerigans of Killogan."

"I know the family," said Stinton. "They are decent *in their way*—but come, my lad, don't lose your temper, and answer me another question. Where were you bringing this whiskey?"

"To a betther man than ever stood in your shoes," replied Condy in a tone of absolute defiance—"to a gintleman anyway," with a peculiar emphasis on the word gintleman.

"But what's his name?"

"Mr. Stinton's his name—gauger Stinton."

The shrewd exciseman stood and fixed his keen eye on Condy for upwards of a minute, with a glance of such piercing scrutiny as scarcely any consciousness of imposture could withstand.

Condy, on the other hand, stood and eyed him with an open, unshrinking, yet angry glance; never winced, but appeared by the detection of his keg to have forgotten the line of cunning policy he had previously adopted, in a mortification which had predominated over duplicity and art.

He is now speaking truth, thought the gauger. He has lost his temper, and is completely off his guard.

"Well, my lad," he continued, "this is very good so far, but who was it sent the keg to Stinton?"

"Do you think," said Condy, with a look of strong contempt at the gauger, for deeming him so utterly silly as to tell him, "Do you think you can make me turn informer? There's none of that blood in me, thank goodness."

"Do you know Stinton?"

"How could I know the man I never seen?" replied Condy, still out of temper; "but one thing I don't know, gintlemen, and that is, whether you have any right to take my whiskey or not."

"As to that, my good lad, make your mind easy—I'm Stinton."

"You, sir," said Condy, with well-feigned surprise.

"Yes," replied the other, "I'm the very man you were bringing the keg to. And now I'll tell you what you must do for me. Proceed to my house with as little delay as possible; ask to see my daughter—ask for Miss Stinton—take this key, and desire her to have the keg put into the cellar. She'll know the key, and let it also be a token that she is to give you your breakfast. Say I desired that keg to be placed to the right of the five gallon one that I seized on Thursday last, that stands on a little stillion under my blunderbuss."

"Of coorse," said Condy, who appeared to have misgivings on the matter, "I suppose I must, but somehow——"

"Why, sirrah, what do you grumble now for?"

Condy still eyed him with suspicion.

"And, sir," said he, after having once more mounted the keg, "am I to get nothing for such a weary trudge as I had wid it, but my breakfast?"

"Here," said Stinton, throwing him half a crown, "take that along with it, and now be off—or stop—Cartwright, will you dine with me to-day, and let us broach the keg? I'll gaurantee its excellence, for this is not the first I have got from the same quarter—that's *entre nous*."

"With all my heart," replied Cartwright, "upon the terms you say, that of the broach."

"Then, my lad," said Stinton, "say to my daughter that a friend—perhaps a friend or two—will dine with me to-day; that is enough."

They then mounted their horses, and were proceeding as before, when Cartwright addressed the gauger as follows : "Do you not put this lad, Stinton, in a capacity to overreach you yet?"

"No," replied the other, "the young rascal spoke the truth

after the discovery of the keg, for he lost his temper, and was no longer cool."

"For my part, hang me if I'd trust him."

"I should scruple to do so, myself," replied the gauger, "but, as I said, these Keerigans—notorious illicit fellows, by the way—send me a keg or two every year, and almost always about this very time. Besides, I read him to the heart and he never winced. Yes, decidedly, the whiskey was for me; of that I have no doubt whatsoever."

"I most positively would not trust him."

"Not that perhaps I ought," said Stinton, "on second thought, to place such confidence in a lad who acted so adroitly in the beginning. Let us call him back, and re-examine him at all events."

Now Condy had, during this conversation, been discussing the very same point with himself.

"Bad cess forever attend you, Stinton agra," he exclaimed, "for there's something surely over you—a lucky shot from behind a hedge, or a break-neck fall down a cliff, or something of that kind. If the ould boy hadn't his croubs hard and fast in you, you wouldn't let me walk away with the whiskey anyhow. Bedad, it's well I thought o' the Keerigans, for sure enough I did hear Barney say that he was to send a keg in to him this week some day; and he didn't think I knew him aither. Faix, it's many a long day since I knew the sharp puss of him, with an eye like a hawk. But what if they folly me, and do up all? Anyway, I'll prevint them from having suspicion of me before I go a toe farther, the ugly rips."

He instantly wheeled about, a moment or two before Stinton and Cartwright had done the same, for the purpose of sifting him still more thoroughly, so that they found him meeting them.

"Gintlemen," said he, "how do I know that aither of you is Mr. Stinton, or that the house you directed me to is his? I know that if the whiskey doesn't go to him I may lave the counthry."

"You are either a deeper rogue or a more stupid fool than I

took you to be," observed Stinton; "but what security can you give us that you will leave the keg safely at its destination?"

"If I thought you were Mr. Stinton, I'd be very glad to lave the whiskey where it is, and even do without my breakfast. Gintlemen, tell me the truth, bekase I'd only be murdhered out of the face."

"Why, you idiot," said the gauger, losing his temper and suspicions both together, "can't you go to the town and inquire where Mr. Stinton lives?"

"Bedad, thin, thrue enough, I never thought of that at all at all; but I beg your pardon, gintlemen, an' I hope you won't be angry wid me, in regard that it's kilt and quartered I'd be if I let myself be made a fool of by anybody."

"Do what I desire you," said the exciseman; "inquire for Mr. Stinton's house, and you may be sure that the whiskey will reach him."

"Thank you, sir. Bedad, I might have thought of that myself."

This last clause, which was spoken in a soliloquy, would have deceived a saint himself.

"Now," said Stinton, after they had re-commenced their journey, "are you satisfied?"

"I am at length," said Cartwright; "if his intentions had been dishonest instead of returning to make himself certain against being deceived, he would have made the best of his way from us; a rogue never wantonly puts himself in the way of danger or detection."

That evening, about five o'clock, Stinton, Cartwright, and two others arrived at the house of the worthy gauger, to partake of his good cheer. A cold frosty evening gave a peculiar zest to the comfort of a warm room, a blazing fire and a good dinner. No sooner were the viands discussed, the cloth removed, and the glasses ready, than their generous host desired his daughter to assist the servant in broaching the redoubtable keg.

"That keg, my dear," he proceeded, "which the country lad, who brought the key of the cellar, left here to-day."

"A keg?" repeated the daughter with surprise.

"Yes, Maggy, my love—a keg. I said so, I think."

"But, papa, there came no keg here to-day."

The gauger and Cartwright both groaned in unison.

"No keg?" said the gauger.

"No keg?" echoed Cartwright.

"No keg, indeed," re-echoed Miss Stinton; "but there came a country boy with the key of the cellar, as a token that he was to get the five gallon——"

"Oh," groaned the gauger, "I'm knocked up—outwitted; oh!"

"Bought and sold," added Cartwright.

"Go on," said the gauger; "I must hear it out."

"As a token," proceeded Miss Stinton, "that he was to get the five gallon keg on the little stillion, under the blunderbuss, for Captain Dalton."

"And he got it?"

"Yes, sir, he got it: for I took the key as a sufficient token."

"But, Maggy—hear me child—surely he brought a keg here, and left it; and of course it's in the cellar?"

"No, indeed, he brought no keg here; but he did bring the five gallon one that was in the cellar away with him."

"Stinton," said Cartwright, "send round the bottle."

"The rascal," ejaculated the gauger; "we shall drink his health."

And on relating the circumstances, the company drank the sheepish lad's health, that bought and sold the gauger.

THE IRISH MIDWIFE.

The village of Ballycomaisy was as pleasant a little place as one might wish to see of a summer's day. It consisted principally of one long street, which you entered from the north-west side by one of those old-fashioned bridges, the arches of which were much more akin to the Gothic than the Roman. Most of the houses were of mud, a few of stone, one or two of which had the honor of being slated on the front side of the roof, and rustically thatched on the back, where ostentation was not necessary. There were two or three shops, a liberal sprinkling of public-houses, a chapel a little out of the town, and an old dilapidated market-house near the centre. A few little by-streets projected in a lateral direction from the main one, which was terminated on the side opposite to the north-west by a pound, through which, as usual, ran a shallow stream, that was gathered into a little gutter as it crossed the road. A crazy antiquated mill, all covered and cobwebbed with gray mealy dust, stood about a couple of hundred yards out of the town, to which two straggling rows of houses, that looked like an abortive street, led you. This mill was surrounded by a green common, which was again hemmed in by a fine river, that ran round in a curving line from under the hunchbacked arch of the bridge we mentioned at the beginning. Now, a little behind, or rather above this mill, on the skirt of the aforesaid common, stood a rather neat-looking whitish cabin, with about half a rood of garden behind it. It was but small, and consisted merely of a sleeping-room and kitchen. On one side of the door was a window, opening on hinges; and on the outside, to the right as you entered the house, there was placed a large stone about four feet high, backed by a sloping mound of earth, so graduated as to allow a person to ascend the stone without any difficulty. In this cabin lived Rose Moan, the Midwife; and we need scarcely inform our readers that the stone in question was her mounting-stone, by which she was enabled to place herself on pillion or crupper, as the case happened, when called out upon her usual avocation.

Rose was what might be called a *flahoolagh*, or portly woman, with a good-humored set of Milesian features; that is to say, a pair of red, broad cheeks, a well-set nose, allowing for the disposition to turn up, and two black twinkling eyes, with a mellow expression that betokened good nature, and a peculiar description of knowing *professional* humor that is never to be met with in any *but* one of her calling. Rose was dressed in a red flannel petticoat, a warm cotton sack or wrapper, which pinned easily over a large bust, and a comfortable woolen shawl. She always wore a long-bordered morning cap, over which, while traveling, she pinned a second shawl of Scotch plaid; and to protect her from the cold night air, she enfolded her precious person in a deep blue cloak of the true indigo tint. Over her head, over cloak and shawl and morning cap, was fixed a black "splush hat," with the leaf strapped down by her ears on each side, so that in point of fact she cared little how it blew, and never once dreamed that such a process as that of Raper or Mackintosh was necessary to keep the liege subjects of these realms warm and water-proof, nor that two systems could exist in Ireland so strongly antithetical to each other as those of Raper and Father Mathew.

Having thus given a brief sketch of her local habitation and personal appearance, we shall transfer our readers to the house of a young new-married farmer named Keho, who lived in a distant part of the parish. Keho was a comfortable fellow, full of good nature and credulity; but his wife happened to be one of the sharpest, meanest, most suspicious and miserable individuals that ever was raised in good-humored Ireland. Her voice was as sharp and her heart as cold as an icicle; and as for her tongue, it was incessant and interminable. Were it not that her husband, who, though good-natured, was fiery and resolute when provoked, exercised a firm and salutary control over her, she would have starved both him and her servants into perfect skeletons. And what was still worse, with a temper that was vindictive and tyrannical, she affected to be religious, and upon those who did not know her, actually attempted to put herself off as a saint.

One night, about twelve months after his marriage, honest Corny Keho came out to the barn, where slept his two farm servants, named Phil Hannigan and Barny Casey. He had been sitting by himself, composing his mind for a calm night's rest, or probably for a curtain lecture, by taking a contemplative whiff of the pipe, when the servant wench, with a certain air of hurry, importance and authority, entered the kitchen, and informed him that Rose Moan must be immediately sent for.

"The misthress isn't well, masther, an' the sooner she's sint for, the betther. So mind my words, sir, if you plaise, an' pack aff either Phil or Barny for Rose Moan, an' I hope I won't have to ax it again—hem!"

Dandy Keho—for so Corny was called, as being remarkable for his slovenliness—started up hastily, and having taken the pipe out of his mouth, was about to place it on the hob; but reflecting that the whiff could not much retard him in the delivery of his orders, he sallied out to the barn and knocked.

"Who's there? Lave that wid you, unless you wish to be shotted." This was followed by a loud laugh from within.

"Boys, get up wid all haste: it's the misthress. Phil, saddle Hollowback and fly—(puff)—fly in a jiffy for Rose Moan; an' do you, Barny, clap a-back sugaun—(puff)—an Sobersides, an' be aff for the misthress's mother—(puff.)"

Both were dressing themselves before he had concluded, and in a very few minutes were off in different directions, each according to the orders he had received. With Barny we have nothing to do, unless to say that he lost little time in bringing Mrs. Keho's mother to her aid: but as Phil is gone for a much more important character, we beg our readers to return with us to the cabin of Rose Moan, who is now fast asleep; for it is twelve o'clock of a beautiful moonlight night, in the pleasant month of August. Tap-tap. "Is Mrs. Moan at home?" In about half a minute her warm, good-looking face, enveloped in flannel, is protruded from the window.

"Who's that, *in God's name?*" The words in italics were added, lest the message might be one from the fairies.

"I'm Dandy Keho's s rvant—one of them, at any rate—an' my misthress has got a stitch in her side—ha! ha! ha!"

"Aisy, avick—so, she's *down*, thin—aisy—I'll be wid you like a bow out of an arrow. Put your horse over to 'the stone,' an' have him ready. The Lord bring her over her difficulties, any way, amin!"

She then pulled in her head, and in about three or four minutes sallied out, dressed as we have described her; and having placed herself on the crupper, coolly put her right arm round Phil's body, and desired him to ride on with all possible haste.

"Push an, avouchal, push an—time's precious at all times, but on business like this every minute is worth a life. But there's always one comfort, that God is marciful. Push forrid avick."

"Never fear, Mrs. Moan. If it's in Hollowback, bedad, I'm the babe that'll take it out of him. Come, ould Hackball, trot out—you don't know the message you're an, nor who you're carryin'."

"Isn't your misthress—manin' the Dandy's wife—a daughther of ould Fitzy Finnegan's, the schrew of Glendhu?"

"Faith, you may say that, Rose, as we all know to our cost. Be me song, she does have us sometimes that you might see through us; an' only for the masther——but, dang it, no matther—she's down now, poor woman, an' it's not just the time to be rakin' up her failin's."

"It is not, an' God mark you to grace for sayin' so. At a time like this we must forget everything, only to do the best we can for our fellow-creatures. What are you lookin' at, avick?"

Now this question naturally arose from the fact that honest Phil had been, during their short conversation, peering keenly on each side of him, as if he expected an apparition to rise from every furze-bush on the common. The truth is, he was almost proverbial for his terror of ghosts and fairies, and all supernatural visitants whatever; but upon this occasion his fears arose to a painful height, in consequence of the popular belief, that when a midwife is sent for, the Good People throw every possible obstruction in her way, either by laming the horse, if she rides, or by disqualifying the guide from performing his duty as such. Phil, however, felt ashamed to avow his fears on these points, but still could not help unconsciously turning the conversation to the very topic he ought to have avoided.

"What war you looking at, avick?"

"Why, bedad, there appeared something there beyant, like a man, only it was darker. But be this and be that—hem, ahem! —if I could get my hands on him, whatsomever he——"

"Hush!h, boy, hould your tongue; you don't know but it's the very word you war goin' to say might do us harm."

"Whatsomever he is, that I'd give him a lift on Hollowback if he happened to be any poor fellow that stood in need of it. Oh! the sorra word I was goin' to say against anything or anybody."

"You're right, dear. If you knew as much as I could tell you—push an—you'd have a dhrop o' sweat at the ind of every hair on your head."

"Be my song, I'm tould you know a power o' quare things, Mrs. Moan; an' if all that's said is thrue, you sartinly do."

Now, had Mrs. Moan and her heroic guide passed through the village of Ballycomaisy, the latter would not have felt his fears so strong upon him. The road, however, along which they were now going was a grass-grown *bohreen*, that led them from behind her cabin through a waste and lonely part of the country; and as it was a saving of better than two miles in point of distance, Mrs. Moan would not hear of their proceeding by any other direction. The tenor of her conversation, however, was fast bringing Phil to the state she so graphically and pithily described.

"What's your name?" she asked.

"Phil Hannigan, a son of fat Phil's of Balnasaggart, an' a cousin to Paddy who lost a finger in the Gansy (Guernsey) wars."

"I know. Well, Phil, in throth the hairs 'ud stand like stalks o' barley upon your head, if you heard all I could mintion."

Phil instinctively put his hand up and pressed down his hat, as if it had been disposed to fly from off his head.

"Hem! ahem! Why, I'm tould it's wonderful. But is it thrue, Mrs. Moan, that you have been brought *on business* to some o' the "—here Phil looked about him cautiously, and lowered his voice to a whisper—"to some o' the fairy women?"

"Husth, man alive—what the sorra timpted you to call them anything but the Good People? This day's Thursday—God stand betune us an' harm. No, Phil, I name nobody. But there was a woman, a midwife—mind, avick, that I don't say *who* she was—maybe I know why, too, an' maybe it would be as much as my life is worth—"

"Aisey, Mrs. Moan! God presarve us! what is that tall thing there to the right?" and he commenced to pray in Irish as fast as he could get out the words.

"Why, don't you see, boy, it's a fir-tree, but sorra movin' it's movin'."

"Ay, faix, an' so it is; bedad I thought it was gettin' taller an' taller. Aye! hut! it *is* only a tree."

"Well, dear, there was a woman, an' she was called away one night by a little gentleman dressed in green. I'll tell you the story some time—only this, that havin' done her *duty*, an' tuck no payment, she was called out the same night to a neighbor's wife, an' a purtier boy you couldn't see than she left behind her. But it seems she happened to touch one of his eyes wid a hand that had a taste of *their* panado an it; an' as the child grew up, every one wondhered to hear him speak of the multitudes o' thim that he seen in all directions. Well, my dear, he kept never sayin' anything to them until one day when he was in the fair of Ballycomaisy, that he saw them whippin' away meal and cotton and butther, an' everything that they thought serviceable to them; so you see he could hold iu no longer, an' says he to a little fellow that was very active an' thievish among them, 'Why do you take what doesn't belong to you?' says he. The little fellow looked up at him—"

"God be about us, Rose, what is that white thing goin' along the ditch to the left of us?"

"It's a sheep, don't you see? Faix, I believe you're cowardly at night."

"Aye, faix, an' so it is, but it looked very quare somehow."

'—An' says he, 'How do you know that?' 'Bekase I see you all,' says the other. 'An' which eye do you see us all wid?' says he again. 'Why, wid the left,' says the boy. Wid that he gave a short whiff of a blast up into the eye, an' from that day not a stime the poor boy was never able to see wid it. No, Phil, I didn't say it was *myself*—I named *nobody*."

"An', Mrs. Moan, is it thrue that you can put the dughaughs upon them that trate their wives badly?"

"Whisht, Phil. When you marry, keep your timper—that's all. You knew long Ned Donnelly?"

"Aye, bedad, sure enough; there was quare things said about—"

"Push an, avick, push an; for who knows how some of us is wanted? You have a good masther, I believe, Phil? It's poison the same Ned would give me if he could. Push an, dear."

Phil felt that he had got his answer. The abrupt mystery of her manner and her curt allusions left him little indeed to guess at. In this way did the conversation continue, Phil feloniously filching, as he thought, from her own lips, a corroboration of the various knowledge and extraordinary powers which she was believed to possess, and she ingeniously feeding his credulity, merely by enigmatical hints and masked allusions; for although she took care to affirm nothing directly or personally of herself, yet did she contrive to answer him in such a manner as to confirm every report that had gone abroad of the strange purposes she could effect.

"Phil, wasn't there an uncle o' yours up in the Mountain Bar that didn't live happily for some time wid his wife?"

"I believe so, Rose; but it was before my time, or any way when I was only a young shaver."

"An' did you ever hear how the reconcilement came betune them?"

"No, bedad," replied Phil, "I never did; an' that's no wondher, for it was a thing they never liked to spake of."

"Throth, it's thrue for you, boy. Well, I brought about——push an, dear, push an. They're as happy a couple now as breaks bread, any way, and that's all they wanted."

"I'd wager a thirteen it was you did that, Rose."

"Hut, gorsoon, hould your tongue. Sure they're happy now, I say, whosomever did it. I named nobody, nor I take no pride to myself, Phil, out o' sich things. Some people's gifted above others, an' that's all. But, Phil?"

"Well, ma'am?"

"How does the Dandy an' his scald of a wife agree? for, throth, I'm tould she's nothing else."

"Faix, but middlin' itself. As I tould you, she often has us as empty as a paper lanthern, wid sarra a thing but the light of a good conscience inside of us. If we *pray* ourselves, begorra she'll take care we'll have the *fastin'* at first cost; so that you see, ma'am, we hould a devout situation undher her."

"An' so that's the way wid you?"

"Aye, the downright thruth, an' no mistake. Why, the stirabout she makes would run nine miles along a deal board, an' scald a man at the far end of it."

"Throth, Phil, I never like to go next or near sich women or sich places, but for the sake o' the innocent we must forget the guilty. So push an, avick, push an. Who knows but it's life an' death wid us? Have you ne'er a spur on?"

"Oh! not a spur I tuck time to wait for."

"Well, afther all, it's not right to let a messenger come for a woman like me, widout what is called the Midwife's Spur—a spur in the head—for it has long been said that one in the head is worth two in the heel, an' so indeed it is—on business like this, any way."

"Mrs. Moan, do you know the Moriartys of Ballaghmore, ma'am?"

"Which o' them, honey?"

"Mick o' the Esker Beg."

"To be sure I do. A well-favored, dacint family they are, an' full o' the world, too, the Lord spare it to them."

"Bedad, they are, ma'am, a well-favored* family. Well, ma'am, isn't it odd, but somehow there's neither man, woman, nor child in the parish but gives you the good word above all the women in it; but as for a midwife, why, I heard my aunt say that if ever mother an' child owended their lives to another, she did her and the babby's to you."

The reader may here perceive that Phil's flattery must have had some peculiar design in it, in connection with the Moriartys, and such indeed was the fact. But we had better allow him to explain matters himself.

"Well, honey, sure that was but my duty; but God be praised for all, for everything depinds on the Power above. She should call in one o' those new-fangled women who take out their Dispatches from the College in Dublin below; for you see, Phil, there is sich a place there—an' it stands to raison that there should be a Fondlin' Hospital beside it, which there is too, they say; but, honey, what are these poor ignorant cratures but *new lights*, ivery one o' thim, that a dacint woman's life isn't safe wid?"

"To be sure, Mrs. Moan; an' every one knows they're not to be put in comparishment wid a woman like you, that knows sich a power. But how does it happen, ma'am, that the Moriartys does be spakin' but middlin' of you?"

"Of me, avick?"

"Aye, faix; I'm tould they spread the mouth at you sometimes, espishily when the people does be talkin' about all the quare things you can do."

"Well, well, dear, let them have their laugh—they may laugh that win, you know. Still one doesn't like to be provoked—no indeed."

---

*This term in Ireland means "handsome"—"good-looking."

"Faix, an' Mick Moriarty has a purty daughter, Mrs. Moan, an' a purty penny he can give her, by all accounts. The nerra one o' myself but would be glad to put my comedher on her, if I knew how. I hope you find yourself aisy on your sate, ma'am?"

"I do, honey. Let them talk, Phil, let them talk; it may come their turn yet—only I didn't expect it from *them*. You! but, avick, what chance would *you* have with Mick Moriarty's daughter?"

"Aye, every chance an' sartinty too, if some one that I know, and that every one that knows her respects, would only give me a lift. There's no use in comin' about the bush, Mrs. Moan— bedad it's yourself I mane. You could do it. An' whisper, betune you an' me it would be only sarvin' them right, in regard of the way they spake of you—sayin' indeed, an' galivantin' to the world that you know no more than another woman, an' that ould Pol Doolin of Ballymagowan knows oceans more than you do."

This was perhaps as artful a plot as could be laid for engaging the assistance of Mrs. Moan in Phil's design upon Moriarty's daughter. He knew perfectly well that she would not, unless strongly influenced, lend herself to anything of the kind between two persons whose circumstances in life differed so widely as those of a respectable farmer's daughter with a good portion, and a penniless laboring boy. With great adroitness, therefore, he contrived to excite her prejudices against them by the most successful arguments he could possibly use, namely, a contempt for her imputed knowledge, and praise of her rival. Still she was in the habit of acting coolly, and less from impulse than from a shrewd knowledge of the best way to sustain her own reputation, without undertaking too much.

"Well, honey, an' so you wish me to assist you? Maybe I could do it, and maybe—but push an, dear, move him an; we'll think of it, an' spake more about it some other time. I must think of what's afore me now—so move, move, acushla; push an."

Much conversation of the same nature took place between them, in which each bore a somewhat characteristic part; for to say the truth, Phil was as knowing a "boy" as you might wish to become acquainted with. In Rose, however, he had a woman of no ordinary shrewdness to encounter; and the consequence was, that each after a little more chat began to understand the other a little too well to render the topic of the Moriartys, to which Phil again reverted, so interesting as it had been. Rose soon saw that Phil was only a *plasthey*, or sweetener, and only "soothered" her for his own purposes; and Phil perceived that Rose understood his tactics too well to render any further tampering with her vanity either safe or successful.

At length they arrived at Dandy Keho's house, and in a moment the Dandy himself took her in his arms, and, placing her gently on the ground, shook hands with and cordially welcomed her. It is very singular, but no less true, that the moment a midwife enters the house of her patient, she always uses the plural number, whether speaking in her own person or in that of the former.

"You're welcome, Rose, an' I'm proud an' happy to see you here, an' it'll make poor Bridget strong, an' give her courage, to know you're near her."

"How are we, Dandy? how are we, avick?"

"Oh, bedad, middlin', wishin' very much for you, of coorse, as I hear—"

"Well, honey, go away now. I have some words to say afore I go in, that'll sarve us, maybe—a charm it is that has great vartue in it."

The Dandy then withdrew to the barn, where the male portion of the family were staying until the *ultimatum* should be known. A good bottle of potteen, however, was circulating among them, for every one knows that occasions of this nature usually generate a festive and hospitable spirit.

* * * * * * *

In the barn the company were very merry, Dandy himself being as pleasant as any of them, unless when his brow became shaded by the very natural anxiety for the welfare of his wife and child, which from time to time returned upon him. Stories were told, songs sung, and jokes passed, all full of good nature and not a little fun, some of it at the expense of the Dandy himself, who laughed at and took it all in good part. An occasional *bulletin* came out through a servant maid, that matters were just the same way; a piece of intelligence which damped Keho's mirth considerably. At length he himself was sent for by the Midwife, who wished to speak with him at the door.

"I hope there's nothing like danger, Rose?"

"Not at all, honey; but the truth is, we want a seventh son who isn't left-handed."

"A seventh son! Why, what do you want him for?"

"Why, dear, just to give her three shakes in his arms: it never fails."

"Bedad, an' that's fortunate; for there's Mickey M'Sorley of the Broad Bog's a seventh son, an' he's not two gunshots from this."

"Well, aroon, hurry off one or two o' the boys for him, and tell Phil, if he makes haste, that I'll have a word to say to him afore I go."

This intimation to Phil put feathers to his heels; for from the moment that he and Barny started, he did not once cease to go at the top of his speed. It followed as a matter of course that honest Mickey M'Sorley dressed himself and was back at Keho's house before the family believed it possible the parties could have been there. This ceremony of getting a seventh son to shake the sick woman, in cases where difficulty or danger may be apprehended, is one which frequently occurs in remote parts of the country. To be sure, it is only a form, the man merely taking her in his arms, and moving her gently three times. The writer of this, when young, saw it performed with his own eyes, as the saying is; but in his case the man was not a seventh son, for no such person could be procured. When this difficulty arises, any man who has the character of being lucky, provided he is not married to a red-haired wife, may be called in to give the three shakes. In other and more dangerous cases Rose would send out persons to gather half a dozen heads of blasted barley, and, having stripped them of the black fine powder with which they were covered, she would administer it in a little new milk, and this was always attended by the best effects. It is somewhat surprising that the whole Faculty should have adopted this singular medicine in cases of similar difficulty, for in truth it is that which is now administered under the more scientific name of *Ergot of Rye.*

In the case before us, the seventh son sustained his reputation for good luck. In about three-quarters of an hour Dandy was called in " to kiss a strange young gintleman that wanted to see him." This was an agreeable ceremony to Dandy, as it always is to catch the first glimpse of one's own first-born. On entering he found Rose sitting beside the bed in all the pomp of authority and pride of success, bearing the infant in her arms, and dandling it up and down, more from habit than any necessity that then existed for doing so.

"Well," said she, "here we are all safe and sound, God willin'; an' if you're not the father of as purty a young man as ever I laid eyes on, I'm not here. Corny Keho, come an' kiss your son, I say."

Corny advanced, somewhat puzzled whether to laugh or cry, and taking the child up with a smile, he kissed it five times—for that is the mystic number—and as he placed it once more in Rose's arms, there was a solitary tear on his cheek.

"Arra, go an' kiss your wife, man alive, an' tell her to have a good heart, an' to be as kind to all her fellow-creatures as God has been to her this night. It isn't upon this world the heart ought to be fixed, for we see how small a thing and how short a time can take us out of it."

"Oh, bedad," said Dandy, who had now recovered the touch of feeling excited by the child, "it would be too bad if I would grudge her a smack." He accordingly stooped and kissed her; but, truth to confess, he did it with a very cool and business-like air. "I know," he proceeded, "that she'll have a heart like a jyant, now that the son is come."

"To be sure she will, an' she must; or if not, *I'll* play the sorra, an' break things. Well, well, let her get strength a bit first, an' rest an' quiet; an' in the meantime get the groanin'-malt ready, until every one in the house drinks the health of the stranger. My soul to happiness, but he's a born beauty. The nerra Keho of you all never was the aiquails of what he'll be yet, plaise God. Troth, Corny, he has daddy's nose upon him, any how. Aye, you may laugh; but, faix, it's thrue. You may take with him, you may own to him, anywhere. Arra, look at that! My soul to happiness if one egg's liker another! Eh, my posey! Where was it, alanna? Aye, you're there, my duck o' diamonds! Troth, you'll be the flower o' the flock, so you will. An' now, Mrs. Keho, honey, we'll lave you to yourself awhile, till we thrate these poor cratures of sarvints; the likes o' them oughtn't to be overlooked; an' indeed they did feel a great deal itself, poor things, about you; an' moreover they'll be longin' of coorse to see the darlin' here."

Mrs. Keho's mother and Rose superintended the birth-treat between them. It is unnecessary to say that the young men and girls had their own sly fun upon the occasion; and now that Dandy's apprehension of danger was over, he joined in their mirth with as much glee as any of them. This being over, they all retired to rest; and honest Mickey M'Sorley went home very *hearty*,* in consequence of Dandy's grateful sense of the aid he had rendered his wife. The next morning, Rose, after dressing the infant and performing all the usual duties that one expected from her, took her leave in these words:

"Now, Mrs. Keho, God bless you an' yours, and take care of yourself. I'll see you again on Sunday next, when it's to be christened. Until then, throw out no dirty wather before sunrise or after sunset; an' when Father Molloy is goin' to christen it, let Corny tell him not to forget to christen it *against the fairies*, an' thin it'll be safe. Good-bye, ma'am; an' look you to her, Mrs.

---

*Tipsy.

Finnegan," said she, addressing her patient's mother, "an' *banaght lath* till I see all again."

The following Sunday morning, Rose paid an early visit to her patient, for, as it was the day of young Dandy's christening, her presence was considered indispensable. There is, besides, something in the appearance and bearing of a midwife upon those occasions which diffuses a spirit of bouyancy and light-heartedness not only through the immediate family, but also through all who may happen to participate in the ceremony, or partake of the good cheer. The moment she was seen approaching the house, every one in it felt an immediate elevation of spirits, with the exception of Mrs. Keho herself, who knew that wherever Rose had the arrangement of the bill of fare, there was sure to be what the Irish call "full an' plinty"—"lashins an' lavins"—a fact which made her groan in spirit at the bare contemplation of such waste and extravagance. She was indeed a woman of a very un-Irish heart—so sharp in her temper and so penurious in soul, that one would imagine her veins were filled with vinegar instead of blood.

"*Banaght Dheah in shoh*" (the blessing of God be here), Rose exclaimed on entering.

"*Banaght Dhea agush Murra ghuid*" (the blessing of God and the Virgin on you), replied Corny, "an' you're welcome, Rose ahagur."

"I know that, Corny. Well how are we?—how is my son?"

"Begorra, thrivin' like a pair o' throopers."

"Thank God for it! Haven't we a good right to be grateful to him, anyway? An' is my little man to be christened to-day?"

"Indeed he is—the gossips will be here presently, an' so will *her* mother. But, Rose, dear, will you take the ordherin' of the aitin' an' drinkin' part of it?—you're betther up to these things than we are, an' so you ought, of coorse. Let there be no want of anything; an' if there's an overplush, sorra may care; there'll be poor mouths enough about the door for whatever's left. So, you see, keep never mindin' any hint *she* may give you—you know she's a little o' the closest; but no matther. Let there, as I said, be enough an' to spare."

"Throth, there spoke your father's son, Corny : all the ould dacency's not dead yet, anyhow. Well, I'll do my best. But she's not fit to be up, you know, an' of coorse can't disturb us." The expression of her eye could not be misunderstood as she uttered this. "I see," said Corny—"devil a betther, if you manage that, all's right."

"An' now I must go in, till I see how she an' my son's gettin' an: that's always my first start; bekase you know, Corny, honey, that *their* health goes afore everything."

Having thus undertaken the task required of her, she passed into the bedroom of Mrs. Keho, whom she found determined to be up, in order, as she said, to be at the head of her own table.

"Well, alanna, if you must, you must; but in the name of goodness I wash my hands out of the business teetotally. Dshk, dshk, dshk! Oh, wurra! to think of a woman in your state risin' to sit at her own table! That I may never, if I'll see it, or be about the place at all. If you take your life by your own wilfulness, why, God forgive you; but it mustn't be while I'm here. But since you're bent on it, why, give me the child, an' afore I go, anyhow, I may as well dress it, poor thing! The heavens pity it—my little man—eh?—where was it?—cheep —that's it, a ducky; stretch away. Aye, stretchin' an' thrivin' an' my son! Oh, thin, wurra! Mrs. Keho, but it's you that ought to ax God's pardon for goin' to do what might lave that darlin' o' the world an orphan, may be. Arrah, if I can have patience wid you. May God pity you, my child. If anything happened your mother, what 'ud become of you, and what 'ud become of your poor father this day? Dshk, dshk, dshk!" These latter sounds, exclamations of surprise and regret, were produced by striking the tongue against that part of the inward gum which covers the roots of the teeth.

"Indeed, Rose," replied her patient, in her sharp, shrill, quick voice, "I'm able enough to get up; if I don't we'll be hard rished. Corny's a fool, an' it'll be only rap an' rive wid every one in the place."

"Wait, ma'am, if you plaise. Where's his little barrow?' Aye, I have it. Wait, ma'am, if you plaise, till I get the child dressed, an' I'll soon take myself out o' this. Heaven presarve us! I have seen the like o' this afore—aye, have I—where it was as clear as crystal *that there was something over them*—aye, over them that took their own way as you're doin'."

"But if I don't get up?"

"Oh, by all manes, ma'am—by all manes. I suppose you have a laise o' your life, that's all. It's what I wish I could get."

"An' must I stay here in bed all day, an' me able to rise, an' sich willful waste as will go on, too?"

"Remember you're warned. This is your first baby, God bless it an' spare you both. But, Mrs. Keho, does it stand to raison that you're as good a judge of these things as a woman like me, that it's my business? I ax you that, ma'am."

This poser in fact settled the question, not only by the reasonable force of the conclusion to be arrived from it, but by the cool, authoritative manner in which it was put.

"Well," said the other, "in that case I suppose I must give in. You ought to know best."

"Thank you kindly, ma'am; have you found it out at last? No, but you ought to put your two hands undher my feet for previntin' you from doin' what you intinded. That I may never sup sorrow, but it was as much as your life was worth. Compose yourself; I'll see that there's no waste, and that's enough. Here, hould my son—why, thin, isn't he the beauty o' the world, now that he has got his little dress upon him?—till I pin up this apron across the windy; the light's too strong for you. There, now; the light's apt to give one a headache when it comes in full bint upon the eyes that way. Come, alanna, come an now, till I show you to your father an' them all. Wurra, thin, Mrs. Keho, darlin'," (this was said in a low confidential whisper, and in a playful wheedling tone which baffles all description), "wurra, thin, Mrs. Keho, darlin', but it's he that's the proud man, the proud Corny, this day. Rise your head a little—aisy—there now, that'll do—

one kiss to my son, now, before he laives his mammy, he says, for a weeny while, till he pays his little respects to his daddy an' to all his friends, he says, an' thin he'll come back to mammy agin—to his own little bottle, he says."

Young Corny soon went the rounds of the whole family, from his father down to the little herd-boy who followed and took care of the cattle. Many were the jokes which passed between the youngsters on this occasion—jokes which have been registered by such personages as Rose, almost in every family in the kingdom, for centuries, and with which most of the Irish people are too intimately and thoroughly acquainted to render it necessary for us to repeat them here.

Rose now addressed herself to the task of preparing breakfast, which, in honor of the happy event, was nothing less than "tay, white bread and Boxty, with a glass of poteen to sharpen the appetite." As Boxty, however, is a description of bread not generally known to our readers, we shall give them a sketch of the manner in which this Irish luxury is made. A basket of the best potatoes is got, which are washed and peeled raw; then is procured a tin grater, on which they are grated; the water is then shired off them, and the macerated mass is put into a clean sheet, or table-cloth, or bolster-cover. This is caught at each end by two strong men, who twist it in opposite directions until the contortions drive up the substance into the middle of the sheet, etc.; this of course expels the water also; but lest the twisting should be insufficient for that purpose, it is placed, like a cheese-cake, under a heavy weight, until it is properly dried. They then knead it into cakes, and bake it on a pan or griddle; and when eaten with butter we can assure our readers that it is quite delicious.

The hour was now about nine o'clock, and the company asked to the christening began to assemble. The gossips or sponsors were four in number; two of them wealthy friends of the family that had never been married, and the two others a simple country pair, who were anxious to follow in the matrimonial steps of Corny and his wife. The rest were, as usual, neighbors, relatives, and *cleaveens*, to the amount of sixteen or eighteen persons, men, women and children, all dressed in their best apparel, and disposed to mirth and friendship. Along with the rest was Bob M'Cann, the fool, who, by the way, could smell out a good dinner with as keen a nostril as the wisest man in the parish could boast of, and who, on such occasions, carried turf and water in quantities that indicated the supernatural strength of a Scotch brownie, rather than that of a human being. Bob's qualities, however, were well proportioned to each other, for, truth to say, his appetite was equal to his strength, and his cunning to either.

Corny and Mrs. Moan were in great spirits, and indeed we might predicate as much of all who were present. Not a soul entered the house who was not brought up by Corny to an out-shot room, as a private mark of his friendship, and treated to an underhand glass of as good poteen "as ever went down the red lane," to use a phrase common among the people. Nothing upon an occasion naturally pleasant gives conversation a more cheerful impulse than this; and the consequence was, that in a short time the scene was animated and mirthful to an unusual degree.

Breakfast at length commenced in due form. Two bottles of whiskey were placed upon the table, and the first thing done was to administer a glass to each guest.

"Come, neighbors," said Corny, "we must dhrink the good woman's health before we ate, especially as it's the first time, anyhow."

"To be sure they will, achora, an' why not? An' if it's the first time, Corny, it won't be the— Musha! you're welcome, Mrs. ——! an' jist in time, too." This she said, addressing his mother-in-law, who then entered. "Look at this swaddy, Mrs. ——; my soul to happiness, but he's fit to be the son of a lord. Eh, a pet? Where was my darlin'? Corny, let me dip my finger in the whiskey till I rub his gums wid it. That's my bully! Oh, the heavens love it, see how it puts the little mouth about lookin' for it agin. Throth you'll have the spunk in you yet, acushla, an' it's credit to the Kehos you'll be, if you're spared, as you will, plaise heavens!'"

"Well, Corny," said one of the gossips, "here's a speedy uprise an' a sudden recovery to the good woman, an' the little sthranger's health, an' God bless the baker that gives thirteen to the dozen, anyhow!"

"Aye, aye, Paddy Rafferty, you'll have your joke any way; an', throth, you're welcome to it, Paddy; if you weren't, it isn't standin' for young Corny you'd be to-day."

"Thrue enough," said Rose, "an', by the dickens, Paddy isn't the boy to be long under an obligation to any one. Eh, Paddy, did I help you there, avick? Aisy, childre; you'll smother my son if you crush about him that way." This was addressed to some of the youngsters, who were pressing round to look at and touch the infant.

"It won't be my fault if I do, Rose," said Paddy, slyly eyeing Peggy Betagh, then betrothed to him, who sat opposite, her dark eyes flashing with repressed humor and affection. Deafness, however, is sometimes a very convenient malady to young ladies, for Peggy immediately commenced a series of playful attentions to the unconscious infant, which were just sufficient to excuse her from noticing this allusion to their marriage. Rose looked at her, then nodded comically to Paddy, shutting both her eyes by way of a wink, adding aloud, "Throth you'll be the happy boy, Paddy; an' woe betide you if you aren't the sweetest end of a honeycomb to her. Take care an' don't bring *me* upon you. Well, Peggy, never mind, alanna; who has a betther right to his joke than the dacent boy that's—aisy, childre: saint's above! but ye'll smother the child, so you will. Where did I get him, Denny? sure I brought him as a present to Mrs. Keho; I never come but I bring a purty little babby along wid me—than the dacent boy, dear, that's soon to be your lovin' husband? Arrah, take your glass, acushla; the sorra harm it'll do you."

"Bedad, I'm afeard, Mrs. Moan. What if it 'ud get into my head, an' me to stand for my little godson? No, bad scran to me if I could—faix, a glass 'ud be too many for me."

"It's not more than half filled, dear; but there's sense in what the girl says, Dandy, so don't press it an her."

In the brief space allotted to us we could not possibly give any thing like a full and correct picture of the happiness and hilarity which prevailed at the breakfast in question. When it was over they all prepared to go to the parish chapel, which was distant at least a couple of miles, the midwife staying at home to see that all the necessary preparations were made for dinner. As they were departing, Rose took Dandy aside and addressed him thus:

"Now, Dandy, when you see the priest, tell him that it is your wish, above all things, 'that he should christen it against the fairies.' If you say that, it's enough. And, Peggy, achora, come here. You're not carryin' that child right, alanna; but you'll know betther yet, plaise goodness. No, avillish, don't keep its little head so closely covered wid your cloak; the day's a burnin' day, glory be to God, an' the Lord guard my child; sure the least thing in the world, where there's too much hait, 'ud smother my darlin'. Keep its head out farther, and just shade its little face that way from the sun. Och, will I ever forget the Sunday whin poor Mally M'Guigan wint to take Pat Feasthalagh's child from under her cloak to be christened, the poor infant was a corpse; an' only that the Lord put it into my head to have it privately christened, the father an' mother's hearts would break. Glory be to God! Mrs. Duggan, if the child gets cross, dear, or misses anything, act the mother by him, the little man. Eh, alanna! where was it? Where was my duck o' diamonds—my little Con Roe? My own sweety little ace o' hearts—ch, alanna! Well, God keep it till I see it again, the jewel!"

Well, the child was baptized by the name of his father, and the persons assembled, after their return from chapel, lounged about Corny's house, or took little strolls in the neighborhood, until the hour of dinner. This of course was much more convivial, and ten times more vociferous than the breakfast, cheerful as that meal was. At dinner they had a dish which we believe is, like the Boxty, peculiarly Irish in its composition; we mean what is called *sthill*. This consists of potatoes and beans, pounded up together in such a manner that the beans are not broken, and on this account the potatoes are well champed before the beans are put into them. This is dished in a large bowl, and a hole made in the middle of it, into which a *miscaun* or roll of butter is thrust, and then covered up until it is melted. After this, every one takes a spoon and digs away with his utmost vigor, dipping every morsel into the well of butter in the middle, before he puts it into his mouth. Indeed, from the strong competition which goes forward, and the rapid motion of each right hand, no spectator could be mistaken in ascribing the motive of their proceedings to the principle of the old proverb, devil take the hindmost. *Sthilk* differs from another dish made of potatoes in much the same way, called *colcannon*. If there were beans, for instance, in *colcannon*, it would be *sthilk*.

After dinner the whiskey began to go round, for in these days punch was a luxury almost unknown to the class we are writing of. In fact, nobody there knew how to make it but the midwife, who wisely kept the secret to herself, aware that if the whiskey were presented to them in such a palatable shape, they would not know when to stop, and she herself might fall short of the snug bottle that is usually kept as a treat for those visits which she continues to pay during the convalescence of her patients.

"Come, Rose," said Corny, who was beginning to soften fast, "it's your turn now to thry a glass of what has never seen wather."

"I'll take the glass, Dandy—'deed will I—but the thruth is, I never dhrink it *hard*. No, but I'll jist take a drop o' hot wather an' a grain o' sugar, an' scald it; that an' as much carraway seeds as will lie upon a sixpence does me good; for, God help me, the stomach isn't at all sthrong wid me, in regard o' bein' up so much at night, an' deprived of my nathural rest."

"Rose," said one of them, "is it thrue that you war called out one night, an' brought blindfoulded to some grand lady belongin' to the quality?"

"Wait, avick, till I make a drop o' *wan-grace** for the misthress, poor thing; an' Corny, I'll jist throuble you for about a

---

* A wan-grace is a kind of small gruel or meal tea, sweetened with sugar.

thimbleful o' spirits to take the smell o' the wather off it. The poor creature, she's a little weak still, an' indeed it's wonderful how she stood it out; but, my dear, God's good to his own, an' fits the back to the burden, praise be to his name!"

She then proceeded to scald the drop of spirits for herself, or, in other words, to mix a good tumbler of ladies' punch, making it, as the phrase goes, hot, strong and sweet—not forgetting the carraways, to give it a flavor. This being accomplished, she made the wan-grace for Mrs. Keho, still throwing in a word now and then to sustain her part in the conversation, which was now rising fast into mirth, laughter and clamor.

"Well, but Rose, about the lady of quality; will you tell us that?"

"Oh, many a thing happened me as well worth tellin', if you go to that; but I'll tell it to you, childre, for sure the curiosity's nathural to yez. Why, I was one night at home an' asleep, an I hears a horse's foot gallopin' for the bare life up to the door. I immediately put my head out, an' the horseman says, 'Are you Mrs. Moan?'

"'That's the name that's an me, your honor,' says myself.

"'Dress yourself, thin,' says he, 'for you're sadly wanted; dress yourself and mount behind me, for there's not a moment to be lost!' At the same time I forgot to say that his hat was tied about his face in sich a way that I couldn't catch a glimpse of it. Well, my dear, we didn't let the grass grow under our feet for about a mile or so. 'Now,' says he, 'you must allow yourself to be blindfoulded, an' it's useless to oppose it, for it must be done. There's the character, maybe the life, of a great lady at stake; so be quiet till I cover your eyes, or,' says he, lettin' out a great oath, 'it'll be worse for you. I'm a desperate man;' an' sure enough, I could feel the heart of him beatin' undher his ribs as if it would bust in pieces. Well, my dears, what could I do in the hands of a man that was strong and desperate? 'So,' says I, 'cover my eyes in welcome; only for the lady's sake, make no delay.' Wid that he dashed his spurs into the poor horse, an' he foamin' an' smokin' like a lime-kiln already. Anyway, in about half an hour I found myself in a grand bedroom; an' jist as I was put into the door he whishpers me to bring the child to him in the next room, as soon as it would be born. Well, sure I did so, afther lavin' the mother in a fair way. But what 'ud you have of it? the first thing I see, lyin' an the table, was a purse of money an' a case o' pistols. Whin I looked at him, I thought the devil, Lord guard us! was in his face, he looked so black and terrible about the brows. 'Now, my good woman,' says he, 'so far you've acted well, but there's more to be done yet. Take your choice of these two,' says he, 'this purse or the contents o' one o' these pistols as your reward. You must murdher the child upon the spot.' 'In the name of God an' his Mother, be you man or devil, I defy you,' says I; 'no innocent blood 'll ever be shed by these hands.' 'I'll give you ten minutes,' says he, 'to put an end to that brat there;' an' wid that he cocked one o' the pistols. My dears, I had nothin' for it but to say *in* to myself a *pather* an' *ave* as fast as I could, for I thought it was all over wid me. However, glory be to God, the prayers gave me great stringth, an' I spoke stoutly. 'Whin the king of Jerusalem,' says I, 'an he was a greater man than ever you'll be—whin the king of Jerusalem ordhered the midwives of Aigyp to put Moses to death, they wouldn't do it, an' God preserved them in spite of him, king though he was,' says I; 'an' from that day to this it was never known that a midwife took away the life of the babe she aided into the world—no, an' I'm not goin' to be the first that'll do it.' 'The time is out,' says he, puttin' the pistol to my ear, 'but I'll give you one minute more.' 'Let me go to my knees first,' says I; 'an' may God have mercy on my sowl, for, bad as I am, I'm willin' to die sooner than commit murdher an the innocent.' He gave a start as I spoke, an' threw the pistol down. 'Aye,' said he, 'an the innocent—an the innocent—that is thrue! But you are an extraordinary woman: you have saved that child's life, and previnted me from committing two great crimes, for it was my intintion to murdher you afther you had murdhered it.' I thin, by his ordhers, brought the poor child to its mother, and whin I came back to the room, 'Take that purse,' says he, 'an' keep it as a reward for your honesty.' 'Wid the help o' God,' says I, ' a penny of it will never come into my company, so it's no use to ax me.' 'Well,' says he, 'afore you lave this, you must swear not to mintion to a livin' sowl what has happened this night, for a year and a day.' It didn't signify to me whether I mintioned it or not; so being jack-indifferent about it, I tuck the oath and kept it. He thin bound my eyes agin, hoisted me up behind him, an' in a short time left me at home. Indeed, I wasn't the betther o' the start it tuck out o' me for as good as six weeks afther!"

The company now began to grow musical; several songs were sung; and when the evening got farther advanced, a neighboring fiddler was sent for, and the little party had a dance in the barn, to which they adjourned lest the noise might disturb Mrs. Keho, had they held it in the dwelling-house. Before this occurred, however, the "midwife's glass" went the round of the gossips, each of whom drank her health, and dropped some silver, at the same time, into the bottom of it. It was then returned to her, and with a smiling face she gave the following toast: "Health to the parent stock! So long as it thrives, there will always be branches! Corny Keho, long life an' good health to you an' yours! May your son live to see himself as happy as his father! Youngsters, here's that you may follow a good example! The company's health in general I wish; an', Paddy Rafferty, that you may never have a blind child but you'll have a lame one to lead it! ha, ha, ha! What's the world widout a joke? I must see the good woman an' my little son afore I go; but as I won't follow yez to the barn, I'll bid yez good-night, neighbors, an' the blessin' of Rose Moan be among yez!"

And so also do we take leave of our old friend Rose Moan, the Irish midwife, who, we understand, took her last leave of the world many years ago.

THE WILL O' THE WISP.

Many years ago, the writer of this, being in the city of Dublin, had the pleasure of hearing the following story from the lips of the far-famed "Zozimus." I have never before seen it in print, and thinking it might perhaps interest your readers, I will endeavor to give it as nearly as possible in the words of its famous narrator, though acknowledging my utter inability to even remotely approach his inimitable style of delivering it. It was told with such earnestness, that I have no doubt whatever that Zozimus himself implicitly believed in the truth of every word he uttered. The story runs:—

In olden times there lived in the northern part of Ireland a blacksmith called William Cooper. Now William was a sort of a loose chap, and the divil entirely at all spoorts. He was noted far and near as the hardest drinker and most reckless dare-divil in the county. Finally his squandering habits plunged him head an' heels in debt, and he had no possible manner of payin'. In his dispare he called on the Ould Boy below to help him, an' shure enough, the divil came at his call. William struck a bargain wid him at once which appeared to satisfy both parties. William was to receive as much goold as he cud spind, but, in return, he was to sell his sowl to the Ould Lad, who was to cum fur him in seven years' time. After William had signed the bond with his blud, the divil disappeared in a flash of blue flame.

William soon got from bad to wurse, spindin' and squanderin' his money in foolishness and dissipation.

But wid all that he wuz no ways mane or stingy in the matter of helpin' a poor nabur, an' many wuz the blessin' he got from their grateful hearts, an' many wuz the prayer offered up fur God to direct him to the right road agin.

Howsomever, it seemed all of no avail, an' it looked as if nothin' wud ever turn him. One day an ould woman whom he cum across axed him fur some alms. He didn't wait to spake, but put his fist in his pocket and drawed out a bright goold guinea, which he handed to her, sayin', "There, me poor woman, an' I hope it will do you more good than it wud do me." The ould woman thanked him kindly, fur you must understhand that a guinea in them days wuz thought a big lot of money entirely by the poor people. So she says to him, "Now, William Cooper, since you have been so kind to a poor ould woman, I will grant you any three wishes you ax fur." You see the ould woman was a fairy— one of the good folks, you know (this was uttered by Zozimus in a low voice and with a confidential manner)—an' she had the power of granting wishes, pervided it wouldn't injure a mortal's sowl.

Well, me brave William spoke up an' says: "Furst ov all, I wish that any one that lifts my sledge to sthrike wid it, must kape on sthrikin' till I take it aff him." "That wish is granted," said the fairy. "Next, I wish that any one that sits down in my arm-chair can never get up out ov it till I relase them." "That wish is also granted," said the fairy. "And now, fur the last one, I wish fur a purse that no one but myself can take anything out ov that I put in it." The fairy immediately drew a purse from her pocket, an' givin' it to William, says:

"Your wishes are all granted," an' thin she disappeared. Some time after this, as William wuz wurkin' away at his forge an' whistlin' to himself, who shud walk in the door but ould Beelzebub. "Ha, ha, William," he sez; "I've cum fur ye at last —time's up, me boy." "All right," sez Will, not alarmed in the laste. "I'm ready to go, av you wait till I finish these plow-irons fur a nabur; I promised him I'd do thim fur him to-day, an' I wudn't like to go down below till I fulfilled me promise, so as not to disappoint him." "All right," sez the divil, "I'll wait." "Take the sledge, thin, an' give me a hand," sez William, "an' I'll be done all the quicker."

So the divil took the sledge an' commenced to strike. Well, he struck, an' struck, an' struck away till he was tired out, an' sick an' sore in every limb, an' there stud Will laughing at him. When he was most ready to drop down, he cries out:

"Will, Will, asthore, av you only take this aff me, I'll not bother you fur five years to cum, an' let you have all the money you want to spind till I cum agin."

"It's a bargain," sed William; so he tuk the sledge aff him an' the divil disappeared.

After this William wint on wurse than ever, an' got so that he wudn't do any wurk at all, until his time was near up. Thin he straightened up a little. One day he was plowin' a small patch of ground belongin' to him, whin the Ould Chap cum fur him agin. "I want you this time," sez the divil. "All right, *ma bouchal*," sez William; "cum to the house wid me till I put on a clane shirt, as I don't like to go into company unless I look dacent."

The divil agreed to this, an' they wint back to the house together.

"*She sheese*," sez William, pushing over his arm-chair, so the divil sat down in it, bud bad scran to the up he cud get agin. Will only laughed at him an' put on a clane shirt, an' off to the market town he wint, where there wuz a fair goin' on. He didn't cum back till late that night, an' there sat the divil still, an' him blue in the face wid his struggles to get out ov the chair.

"Oh, Will!" he cried, "let me out of this, and I won't cum agin fur another five years."

"All right," says Will, an' he let him go; but on account of his bein' half drunk, he didn't notice that the divil promised him no money this time. Will soon found to his grief that what money he had didn't last long, an' people wud give him no work to do on account of his bad ways. So the long and short of it wuz, that Will at last had to beg his bit from door to door. When the time cum round agin, the divil appeared, an' poor Will sez, "I'm glad you cum, fur I'm tired an' sick of livin', anyhow."

"Ah ha!" sez the divil, "you haven't got me in your house or forge now, have you?"

"No," sez Will, "I am not thinkin' av playin' any more thricks on you."

"I doubt that ye cud," sez the divil. So aff they marched together.

After awhile they passed a public house, an' poor Will sez, "Many's the time I had a good drink there, an' I'd like to have one partin' drink before lavin' this world, but I haven't a farden. I have aften heard," he sez to the divil, "that you cud change yourself into any shape you like. If you can, just change yourself into a sovereign, an' I can go in an' get a drink, an' thin I'm ready to go anywhere you take me."

"All right," sez the divil, "I'll oblige you now, as it's the last time an' I'm sure av you."

So he changed himself into the coin and Will put him into his purse. Then he wint into the tap-room, an' throwin' the purse on the table called for some poteen; after drinking several times the tapster axed for his money, an' Will told him to take it from the purse; bud av he wuz tryin' from thin till now, av coorse he cudn't take it out. Will sez, "I've offered you the money an' ye wudn't take it, so I'll keep it myself;" an' he put the purse in his pocket, and they bundled him out. Back he marches to his forge an' put the purse on the anvil. Liftin' his sledge he began to belt away at it, till the ould laddie buck widin it begged fur mercy. At last he sung out: "Will, asthore, av you let me out av this, I'll niver cum next or near ye agin, an' I'll give ye money enough to last you your life-time."

"Agreed," sez William, an' he released him, an' the divil flew away yellin' from the batin' he got.

After this Will lived nice an' comfortable, an' give away a grate dale in charity, besides buildin' up a fine town called Ballymully. At last, however, he had to die, like we all have, so he dropped off. He marched to the gate of heaven and axed to get in; bud whin he told his name, they sed he had dalings wid the Avil One, an' he cudn't get in there. So they packed him off. Back he marched till he got to the door of the other place, an' axed to get in. They axed him who wuz there, an' he sed William Cooper.

"Oh ho! don't let him in," sed the *Ould* Divil, "or he'll get the best ov us all here; he bested me whin he wuz on airth, an' av he got in, he'd best me here too. Pack him off; we don't want him."

So they threw him out a lighted wisp of straw, an' from that day till this he has been wanderin' around the world with his lighted wisp, trying to find some place to get rest.

THE FLOWER OF THE WELL.

A STORY OF MAY-DAY.

Amongst the many singular superstitions once so popular in the remote country districts, "skimming the well," on May morning, was not the least curious. With the first light of daybreak a person repaired to some famous spring, where, by taking the "cream" from the surface, whilst uttering a strictly conventional incantation, it was supposed that his or her neighbor's cows would cease to yield butter, their falling off being compensated for by the sudden increase in the yield of their own. The ceremony falls under the general name of *pishogues*, that is to say, charms, by which the "good people" were propitiated in behalf of the celebrant. Countless stories and legends have this odd custom for a common basis; and, as in all proceedings where the supernatural element is supposed to be invoked, fairies have been described as taking a share in the process.

Every one in Drumshawn, from Bill Hagarty, whose forge stood at the east of the village, to Johnny Walker, the "teaman," whose "general grocery and spirit establishment" was situate at the west, knew Grace Lanigan. She was a little, wiry-limbed, blear-eyed old woman, who went about the village in a red hood and a check apron, her feet encased in a pair of high-sounding brogues. Grace betrayed in her attire a gipsyish fondness for plaids and bright colored fabrics, in consequence of which she was popularly known by the nick-name of "the ould dandy." Amongst her other peculiarities, she was passionately addicted to the use of a short, black pipe, which it was believed was scarcely absent from her mouth even when she slept. In all matters of witchcraft, spells and charms, Grace was an able and illustrious proficient. She could tell fortunes by a process which these pages do not afford room to describe; she cultivated the house leek in the thatch of her cottage, and had a horse-shoe nailed to the side-post, as a protection from the imps and elves that do mischief by night. No season of the year passed over without its special superstitious observance—Shrovetide, Midsummer, Halloween, each had its peculiar rite. Much has been written to fasten the charge of gross impiety on educated persons of the class to which Grace belonged; yet it is not too much to say that learning and logic are misused when thus applied, and that the world will persist in believing that the evil of our superstitions is more than counterbalanced by their poetry and imaginativeness.

Grace had once been well-to-do in the world, but dark days had befallen her. She used to look back with grief to the day when ten cows were milked, morning and evening, in her bawn, and she was mistress of a farm of between forty and fifty acres. It was not imprudence which had brought about the change, but the badness of the times and harvests. All her spells could not prevent her cattle dying, her corn rotting before it had ripened. Disaster, as Mr. Poe has it, followed disaster, until Grace was left but a patch of land and a single cow. Those she had, and nothing more.

We omitted from this brief inventory, Nick Lanigan, her only son, a youth of some twenty summers, who had never done any good; and intended, if appearances meant anything, to carry out that useful programme to the end of his days. Nick stood nearly six feet in his vamps, and was as fine a specimen of the rawbone type of manly beauty as could be found in the province. He had a head of reddish colored hair, which fell in two great shocks over his temples, and covered his scalp with a bluff crop resembling sunburnt brushwood. The lid of his right eye depended permanently to such an extent that it almost covered the orb below it, and lent his face a winking expression which, in combination with the solemn grotesqueness of his mouth and the receding lines of his chin, constituted a physiognomy at once ludicrous, helpless and impotent. Nick had the reputation of being a fool, and to some extent the popular belief was countenanced by his acts and sayings. It was said that he slept on the floor in a sack, and that no amount of instruction could induce him to remember the exact number of pence in a shilling. He went hatless and shoeless in all weathers, turning up the ends of his trousers so as to expose a pair of lean calves, floridly colored by exposure to fire and weather. Yet, in the main, Nick was no fool, and what is better, no coward. He was wise enough to refuse all belief in his mother's spells and charms, and wicked enough to provoke her by expelling her pishogues. If only rebuked for a misdemeanor, he would place his back to the wall, and laugh like a tickled griffin until the tears started into his eyes, and his sides ached from shaking. But whenever his mother's displeasure sought an outlet in blows, Nick would "make" for the door, and betake himself to a neighboring lime-kiln, where he lived on roasted potatoes, often for three consecutive days, until the storm blew over.

At last he sinned grievously against the parental authority, and was driven from the house with a volley of injunctions "never to darken the door after during the rest of his mortal life." The expulsion cost the hopeless youth little anxiety. As he said himself, "he was used to it;" and he returned to his old quarters with a sobriety of temper and an alacrity of pace which would have done honor to a greater philosopher. The cause of the fracas was this. One May-day, Grace, who had been mysteriously absent in the morning, returned home about noon, drew her creepeen to the fire, and having lighted her black pipe, took a meditative smoke up the chimney. Mother and son were silent for many minutes—the one enjoying her pipe, the other profoundly engaged in the manufacture of bird-lime. Any one looking at the two would have guessed that no common anxiety lay at Grace's heart—an anxiety in which Nick had more share than he wished should be made public. Eventually, Grace began to rock herself from side to side, a proceeding which always gave Nick considerable displeasure, and often forced him to leave the house.

"Musha, mother," he asked, at last, lifting his head from the bird-lime and casting a malicious look at the old woman, "isn't that child asleep yet?"

Grace, who fully appreciated the force of the joke, raised her head for a moment, and slowly resumed her rocking movement.

"Nick," she said, after a short pause, "you must soon go out and turn a hand for yourself. Things is going to the bad—worse and worse—and if I can make out a bit an' sup for myself, it's more than I'll be able to do for you, you idlin' vagabone."

"Why, then, isn't your frinds, the good people, goin' to befrind yez a bit, aither, afther yer thrubble to plaze them—eh, mother?"

Grace took a long whiff and knocked out the ashes of her pipe on the hob. "Faix, avourneen, I believe they're just as hard up as ourselves, the crathurs, an' more's the pity."

"Musha, don't be runnin' away wid yer seven senses entirely, mother. Av coorse, * *Ni ghuil saoi gam locht*, and that's nayther here nor there wid people that have oceans of goold and silver to do as they likes wid. I'll be bail now, an' the cow runnin' as dhry as a cart wheel, yez didn't skim the well this mornin'."

Grace groaned profoundly and crossed her arms on her knees. "It's not the first good thing a fool said," she answered, "and I did thry to skim the well this morning, but I might as well be attemptin' to prod the blessed moon with a knittin'-needle."

"Is she in her right mind at all?" said Nick, by way of an apostrophe addressed to a third party. "Horns and knittin'-needles, inagh!"

"Yerra, you *omadhaun*, sure 'tis hard enough to get any on derstandin' into that red head iv yerz. Afther all my thrubble, I might as well be pratin' to the griddle, as thryin' to learn yez."

---

* No one's without a failing.

"Ai, thin, does yez hear her?" continued Nick, with a most unfilial interruption. "Isn't it as aisy for you to say, wanst for all in all, av yez skimmed the well this mornin'? Begor, if yez didn't, give the cow a goold meddle and pinsion her off dacently, this minute."

"Haven't I towld yez I was up and skimmed it airly enough, you bosthoon?" shouted Grace, whose temper was visibly declining in the wrong direction.

"Now, that's a plain answer," rejoined Nick, suppressing a laugh. "Av yez said that at fust see all the thrubble ye'd spare yerself. Why thin, mother, now that yer comin' out raisonable, tell us all about it, won't yez?"

"Until yez bell it all over the parish, I suppose," said Grace, with a little bitterness.

"Is it me, mother! Dickens the word then they'll hear iv it from me, I be bail."

Grace having been repeatedly assured that Nick would preserve her secret inviolably, and impelled by the natural desire we all feel to lighten our burdens by sharing them with others, took her pipe from her mouth and began as follows:

"Yez see, Nick, as the ould cow, bad scannin to her, was makin' up her mind to give up milkin' completely, I sez to myself that I'd see what could be done by setting a charm to take away Biddy Grady's crame and butther and bring it back to ourselves. May-mornin', you know, great a fool as you are, is the only time of the year to set the rale charm; so I got up before the cock was crowin', and set off to Tubher-ahina with the new skimmer in my pocket. An' when I got to the brink iv the well, lo and behold you! what was sittin' there foreninst me on the top iv a bulrush but an ould crather about the hoith of a piggin! Arrah, yez should see his nose! 'twas as long an' as sharp as Paddy Crosby's shears, and on the top iv his shoulders he had a hump like a sergeant's knapsack. There he was sated as nate as tuppence, and as grand as a lord.

"'Mornin',' ma'am,' sez he, winkin' at me wid his two eyes.

"'Musha, the same to yerself,' sez I, 'if there's no offince in wishin' it.'

"'Troth an' there's not, ma'am,' sez my ould laddo. 'Isn't it airly yer out?' sez he agin'.

"'Every one to his taste,' sez I, 'as the lady said when she kissed her cow.'

"'Indeed,' sez he, 'indeed! Is it any harm to ask when yerself kissed yer cow last?'

"'Oh, faix, as for that matther,' sez myself, makin' answer to him, ''tis as the fit comes an' goes. It isn't every day a heifer can dhry her mouth,' sez I; 'wid a cambric handkercher.'

"'Thrue for you, Mrs. Lanigan,' says he, giving a twist atop iv the bulrush. 'Are yez makin' much by your butther these times?'

"'As yez asked the kushtion civil, agregal,' sez I, 'I'd be sorry to desave yez. Why thin, I'm bate intirely this sayson. Yez might as well be milkin' a milestone as to persuade the cow to do her duty; an',' sez I, followin' up the discoorse, 'if somethin' don't turn up this mornin', I'll have to give up house and home, and go weedin', or bindin', or somethin' iv that sort.'

"'Skim away,' siz he, 'skim away, Mrs. Lanigan, and the divil is in it,' says he, scratchin' his head, and takin' a pinch iv snuff, 'if yez don't do betther nor yer doin'.'

"'More power to yez,' sez I to him, dippin' the new skimmer into the well; and faith, it was hardly wet, when I hears a great hallooin' over head, and on lookin' up, does yez see, what was there above me, flyin' about in the air, but two or three foine leedles, galavantin' wid aich other, and makin' the curiorsest noise I ever heerd. Well, whilst they kept ginglin' and turnin', all iv a sudden, as Murty Regan's mare broke her leg, they set up a cry of 'Butther is goin', butther is comin'; alew!' I cocks my eye at thim, and sees that, barrin' the quare way they had of fluttherin' up and down, they were nate lookin' girls, dressed in poplin from top to toe, only that it was a bit thin and shaky from bein' washed so often. The ould gintleman that was forninst me was gone asleep when I wanted to ask him who they were, but jest straight at his back I seen another couple iv boyos roostin' atop iv the sedges. One iv them was smokin' a pipe a bit shorter than my own dudheen, and to see his ould shrivelled-up face workin' in and out as he tuk his blast, would make a milestone burst with laughter. But the thing that was wid him banged anythin' I iver dhremt iv. Yerra, Nick, he had a head on his shoulders for all the world like a carrot, and out iv it was two horns, turned round and round like a cat's tail at the inds.

"'Takin' yer smoke,' says myself to the gorsoon wid the pipe.

"'Musha, who gave yez yer knowledge?' sez he, puttin' down the ashes wid the butt of his little finger. 'Dickens shoot me, Mike,' sez he, turnin' to the other gorsoon, 'but those ignoramuses will bate us clane out iv the country before Shrovetide.'

"'Sure, arry one harkenin' to yez would think 'twas the schoolmasther was spakin',' sez I, 'barrin' he'd hang a dozen iv yer seed and breed in the ink-bottle at his button-hole.'

"'Didn't I tell yez, Mike?' sez he, turnin' round agin to the chap wid the horns. 'We won't stand it no longer,' sez he, takin' the pipe from his mouth. 'And what ill wind blew yez here so airly, Mrs. Lanigan?' sez he.

"'I'd be sorry to desave yez,' sez I, 'though I wish it was some one else put the kusthun. Isn't it as plain as the pipe in yer ugly gob that 'twas no good wind dhruv me where you are?'

"'Butther is goin', butther is comin',' cried the girls hoigh above us.

"'Does yez hear that, Mrs. Lanigan?' sez my neighbor—'are yez listenin' to that?' sez he, wid a grin that went from ear to ear. 'If yez hasn't lost all yer teeth, skim the well, and take to yer shankers,' sez he, 'or the devil resave the bit of butther ye'll see whilst yer name's Grace.'

"''Tisn't the first time somebody, I won't mintion, gave a good advice,' sez I, 'and here's at yez;' and wid that I dipped the skimmer agin into the well, but I might as well thry to lift the wather into a sieve, for it all ran out through the bottom.'

"'Begor, yer-done for at last,' sez the ould bosthoon, cacklin' to himself wid divarshin. 'Thry it agin,' sez he, 'there's many a slip 'tween the cup and the lip, Mrs. Lanigan, darlint.'

"'What makes the wather run through the skimmer?' sez I, gettin' angry.

"'Don't you see the rayson,' sez he—'arrah, because it won't stop in it, Mrs. Lanigan.'

"'Y'ev been to school, masther,' sez I to him, 'and by the same token, yez always sat on the windy side av the hedge, and didn't hear much iv the larnin', ma bouchal.'

"'Ah, thin, Grace,' sez he, lookin' as sayrious as a bed-post, 'there's a pair av us there, ai?' And wid that the pair of geese set up a screech of laughin' that set me dancin' in the tan-thrums.

"'Butther is goin'—butther is comin',' sez the ladies.

"'Yez betther cut your stick, Grace,' says the ould fellow, 'or skim the well at wanst. Take another dip, agragal, and who knows the luck yez may git?'

"So I took him at his word, and put the skimmer down a succond time, but keepin' out the tide wid a pitchfork was divarshin to thryin' to take up the crame wid a skimmer that wouldn't hould chaney-alleys.

"The boyos began laughin', my dear, agin, and siz they, 'Grace, did yez meet 'eer a red-haired woman this mornin'?'

"'Troth, no,' siz I.

"'Did yez come across 'eer a magpie?' siz they.

"'Troth, I didn't,' sez I agin.

"'Maybe you overlooked Nick's throwin' an ould shoe afther yez, as yez left the house,' says the lad wid the horns.

"'Begannys, yer right, my bucko,' sez I, remimberin' it all of a hape.

"'Then,' sez he, 'yez might as well be bailen' out the green bay with a bottomless thimble. Lave it alone, acushla, and betther luck next time.'

"The words was hardly out av his mouth when I hears a great hallooin' in the air, and on lookin' up, may I never turn another sod av turf if the air for a mile round wasn't thick wid fairies, flyin' from all quarters, wid keelers of milk fastened to their backs. Arrah, to see them was a thrate worth walkin' a distance for. Some av them had tails, and some av them no tails at all; some av them had beards cockin' stiff out av their chins, and some had no more beard on thim than yerself, avic. You needn't be scrapin' yer chin, Nick, 'tis as bare as the dale table there. Such noses and faces I never seen before ; and whilst they were batin' about the bushes, the girls set up the ould song agin, ' Butther is goin'—butther is comin'.' Immediately all the gorsoons rowled the full of their keelers into a big tub, and sez one, ' Let Grace Lanigan look out now,' sez he, ' for if her cow was as ould as Methusala, she'll milk as much now as a pratystalk.' Hearin' this discoorse, I made another dip iv the skimmer, and no sooner I missed it agin than Larry Hayes' cock (divil choke him) began crowin', and all the fairies vanished from my sight. So, Nick, darlint, look out for yerself, av yez have look at your side. I've towld yez all, lock, stock and barrel. There'll be no more milk, no more nothing ; troth, I see——"

"Wait a bit, mother," exclaimed Nick, and as he spoke he took up a position between her and the door. " Have yez the skimmer about yez ? "

" Faix, I have, safe and sound in my pocket, alanna."

" And did yez look at the bottom av it when yer set off to skim the well this morning ? "

" 'Deed, thin, I didn't."

"Well, thin, look at it now, and ye'll find three round holes burned wid a red hould-fast in the bottom av it."

Grace held the skimmer between her eyes and the cloudy light that came through the window. A brief examination of the utensil verified Nick's statement.

" Ah, thin, who done this, alanna ?" she asked, "ai, who done this ? Tell me."

" Musha, faith, mother, 'twas me, for the fun av it," replied her hopeful son.

Grace grasped the bent hoop which served for a tongs in her humble household, and rushed at her guilty offspring. Nick, who evidently anticipated such a movement, escaped from the house and stood " mopping and mowing " before the door.

"And, mother, does yez know why the ould cow's milk ran short? Shure yez ud never guess—faith, bekase I dhrank it."

A suppressed scream was Grace's only answer. "While there's life in yer body," she shouted, " shun this house, I warn yez, mind, I warn yez;" and with these words she closed the door, and reseated herself on the creepeen.

Nick, we are told, stayed away for three weeks, and in his absence, so considerable was the increase in the yield of milk, that Grace recovered her temper, forgave her undutiful son, and thenceforth grew somewhat credulous in the potency of charms, though she clung faithfully to her old belief in the world of Faëry.

PUBLICATIONS
OF
P. J. KENEDY,
EXCELSIOR
Catholic Publishing House,
5 BARCLAY ST., NEAR BROADWAY,
Opposite the Astor House,
NEW YORK.

Adventures of Michael Dwyer. **$1 00**
Adelmar the Templar. A Tale.. **40**

Ballads, Poems, and Songs of
   William Collins.................. **1 00**
Blanche. A Tale from the French... **40**
Battle of Ventry Harbor......... **20**
Bibles, from $2 50 to............. **15 00**
Brooks and Hughes Controversy **75**
Butler's Feasts and Fasts....... **1 25**

Catholic Prayer-Books, 25c., 50c., *up to* **12 00**

☞ Any of above books sent free by mail on receipt of price. Agents wanted everywhere to sell above books, to whom liberal terms will be given. Address
P. J. KENEDY, Excelsior Catholic Publishing House, *5 Barclay Street, New York.*

Publications of P. J. Kenedy, 5 Barclay St., N. Y.

Blind Agnese. A Tale............	$0 50
Butler's Catechism..............	8
" " with Mass Prayers.	30
Bible History. Challoner..........	50
Christian Virtues. By St. Liguori.	1 00
Christian's Rule of Life. " "	30
Christmas Night's Entertainments...........................	60
Conversion of Ratisbonne.......	50
Clifton Tracts. 4 vols............	3 00
Catholic Offering. By Bishop Walsh...........................	1 50
Christian Perfection. Rodriguez. 3 vols. *Only complete edition*......	4 00
Catholic Church in the United States. By J. G. Shea. Illustrated.	2 00
Catholic Missions among the Indians........................	2 50
Chateau Lescure. A Tale.........	50
Conscience; or, May Brooke. A Tale	1 00
Catholic Hymn-Book............	15
Christian Brothers' 1st Book....	13
" " 2d " ...	25
" " 3d "	63
" " 4th "	88
Catholic Primer.................	6

Catholic Prayer-Books, 25c., 50c., *up to* 12 00

☞ Any of above books sent free by mail on receipt of price. Agents wanted everywhere to sell above books, to whom liberal terms will be given. Address

P. J. KENEDY, Excelsior Catholic Publishing House, *5 Barclay Street, New York.*

Publications of P. J. Kenedy, 5 Barclay St., N. Y.

Irish National Songster	$1 00
Imitation of Christ	40
Keeper of the Lazaretto. A Tale.	40
Kirwan Unmasked. By Archbishop Hughes	12
King's Daughters. An Allegory	75
Life and Legends of St. Patrick.	1 00
Life of St. Mary of Egypt	60
" " *Winefride*	60
" " *Louis*	40
" " *Alphonsus M. Liguori.*	75
" " *Ignatius Loyola.* 2 vols.	3 00
Life of Blessed Virgin	75
Life of Madame de la Peltrie	50
Lily of Israel. 22 Engravings	75
Life Stories of Dying Penitents.	75
Love of Mary	50
Love of Christ	50
Life of Pope Pius IX.	1 00
Lenten Manual	50
Lizzie Maitland. A Tale	75
Little Frank. A Tale	50

Catholic Prayer-Books, 25c., 50c., *up to* 12 00

☞ Any of above books sent free by mail on receipt of price. Agents wanted everywhere to sell above books, to whom liberal terms will be given. Address
P. J. KENEDY, Excelsior Catholic Publishing House, *5 Barclay Street, New York.*

Publications of P. J. Kenedy, 5 Barclay St., N. Y.

Little Catholic Hymn-Book...$0 10
Lyra Catholica (large Hymn-Book).. 75

Mission and Duties of Young
  Women........................... 60
Maltese Cross. A Tale........... 40
Manual of Children of Mary.... 50
Mater Admirabilis...............1 50
Mysteries of the Incarnation.
  (St. Liguori.)................... 75
Month of November............... 40
Month of Sacred Heart of Jesus. 50
  "   " *Mary*................. 50
Manual of Controversy........... 75
Michael Dwyer. An Irish Story of
  1798 ....1 00
Milner's End of Controversy.... 75
May Brooke ; or, Conscience. A
  Tale............................1 00

New Testament................... 50

Oramaika. An Indian Story....... 75
Old Andrew the Weaver........... 50

Preparation for Death. St. Liguori........................... 75

Catholic Prayer-Books, 25c., 50c., up to 12 00

☞ Any of above books sent free by mail on receipt of price. Agents wanted everywhere to sell above books, to whom liberal terms will be given. Address
P. J. KENEDY, Excelsior Catholic Publishing House, 5 Barclay Street, New York.

Publications of P. J. Kenedy, 5 Barclay St., N. Y.

Prayer. By St. Liguori. $0 50
Papist Misrepresented............ 25
Poor Man's Catechism........... 75

Rosary Book. 15 Illustrations. 10
Rome: Its Churches, Charities, and Schools. By Rev. Wm. H. Neligan, LL.D.......... .... 1 00
Rodriguez's Christian Perfection. 3 vols. *Only complete edition..* 4 00
Rule of Life. St. Liguori........... 40

Sure Way; or, Father and Son. 25
Scapular Book.................... 10
Spirit of St. Liguori.............. 75
Stations of the Cross. 14 Illustrations................................ 10
Spiritual Maxims. (St. Vincent de Paul)............................. 40
Saintly Characters. By Rev. Wm. H. Neligan, LL.D................1 00
Seraphic Staff.... 25
" *Manual*, 75 cts. to......3 00
Sermons of Father Burke, plain. 2 00
"   "   " gilt edges.3 00
Schmid's Exquisite Tales. 6 vols.3 00
Shipwreck. A Tale 50

Catholic Prayer-Books, 25c., 50c., *up to* 12 00

☞ Any of above books sent free by mail on receipt of price. Agents wanted everywhere to sell above books, to whom liberal terms will be given. Address

P. J. KENEDY, Excelsior Catholic Publishing House, *5 Barclay Street, New York.*

Publications of P. J. Kenedy, 5 Barclay St., N. Y.

Savage's Poems $2 00
Sybil: A Drama. By John Savage.... 75

Treatise on Sixteen Names of
Ireland. By Rev. J. O'Leary, D. D. 50
Two Cottages. By Lady Fullerton.. 50
Think Well On't. Large type...... 40
Thornberry Abbey. A Tale....... 50
Three Eleanors. A Tale.......... 75
Trip to France. Rev. J. Donelan.. 1 00
Three Kings of Cologne.......... 30

Universal Reader................ 50
Vision of Old Andrew the
Weaver...................... 50
Visits to the Blessed Sacrament. 40

Willy Reilly. Paper cover......... 50
Way of the Cross. 14 Illustrations. 5
Western Missions and Mission-
aries............... ....2 00
Walker's Dictionary............ 75

Young Captives. A Tale.......... 50
Youth's Director................. 50
Young Crusaders. A Tale........ 50

Catholic *Prayer-Books*, 25c., 50c., up to 12 00

☞ Any of above books sent free by mail on receipt of price. Agents wanted everywhere to sell above books, to whom liberal terms will be given. Address

P. J. KENEDY, Excelsior Catholic Publishing House, *5 Barclay Street, New York.*

8

www.ingramcontent.com/pod-product-compliance
Lightning Source LLC
Chambersburg PA
CBHW030743230426
43667CB00007B/821